Understanding
The Grapes of Wrath

The Greenwood Press "Literature in Context" Series
Student Casebooks to Issues, Sources, and Historical Documents

UNDERSTANDING
The Grapes of Wrath

A STUDENT CASEBOOK TO ISSUES, SOURCES, AND HISTORICAL DOCUMENTS

Claudia Durst Johnson

The Greenwood Press
"Literature in Context" Series

GREENWOOD PRESS
Westport, Connecticut • London

Library of Congress Cataloging-in-Publication Data

Johnson, Claudia D.
    Understanding The grapes of wrath : a student casebook to issues,
sources, and historical documents / Claudia Durst Johnson.
        p.   cm.—(The Greenwood Press "Literature in context"
series, ISSN 1074–598X)
    Includes bibliographical references and index.
    ISBN 0–313–30575–7 (alk. paper)
    1. Steinbeck, John, 1902–1968. Grapes of wrath—Handbooks,
manuals, etc.   2. Migrant agricultural laborers in literature.
3. Labor camps in literature.   4. California—In literature.
I. Title.   II. Series.
PS3537.T3234G8565   1999
813'.52—dc21   99–17854

British Library Cataloguing in Publication Data is available.

Library of Congress Catalog Card Number: 99–17854
ISBN: 0–313–30575–7
ISSN: 1074–598X

First published in 1999

Greenwood Press, 88 Post Road West, Westport, CT 06881
An imprint of Greenwood Publishing Group, Inc.
www.greenwood.com

Printed in the United States of America

(∞)™

The paper used in this book complies with the
Permanent Paper Standard issued by the National
Information Standards Organization (Z39.48–1984).

P

Copyright Acknowledgments

The author and publisher gratefully acknowledge permission for the use of the following material:

From "Broke at Fifty," by Frank Moorhead. Reprinted with permission from the May 13, 1931 issue of *The Nation* magazine.

Excerpts of interviews with J. R. Davison and Melt White from WGBH's *The American Experience* "Surviving the Dust Bowl" Web site <www.wgbh.org>. Reprinted by permission of WGBH.

From *Factories in the Field*, by Carey McWilliams. Reprinted by permission of Harold Ober Associates Incorporated. Copyright © 1939 by Carey McWilliams. Copyright renewed.

From "Concentration of U.S. Riches" and "Wage-Hour Law Provisions," *Oakland Tribune* October 19, 1938. Reprinted by permission of the *Oakland Tribune*.

From "Pretty Boy Floyd Slain," *New York Times* October 23, 1934. Copyright © 1934 by the New York Times Co. Reprinted by permission.

From "20,000 Attend Burial of Floyd in Oklahoma," *New York Times* October 29, 1934. Reprinted by permission of the Associated Press.

From "Chavez Ends Symbolic 25-Day Fast," *San Francisco Chronicle* March 11, 1968. © San Francisco Chronicle. Reprinted by permission.

From "America's Secret Child Labor Force," by David Foster and Farrell Kramer. New York: Associated Press, December 14, 1997. Reprinted by permission of the Associated Press.

From "From Fields and Factories, Children's Voices Emerge," by Verena Dobnik and Ted Anthony. New York: Associated Press, December 9, 1997. Reprinted by permission of the Associated Press.

Every reasonable effort has been made to trace the owners of copyright materials in this book, but in some instances this has proven impossible. The author and publisher will be glad to receive information leading to more complete acknowledgments in subsequent printings of the book and in the meantime extend their apologies for any omissions.

Contents

Introduction

In 1939, as the nation continued to suffer from an economic depression regarded as one of the most devastating events in its history, a young California writer named John Steinbeck saw into print a novel about a family of migrant agricultural workers who had fled Oklahoma to find a new life in California. The novel, titled *The Grapes of Wrath*, had an immediate and explosive effect on the public. In some quarters, especially in the fields of California where he had worked alongside migrant laborers, Steinbeck was regarded as a hero who had had the courage to portray appalling conditions as they really were.

The demand for the book by the reading public made it an instant best-seller. It has often been observed that *The Grapes of Wrath* was the *Uncle Tom's Cabin* of its time, creating an immediate sensation. Even in Oklahoma, where Steinbeck's novel was roundly denounced, it was the biggest selling novel since the widely popular *Gone with the Wind*. In 1940, the novel was made into a film—directed by John Ford and starring Henry Fonda—that is still regarded as a classic.

Yet, the novel was not received with universal admiration by any means. In California, growers and politicians alike called the author the most dangerous man in America. As soon as the book appeared on library shelves in California, it was ordered removed.

In Oklahoma, Steinbeck was attacked by politicians and ordinary citizens for defaming the state and presenting its people as uncivilized and immoral.

In other parts of the country, the book was condemned on the grounds that it was pornographic. Leading churchmen, like Roman Catholic Cardinal Spellman, found it to be a filthy abomination that devout Catholics were urged to avoid at any cost.

Despite the controversy, the novel brought attention to the problem of migrant farmworkers and was eventually instrumental in bringing about some improvements in their situation. As a work of literature, it has sustained its appeal throughout the twentieth century. It has never been out of print in its sixty-year history.

More often than not, historians have neglected the long struggle of the people whose backbreaking and underpaid work puts food on the nation's tables. It is the power of Steinbeck's novel, however, that has kept the subject alive. And because of its timely setting in the Depression, few works lend themselves so readily to contextual study.

The first chapter is an analysis of the novel in "New Critical" fashion, its construction, images, and philosophy presented with little reference to social background. The chapters that follow present the novel within the times in which it appeared. Chapter Two is an examination of the financial causes and results of what has come to be called the Great Depression. The history of farming in the early twentieth century and the particular character of agribusiness in California is the subject of Chapter Three. Chapter Four is a close examination of the migrant farmworker in 1930s California. The attempts to organize farmworkers and the major agricultural strikes of the period are examined in Chapter Five. The subject of Chapter Six is lawlessness on the part of law-enforcement officers in so many of their dealings with working-men, especially union members, and the admiration that many working people had for the notorious outlaws of the 1930s. The final chapter in the work concerns issues regarding the working and living conditions of the farmworker that have persisted long after the publication of *The Grapes of Wrath*. This chapter deals with the rise of Cesar Chavez and the United Farm Workers (UFW). His tireless work to win union recognition for agricultural laborers for the first time continues to inspire over thirty-five years later.

Among the documents used to illuminate the novel are:

- firsthand accounts and investigative reports of the causes and effects of the Depression,
- letters written to First Lady Eleanor Roosevelt and Secretary of Labor Frances Perkins,
- flyers intended to provoke farmers to organize and act,
- interviews with eyewitnesses to the Dust Bowl,
- government studies of the problems of agri-business,
- portions of a diary and an autobiography of migrant workers in the 1930s,
- transcripts of congressional committee testimony,
- excerpts from a book attacking *The Grapes of Wrath*,
- a Wobbly song about a farmworkers' riot,
- tables showing major strikes in the 1930s,
- affidavits by union activists who were attacked by lawmen and vigilantes,
- minutes from meetings of lawmen and growers' associations,
- an open letter, a speech, and a prayer by Cesar Chavez,
- a press release from the 1998 California legislature on the problems of farmworkers.

Page references are to a Penguin Books edition of *The Grapes of Wrath* (New York, 1967).

1

A Literary Analysis of *The Grapes of Wrath:* Suffering and Sacrifice

In the 1930s, the United States endured one of the greatest traumas in its history, at the time second only in magnitude of suffering to the Civil War. It was known as the Great Depression. The stock market crash of 1929, after years of rampant financial speculation, spending, and a variety of natural disasters, resulted in widespread financial collapse and crop failures that led to unemployment, hunger, and homelessness on a massive scale. It brought the United States closer to social and political revolution than it had ever been since the country's founding in revolution some 150 years before. The capitalistic ideas on which the nation rested were not only useless in stopping the injustice and suffering, but were actually worsening the situation to which they had contributed. Many Americans believed that nothing less than the overthrow of the whole structure of society would remedy the intolerable situation. Two courses of action eventually brought the nation back from the brink: the radical economic measures put in place by the administration of Franklin D. Roosevelt and the outbreak of World War II.

One novel stands above all others as a record and interpretation of the experience of the 1930s: John Steinbeck's *Grapes of Wrath*. Published in 1939, it is a stark picture of the social conditions in which so many Americans struggled. So rooted is the novel in the context of the thousands of agricultural migrants who had journeyed to California, that it lives in the public memory as the consummate novel of social protest. Yet, its social message is couched in terms made universal with references to biblical stories of suffering and sacrifice. The setting, plot structure, and characterization are the first subjects in the analysis that follows. Following the literary attributes of the novel, we will examine its social message as it is unveiled in the "interchapters." The focus will then turn to the more universal and philosophical themes of the novel, including the many ironies that strengthen its message. The analysis closes with a discussion of a few of the controversies relative to interpretation of the novel.

THE SETTING

The account of the Joad family's journey begins in the summer heat of the mid-1930s, and ends less than a year later in the winter. It begins in a period of killing drought, just after dust storms have smothered the Mid- and Southwest, and ends with the destructive rains that seem as if they will never cease.

The story opens in eastern Oklahoma, moves along with the travelers across the United States, and ends in California, as the Joads follow the dream of plenty in the West that had inspired thousands of Americans before them from the Gold Rush days of the nineteenth century. The Americanness of the journey, underscored by particularizing the course of their journey, can easily be plotted on a map of the United States. They depart from Sallisaw, Oklahoma, about ten miles from the Arkansas town of Fort Smith. Southwest of the Joad's farm in Sallisaw lies McAlester, Oklahoma, where Tom Joad served time in prison for homicide.

From Sallisaw, the family travels west on a highway now superseded by Interstate 40, going through Gore (24 miles from home); Warner (13 more miles); Checotah (14 more); Peden (25 more miles); Meeker (13); Harrah (14); until after 27 more miles, they reach Oklahoma City. Here, where migrants from all over the Midwest and South converge, they join Highway 66, known as the Migrant Road. In Bethany, Oklahoma, 14 miles from Oklahoma City, they stop for their first night on the road. The next day they go through El Reno, Bridgeport, Clinton, Elk City, Sayer, and Texola—all in Oklahoma—before reaching Texas. In Texas, they drive through the Panhandle—Shamrock, Alanreed, Groom, and Yarnell—and camp just on the western border in the evening. On the third day, after driving through Wildorado, Vegas, Boise, and Glenrio, Texas, they reach New Mexico. About 100 miles from the border, they cross the Pecos River. Between Santa Rosa and Albuquerque, they spend the night.

They cross into Arizona near the Petrified Forest and travel through Holbrook, Winslow, and Flagstaff. They drive all night to Oatman, Arizona, on the California border, stopping finally at Needles, California, where they bathe in the Colorado River. Late in the afternoon they start on their last 300 miles, which will take them across the Mojave Desert. They reach Daggett at midnight. After the towns of Barstow, Mojave, and Tehachapi, they reach their destination of Bakersfield, California, while it is still morning.

They camp for a short period in a Hooverville outside Bakersfield and then head south on Highway 99 to Highway 223. Traveling east for a few miles they reach the government camp at Weedpatch. When after several weeks they are forced to leave Weedpatch to look for work, they travel north on Highway 99 to a ranch just east of Pixley. After only a couple of days at the Hooper Ranch, they take back roads, going north for about twenty miles to a boxcar camp near Tulare. The novel ends in a barn on a highway near a stream in the region of Tulare.

THE STRUCTURE

On this geographical map running from east Oklahoma to central California, Steinbeck locates his story, using a structure as unconventional as his subjects and point of view. Interlaced throughout the narrative are documentary chapters explaining the general situation in America at the time, pertinent to the Joads' experience in the chapters that follow. The interchapters are generalized accounts, written in a journalistic style, of dust storms, mechanization, the breakup of households, the buying of cars to carry families west, and the agricultural situation and migrants' living conditions in California. Each of these chapters provides the reader with factual background, forming a structure similar to that used by such writers as Leo Tolstoy in *War and Peace*, and in other novels of social protest such as *USA*, by John Dos Passos. One of the most powerful interchapters is Chapter Twenty-Five, in which the dumping and poisoning of food to force an increase in produce prices is described. Drawing on newspaper reports of the time, the author describes how mountains of oranges, dumped on a garbage heap, are sprayed with kerosene to keep the hungry migrants from eating them. Potatoes are dumped in a river, and armed men guard the banks to keep starving people from fishing them out.

The novel departs from the usual tight narrative structure containing an initiating circumstance, rising action, climax, and conclusion. Instead, it has a modified picaresque structure in that the characters journey from place to place, episode to episode, characters to new characters. Much of what is introduced in one episode may have little direct bearing on what follows, as, for example, the introduction early in the journey of the Wilsons, who never appear again. Nor does the novel have the usual closure when all the loose ends are gathered up. For example, we never know what really happens to the Joads. Is Tom successful as a labor organizer? Does he get caught? How do Ma and Pa survive the three months ahead of them when no work is available? Do they ever see Tom or Al again? The reader never learns the answers to these questions.

Such an unconventional way of putting the novel together buttresses the fabric of the tale, reflecting the uncertainty in the lives of the characters who find that the old traditional centers of their lives—home, family, work—have collapsed.

Although the novel lacks a traditional narrative structure, it does have a three-part form: Chapters One through Eleven take place in the old home in Oklahoma and reveal the necessity for the journey; Chapters Twelve through Eighteen make up the trip, a link between home and intended destination. Chapters Nineteen through Thirty take place in California.

The primary episodes in Part One include Tom's homecoming, the killing of hogs, selling of belongings, and packing to leave. Part Two—the journey itself—includes the deaths of the dog, Grampa, Sairy Wilson, and Granma, the breakdown of the car, the disappearance of Noah, the first encounters with police, and the conversation in the river that warns them of trouble in the paradise they are traveling to. Part Three takes place in four major locales in California: the first Hooverville where Connie disappears and Casy is arrested; the government camp at Weedpatch, a picture of humane treatment and the residents' ability to govern themselves; the Hooper Ranch where Casy is killed and Tom becomes a fugitive; and the boxcar camp where Rose O'Sharon gives birth to a dead baby, and the Joads are driven out by floods.

CHARACTERIZATION

There are no exalted regal heroes in *The Grapes of Wrath*. Its people are from the humblest ranks of society and, like proletarian or working-class works of literature, our attention is drawn, not to a single hero, but to the group, as if to emphasize one of the novel's messages—that strength, even survival, lies in unity. *The Grapes of Wrath* is not first and foremost the story of Tom Joad; it is the story of the Joad *family* and all the people they draw into their family circle.

At the same time, each member of the Joad family has his or her own clear identity. Ma is the strongest one even from the first, a character who grows in strength as the journey proceeds and adversities multiply. It is she who directs the brutal business of packing and discarding cherished possessions for the trip; she who orders the family to stay together when the car breaks down; she who sleeps all night beside the corpse of Granma so the others will not be alarmed and lose sleep; she who stands up to the bullying policeman. Ma is also the most benevolent character from beginning to end—the first to insist that the preacher be allowed to join the group, the one who sees the need for Rose of Sharon to save a starving man. And she is the one who realizes important truths of the novel: that "we" are one people and that the more a person suffers, the greater must be his effort to help others. Ma's real change comes in her broadened view of family. At first, though she is charitable to all, she has a fierce sense of her own biological family. By the end, Ma, who once believed family came first, now says of family, "It's anybody" (569).

Tom Joad, her son, is her nearest match in strength by the end of the novel. Tom comes into the novel having been toughened by prison life. And although he has become a wiser man, his self-respect and sense of injury will not allow him to be completely quiet and acquiescent when he is insulted or when he sees gross injustice, even though he knows he takes the risk of returning to prison if he reacts. As a result, he trips up a contractor who threatens one of the migrants, and kills the man who kills Casy. Nevertheless, more than any other character, Tom listens, observes, and learns. By the novel's end, he has decided to become active in the fight against the abusive agricultural system in California. Like Ma, he, too, embraces all the migrants as his family.

Tom's inspiration is Jim Casy, the ex-preacher who joins the Joads on their journey west. Casy is the character who first expresses a philosophy that other characters come to feel rather than intellectualize. Perhaps he is Steinbeck's mouthpiece or, at least, Steinbeck's portrait of a saintly social activist and a tribute to many men and women who unselfishly risked their lives for the poor in the 1930s. After a period of solitude in the wilderness, which has occurred before the novel begins, Casy's religious beliefs have changed so decidedly that he insists from the opening scenes of the novel that he is no longer a minister. He subsequently says that he has no God and that he does not believe in prayer, though he is called upon several times to pray. Casy has, in effect, traded in his evangelical religion for the belief that the ultimate importance in life is one's relationship with other people, rather than with God: " 'Why do we got to hang it on God or Jesus? 'Maybe,' I figgered, 'maybe it's all men an' all women we love; maybe that's the Holy Sperit—the human sperit—the whole shebang' "(31).

Once in California, Casy takes all the blame and is arrested after a fight that he, Tom, and another young migrant have with a sheriff. In jail he comes to realize that strength comes in union and, when he gets out, devotes himself to bettering the conditions of migrant workers.

Another of the Joad children, Rose of Sharon, and her husband Connie are little more than children when they start out on the journey, even though Rose is expecting a child. She dutifully undertakes the chores expected of her, but as difficulties increase (and Connie deserts her), she begins a physical and emotional decline, blaming her family for her husband's desertion and complaining about the lack of food and milk that she knows will have an effect on her unborn child. Yet, the day before she goes into premature labor, when she is sick and weak, she insists on going to help in the cotton fields. The novel ends on her act of life-giving beneficence.

Another member of the Joad family who is with them to the end is Uncle John, a character consistently characterized by excruciating, hand-wringing guilt as well as his generosity to his brother's family. At the beginning of the journey, the reader learns that Uncle John is tortured by his part in causing the deaths of his young wife and child. He looks on himself as a curse and offers repeatedly to take himself out of the scene so that his guilt will not bring greater misfortune on the family. At the novel's end, he is the man chosen to dispose of the body of his niece's stillborn child. His words in the scene show that he has moved beyond guilty self-absorption to dismay and horror at the migrants' treatment at the hands of those in power.

John's brother, Pa Joad, is overshadowed by his strong wife and son, Tom. Yet he is a consistent steadying presence throughout the journey—earthy, profane, usually competent and clearheaded, and always generous, as when he gives some of his limited funds to Mr. Wilson, a man he has known for just a few days. His quiet strength is shown in his ability to let Ma take the reins of the family when it becomes necessary. His intelligence and drive are shown in his determination to build a dam against the flood—a dam almost immediately destroyed by a falling tree. And his great suffering and great heart are shown in his kneeling by the bed of his daughter, who has just lost her baby, to plead with his wife, "Did we slip up? . . . Is there anything we could of did?" (567)

Other important characters include the senile Granma and lusty Grampa, both of whom die not long after the family embarks on the journey; a Joad son named Noah and Rose O'Sharon's husband Connie, both of whom desert the family; Muley Graves, a farmer who refuses to follow his neighbors out west; the Wilsons, who offer their bed to the dying Grampa; Floyd, a young migrant husband and father who stands up to the crooked labor contractors; Jim Rawley, the benevolent and wise manager of the Weedpatch government camp; and the Wainwrights, one of the many examples of the unselfishness of migrant families.

A SOCIAL NOVEL

There is no doubt that *The Grapes of Wrath* is a novel with a message. It is intended to enlighten the reader about a situation that existed at the time of the novel's writing, to change the way people regard that situation, and to inspire them to corrective action. While journalistic accounts of the socioeconomic conditions in the interchapters appeal to one's intellect, the story of how these conditions affect the Joads, in chapters that follow the accounts, appeal to the heart.

The title of the novel comes from Julia Ward Howe's "The Battle Hymn of the Republic," which John Steinbeck at first wanted reprinted in his novel. The specific lines about the union cause to wipe out slavery through sectional bloodshed—the American Civil War—are as follows: "He is trampling out the vintage where the grapes of wrath are stored." In these lines, he refers to God. The grapes of wrath refer to the anger that has built up for years among slaveowners and their opponents over the very existence of slavery in the country and the horrors that came from slavery. In parallel fashion, one sees in the novel, the anger—"the grapes of wrath"— that is growing over the treatment of agricultural workers by the government and the growers. Steinbeck suggests in the novel that anger and resentment will continue to grow until a virtual war breaks out. The phrase is especially apt in Steinbeck's novel because the setting is California with its immense grape-growing areas where migrant labor is necessary to the harvest.

In the first part of the novel, the author addresses the conditions of the small farmowner and sharecropper of the Midwest and South, illustrated by Oklahoma and the trek west. In the last part, he dramatizes the conditions faced by migrant workers in California. Chapter One, about the Dust Bowl, describes the natural disaster that struck farmers who had already been destroyed economically. In May 1934, after the crops had been planted and were already growing in the fields, all rain ceased. The sun began parching the earth. By mid-June, the soil was hard and dry and the winds began to blow, and by mid-July the crops had withered. As if to deal the death blow, dust blew so fiercely across the fields that it created a blizzard, coating everything and everyone, inside and outside the buildings. Crops were ruined, and the topsoil blew away. Those who were used to subsisting on the land now had nothing to eat.

In Chapter Five, Steinbeck turns his attention to the man-made disasters that changed the natural disaster into a killing tragedy. By 1939, the time of the novel, years of failing crops and bank foreclosures resulted in putting land ownership in the hands of large agri-businesses or banks. Very often, they were faceless owners who did not live on the farms, and had never seen the land they owned. Sometimes they controlled the farms in Oklahoma from as far away as New York City. Many families who had owned small farms lost them and had to became tenant farmers or share-croppers, and either rented their land and houses or were given a percentage of the farm's produce in exchange for growing crops that now belonged to somebody else.

After the dust storms, the banks and corporations that owned most of the land were determined to turn a significant profit from their investments. They decided that the best way to do this was to abandon growing a variety of foodstuffs and animals (corn had been the key staple) and to plant one money crop only—cotton. Furthermore, the owners could now turn to farm machinery—die-sel tractors—to replace plowing with horses and mules. This meant two things: (1) that all the various food crops, and even the yards and houses of the tenants would be plowed under by the tractors (even before families moved out) to make way for more land to grow cotton, and (2) that one man on a tractor could replace sixty or seventy farmhands among the sharecroppers. So, the families were driven off the land.

Steinbeck's target in this chapter, as in subsequent ones, is the corporations, the banks, and the government that sustains them, a combination that bleeds rather than serves individuals, and is determined to make a profit at the cost of human life. In short, his target is capitalism gone mad.

In Chapters Seven, Nine, Eleven, and Twelve, the author attacks the men who run smaller businesses and capitalize on the misfor-tunes of the uprooted farmers—the car dealers, the used furniture and tool dealers, the service stations. At the same time, he recog-nizes that these smaller business are all at the mercy of bigger ones.

Chapter Fourteen enlarges on a social note that is sounded throughout the novel: in this greedy climate and given these in-tolerable working and living conditions of starvation and physical abuse, revolution is brewing.

The second half of the social theme, devoted to the conditions of migrant workers in California, takes place in a so-called paradise, where fertile land and abundant rain and sun have allowed farmers to grow many different kinds of crops for mass consumption. Here as well, corporations control large tracts of land, a significant part uncultivated. Here again, as in Oklahoma, the owners' sole motive is the greatest possible profit. In Chapter Nineteen, Steinbeck writes that corporate greed has turned landholders into slaveholders, taking advantage of the dispossessed farmers pouring into the state, hiring the cheapest labor possible, providing them with inhumane living conditions, luring thousands with the promise of work when they will only hire several hundred at rock-bottom pay.

In the mad pursuit of profit, food is dumped and destroyed to drive up prices, even with starving children watching. Hoovervilles, named for President Herbert Hoover, sprang up on the edge of towns, where destitute families lived in ragged tents without toilets or running water.

Another result of the owners' greed was the hiring of lawmen by the corporations. The aim of these men was not to uphold the law but to harass and terrorize the migrants, who were hated and feared by the general populace.

Chapter Twenty-One enlarges on the migrants' problems and the growing empires of the growers, who, to collect even more profit, bought canneries, keeping the cost of fruit down and the cost of canned goods up. As in Oklahoma, so it was in California: the smaller farmers were put out of business as a result of this development.

In Chapter Twenty-Five, Steinbeck writes of the deadly inhumane policies that are in evidence in the spring when fruit ripens, namely, the starvation wages paid to migrant pickers who have no choice if they need to work, and the wholesale dumping of food to keep prices up.

After the fruit harvest is over, cotton picking begins. This is the subject of interchapter Chapter Twenty-Seven. Abuses continue as the cotton is picked, but this opportunity for work, hard and ill-paid as it is, will soon disappear with the gradual introduction of the picking machine in the 1930s.

When cotton picking ends, the real terror begins in the winter in California, not so much because of the cold, but as Steinbeck reports in Chapter Twenty-Nine, because of the endless flooding rains and the realization that there will be no work at all for three months. At no time was life harder, the necessity of thievery greater, the deaths by hunger more numerous, and the prospect of revolution in America more imminent.

There is an appeal in the novel for immediate relief for the migrants: more humane camps like the one at Weedpatch, stopping the practice of destroying food that could feed hungry people, and putting an end to police harassment. These atrocities are, however, only symptoms of a dire national disease. The poor and the dispossessed were going to learn that power came in unionizing—power that could be turned against the system and the people who profited from abusing those who had lost everything. For this reason, the people in power, particularly the large ranch owners, regarded *The Grapes of Wrath* as a blatant piece of propaganda and Steinbeck as one of the most dangerous men in America.

BIBLICAL ALLUSIONS AND THE UNIVERSALITY OF *THE GRAPES OF WRATH*

Steinbeck locates his social protest within a narrative of suffering and sacrifice, made universal with biblical allusions. The novel has traditionally (though not universally) been seen as a human struggle against death and despair, over which hope and renewal ultimately triumph. It is generally agreed that the major characters, especially Casy, Tom, Uncle John, Al, and Rose of Sharon, change and grow, although there is disagreement about how these changes are to be interpreted. The most significant character change is from self-concern to union—oneness—of something much larger than self or family. Critic Stephen Railton defines social and personal changes in religious terms, as a series of "conversions."

In looking at allusions to help reach the more philosophical meaning of the novel, we find several unmistakable and direct biblical references that lead the reader to explore further parallels. The first reference, and a pervasive one, is found in the character of Jim Casy, the ex-preacher who, from his entrance into the story until the end of his life, casts his unorthodox religious speculations in biblical terms. When the reader is first introduced to him, he is singing "Jesus is my Savior now," set to the music of a popular song (24). We immediately learn, however, that although he has been a charismatic preacher, he is now struggling with some unorthodox ideas. His former mixing of sex and religion disqualified him for his calling, yet he cannot accept that sex is from the devil, as he has been taught. He also tells Tom that he has decided that sin and virtue do not exist; that he does not love Jesus—he loves people; and that the Holy Spirit is really the love of other people.

Later he claims that he has no God and that he does not believe in prayer.

In Casy's second monologue in the novel, when he is forced to deliver a prayer before a meal in the Joad house, he is identified with Jesus, though he protests that he is not like Jesus: "I ain't sayin' I'm like Jesus. . . . But I got tired like Him, an' I got mixed up like Him, an' I went into the wilderness like Him" (105). He goes on to explain what he learned in the desert: that holiness is people working together. From these references, the reader can deduce other parallels between Jesus Christ and Jim Casy (that their initials are identical has not gone unnoticed by critics). For one thing, Casy gathers disciples around him whom he teaches and leads. The first of these is Tom Joad, who will eventually decide to follow in Casy's footsteps, devoting himself to helping all migrant workers. At the Hooper Ranch, we see that Casy's band of disciples has broadened into a small group of strikers.

As in the biblical story of Jesus, twice Casy sacrifices himself for others. Once he takes all the blame for an assault on a crooked labor contractor in the first Hooverville they stay at, and goes to jail to prevent law-enforcement officers from arresting other migrants. And in the act that costs him his life—organizing a strike of peach pickers—he stands up to the vigilantes who come after him, echoing Jesus' words, "They know not what they do" (Luke 23:34). Just before he is killed, Casy says, "You fellas don' know what you're doin'. You're helping to starve kids. . . . You don' know what you're a doin' " (495).

Another suggestion of the ex-preacher's identification with Jesus Christ can be found in Matthew 28:20, when Jesus tells his disciples, "Lo, I am with you alway[s]." A similar idea is expressed by Casy to Tom just after he first meets him: "Yeah, I'm goin' with you. An' when your folks start out on the road I'm goin' with them. An' where folks are on the road, I'm gonna be with them" (73). Later, after many trying experiences, Tom Joad, who had been teased in prison with the name "Jesus Meek" (33), echoes the same sentiment as Casy's disciple:

> Then I'll be all aroun' in the dark. I'll be ever'where—wherever you look. Wherever they's a fight so hungry people can eat, I'll be there. Wherever they's cop beatin' up a guy, I'll be there. If Casy knowed, why, I'll be in the way guys yell when they're mad an'—I'll be in

the way kids laugh when they're hungry an' know supper's ready. An' when our folks et the stuff they raise an' live in the houses they build—why, I'll be there. (537)

These allusions emphasize the benevolence and love of the sainted Casy's philosophy, the oneness he feels with the rest of humanity, which he has managed to convey to Tom.

There are other unmistakable biblical references. Two of the Joad children, for example, have names peculiar to scripture: Rose of Sharon and Noah. The biblical source for Rose of Sharon is Song of Solomon, a collection of erotic love songs, replete with pictures of a lush countryside in spring where ripe, tropical fruits, including grapes, abound. Perhaps coincidentally, the place called Sharon is an area in the Holy Land south of Carmel, and the lush agricultural region where the Joads pick fruit is in an area south of Carmel, California. By the close of the novel, Rose of Sharon has become a central character. As the rains begin to diminish, springtime, like that described in Song of Solomon, is just around the corner, and Rose of Sharon becomes part of the life affirming and hope of renewal. If she cannot save her baby, at least she can save another human being, who, ironically, has sacrificed himself for his son by refusing food so that his boy can eat.

There is another direct, but ironical, biblical reference in the son named Noah. In Genesis one finds the story of Noah, a righteous man who was instructed by God to build a great boat, or ark, to escape a mighty flood that would destroy the world as punishment for mankind's wickedness. After drifting for forty days and nights in the ark, Noah and his family see a herald of hope in the form of a dove, find that the boat has come to rest on dry land, and live to see the renewal of the earth. In *The Grapes of Wrath*, this Noah also escapes the flood, but by deserting rather than saving the family. The interpretation here, in keeping with the theme of the novel, may be that the most holy actions, as Casy calls them, are not to isolate and save only one's self and one's family as Noah does, but to embrace and help the rest of humankind as well. Unlike the biblical Noah's successful venture of building an ark to survive the flood, Pa Joad's plan to build a dam against the flood ends in disaster as a tree bashes it in and the water washes it away.

Other religious and biblical references in the novel are numerous and ironical. Throughout, for example, the family encounters people who make known their adherence to scripture. Invariably, these are people the Joads want to avoid.

In searching for meaning in *The Grapes of Wrath*, the pervasiveness of religious references leads us to explore further, less-apparent biblical parallels. One of the most important is the three-part journey itself that critics have compared to that of the Israelites, who fled slavery in Egypt, endured adversities in their journey toward Canaan, and eventually reached the Promised Land, where they initially encountered hostilities. Like the Israelites, who were slaves to Pharoah in Egypt, the Joads and other migrants have become virtual slaves to corporate landowners and banks in Oklahoma. Also, like their Egyptian counterparts, they have seen plagues and starvation. In Chapter 8 of Exodus, one reads of the plagues of frogs, dust, lice, and flies. In 1930s Oklahoma, the people suffer from drought and dust storms.

The Israelites flee Egypt and travel toward the Promised Land in a journey called an exodus. The Joads flee to California toward what they perceive as a land that advertisements have promised as an Eden for families who need work. Like the Israelites, the migrants die along the way and suffer from hunger and lack of water.

As Moses, the leader of the Israelites, brought the Ten Commandments down to the people traveling to Canaan, so Ma Joad lays down the law—the law that the family will stay together. She does this on their journey when family members suggest that they split up temporarily to get the car fixed. Ma angrily brandishes a jack handle, like Moses angrily breaking his tablets of stone.

The Grapes of Wrath contains another unmistakable allusion to Moses near the end. In Exodus, Chapter 2, the story is told of Moses' mother, an Israelite and a slave, placing her newborn son in a cradle and setting it in the water among weeds to save him from being killed in accordance with Pharoah's directive to kill all male children of the Israelites. Moses is plucked from the water by Pharaoh's daughter. "[S]he took for him an ark . . . and put the child therein; and she laid it in the flags by the river's brink" (Exodus 2:3). Moses, of course, grows up to be a bearer of truth. In a perverse twist to this story, Uncle John places, not a live child, but a dead one, in the current of the flood, hoping that it will be carried into the town as a message about the migrant workers' plight: "And then he leaned over and set the box in a stream. . . .

He said fiercely, 'Go down an' tell 'em. . . . Go on down and lay in the street. Maybe they'll know then' " (571, 572).

One of the less-obvious echoes of scripture that Steinbeck uses is in the last name of his major characters. Joad has the sound of the grand sufferer from the Old Testament—Job, pronounced as if it rhymes with robe. Job lost not only all his material possessions, but his children and his health. Like Job, the Joads are visited with unbearable adversities—the loss of their farm and home, the death of Grampa and Granma, the desertion of Noah and Connie, the sickness of Winfield, the necessary separation from Tom, the death of Rose of Sharon's baby, the failure to find work, the constant hunger, the flood. As with Job, just as they believe they have suffered beyond endurance, another trial comes along to test them.

In the novel's conclusion the reader finds another veiled biblical allusion. This time it is the New Testament story of the birth of Jesus. According to tradition, Joseph and Mary, the parents of Jesus, are unable to find a room in an inn after their long journey to Bethlehem, but are allowed to stay in a stable, where Mary gives birth to Jesus. In comparison, the Joads find shelter in a barn after a difficult journey. The novel ends with Rose of Sharon, having given birth to a dead child only hours before, nursing a starving man in place of her baby. Luke 2:19 reads: "But Mary kept all these things and pondered them in her heart." The parallel lines about Rose of Sharon are the last lines of the novel: "She looked up and across the barn, and her lips came together and smiled mysteriously" (581). As with all such parallels to the Bible in the novel, the effect is to give the lowly Joads biblical dignity and meaning. In the case of this scene, we see what many critics interpret as the hope and renewal that comes after great suffering.

The Joads and those like them are biblical in stature, not only because of their suffering, but because of their sacrifices. As we have seen, Casy is the classic example in the novel. But there are other instances, both large and small, in which the dispossessed give up something of themselves to help others. At the end, Tom, learning from Casy, decides to put his life at risk to help other workers resist mistreatment. Sairy Wilson gives up her sickbed to Grampa, a total stranger, who is dying after a stroke. Her husband, Mr. Wilson, gives up an opportunity to travel with a supportive family so that he and his wife will not slow them down. Pa gives up some of the precious little money he has to help Mr. Wilson. Even though it will mean less money for them, men often share news of work with others, women share their tiny store of food with strangers, and make sacrifices to help the sick.

CONVERSIONS

The conversions that occur in the course of the novel or those that will inevitably occur, are personal and social. Both are conversions to sympathetic human union. On the social level, workers inspired by men like Casy are united to protest the living and working conditions of agricultural workers in California. It is, the narrator says, the beginning of a conversion from "I" to "we" (194). When a farmer who has been stripped of his land and must scramble for labor in a hostile environment begins to talk about what they did to "us," instead of what they did to "me," he and those like him become empowered.

On a personal level, individuals convert from selfish and clannish loyalties to the considerations of a larger community. The Joads have never been stingy especially when they insist that Casy and the Wilsons come along with them, but from Ma Joad's powerful protectiveness of her family, she gradually converts to what seems to be the notion that the whole group of migrant workers are part of a larger family: "Use' ta be the fambly was fust. It ain't so now. It's anybody. Worse off we get, the more we got to do" (569). Casy converts from a preoccupation with his own sinfulness and his own spiritual journey in the wilderness, to a devotion to action on behalf of others. Uncle John, who dwells excessively on his own sin and guilt at contributing to the death of his wife and infant, converts to thinking about the suffering of others as he sends the baby's body forth as a message. Al, who is self-obsessed with "tom-catting," converts to a husband to be, making a strong commitment to his bride and her family. Tom converts to take on a saintly mission to labor in the fields for the poor. And Rose of Sharon, who had lashed out at other family members for endangering her and her baby and complaining that she did not have enough milk, takes on a certain authority, caring for a person she has just seen for the first time as if he were her child.

IRONY

The story of so-called simple people and the socioeconomics of the larger world of the 1930s that determines their lives is given a complex dimension with the use of multiple, often cruel, ironies that denote a world turned upside down. Some of the chief illustrations are set out below.

In Oklahoma, those who love the land and farm it with their own hands are thrown off the land, and those who may have never even seen the land, much less farmed it, own it. Another irony is that improvements in technology—the diesel tractor, for instance—are a detriment to human progress, when farmers are put out of work. The man who improves his own life and takes better care of his family by taking a job driving a tractor, helps destroy life for other farmers and their families. To save Grampa, the Joads take him on a journey that kills him. Ma Joad, who more than anything wants to keep the family together, sees both grandparents die and will, before the novel's end, be separated from three of her six children.

It is ironic that the Joads travel toward what they think is paradise and instead find hell. In California, the more that the rich terrorize the poor to protect their lucrative holdings, the more apt the poor are to organize to challenge the power of the rich. Those who are supposed to enforce the law and protect the innocent are actually outlaws who harm the innocent. In a state like California, where many families are desperate for land to farm, land lies uncultivated. The various communities castigate the migrants for not being able to take care of themselves, but leave no way for the migrants to become self-sufficient. For one thing, they pay families who agree to work, too little. In this land where everything grows, people are starving and food is disposed of in such a way that the hungry cannot have it. It is ironic that horses and cars are treated better than humans.

There are further ironies as the novel ends: the less a family has, the more it is prepared to share; the rain that usually renews the earth actually brings death; and the ex-convict who has murdered two people gives promise of becoming a saint.

CRITICAL CONTROVERSIES

At least three critical controversies have emerged over the years about interpreting *The Grapes of Wrath*. These include disagreements about the social intent of the novel, about the religious point of view that emerges, and about whether the novel is one of hope or of pessimism. Critics have been of two minds about the social intent of the novel, specifically about whether Steinbeck intended to spur agricultural workers to revolt or whether he was simply sounding a warning to government and growers of what could happen if they failed to act.

Oklahoma landowners and California growers and Chamber of Commerce members in the 1940s had no doubt that John Steinbeck's message was clear: the novel encouraged migrant workers to mount a revolution and overturn the whole capitalistic system. To this end, they argued, Steinbeck exaggerated the awful lot of agricultural workers and their treatment at the hands of those in control. Furthermore, in the journalistic interchapters, workers are told about the strength they will find in numbers, and in the novel itself, the most sympathetic characters learn that there is a need to organize and resist. The Reds and Bolsheviks mentioned occasionally in the novel seem to be on the side of good rather than evil.

Taking a different position, others have argued that Steinbeck's purpose was not to encourage workers to revolt, and that he was making a public effort to put distance between himself and Communism. The language of the novel as well as Steinbeck's own refusal to make political statements in support of any political persuasion, have led many readers to argue that his purpose was instead to sound a warning to the owners and the government: to tell them that they must do something to help the migrant worker if they wanted to avoid rebellion, which, if it occurred, would be entirely predicable and justified (194).

Another disagreement in interpretation of the novel is about the philosophical vision of the world that lies behind it. Some of the earliest critics found the novel to be in the tradition of Ralph Waldo Emerson, America's great transcendental philosopher. Emerson believed that human beings are trapped in the everyday life of human society and civilization, but long to know a truth that is only available in the realm of spirit. One aspect of that truth is a feeling of oneness with the universe. It is usually perceived as the ego diminishes and the individual reaches something like a glimpse of spirit through meditation or religious experience. In such moments, one realizes the need to concentrate on the reformation of the self rather than the reformation of society. Meaningful and lasting social improvements can only flow from self-reformation. In transcendentalism, there is little stress on right and wrong; instead, divisions run along the lines of spirit as opposed to society and the world changed by man. The emphasis is always on the individual spirit rather than society.

The argument for the Emersonianism of the novel comes primarily from interpretations of Casy's character and statements made by Ma and Tom about the oneness of the people. Like the Emersonians, Casy casts off conventional religion. He has no God in the accepted sense (281), nor does he seem to believe in prayer, though he consents to offer prayers over their last meal in Oklahoma, at the graveside of Grampa, and at the bedside of the dying Sairie. Through a solitary wilderness experience similar not only to that experienced by Jesus, but one very transcendental in nature, he has arrived at some truths that guide his actions. Both he and Jim Rawley, the government camp manager, have come to the conclusion that there is no right or wrong—a very transcendental idea and one that stresses the union with nature over customary beliefs in right and wrong. Instead, Casy believes that " 'All that lives is holy' " (184). Reflecting the idea that God flows all through nature, Ma comes to believe that bearing children and dying are two pieces of one thing (270). And Tom, alluding to his conversations with Casy, talks about all people being just one piece of a larger soul (537).

More recent critics, however, argue that the novel rejects transcendentalism and religion in favor of humanism—the belief that the human being is the measure of all things and that the alleviation of pain in this life is man's greatest mission. Casy has obviously exchanged his traditional beliefs for a new kind of humanism: holiness is not something spiritual having to do with a god in the older religious sense; holiness is men working together in a common cause (105). Even Ruthie's childhood prayer thanking God, instead holds an especially pertinent message for the everyday world about the poverty of the times: her devotion, "Now I lay me down to sleep," ends with the nursery rhyme, "When she got there the cupboard was bare" (176). Casy's prayer over the dead Grampa is essentially a few words directed to the living: "But us, we got a job to do, an' they a thousan' ways, an' don' know which one to take" (184). In Casy's last conversation with Tom, Tom says, "Prayer never brought in no side-meat," and Casy concurs, "And Almighty God never raised no wages" (322).

Furthermore, the people devoted to religion—the Jehovites who want to pray over the dying Granma, and Lizbah, the religious fanatic who has to be ordered away from the Joad's tent at Weedpatch—are neither helpful nor admirable. The preacher who baptizes migrants (424, 425) seems to be an exploiter and charlatan, the young people inspired to ask after the emotional camp meeting, "Wisht I knowed what all the sins was, so I could do 'em" (425). In these portraits, as well as in Casy's renunciation of his former calling as preacher, we see a rejection of what is portrayed as the judgmental sin-and-guilt obsession and exploitation found in the church and religious tradition. In its place is Casy's religion of human love and nature.

The cornerstone of Emersonian transcendentalism is that of individuality as opposed to society. But the message of *The Grapes of Wrath* is the opposite—a union of human beings in society who no longer think of I but of we.

Finally, there is a disagreement about whether the novel is one of hope. Many readers have found hope in Tom's conversion to social action, in the symbolic promise of spring, in Al's impending marriage, and in the scene of renewal played out as Rose of Sharon nurses a man dying of starvation. Throughout the novel, an expression of faith emerges that from the depths of suffering, improvement in the human condition will inevitably come forth, that people in desperate straits will gain the incentive in union to make the lives of all better. But others see it as a pessimistic story of the constant battle for survival that will never be anything other than a struggle. At the end, perhaps the most powerful symbol of the novel is not Rose of Sharon's gesture toward the starving man, but her stillborn child. The Joads are homeless, without a car or possessions or food, and they face three months with no possibility of work. They also face a future in which, realistically, they will never be reunited with the other members of their family from whom they have been separated. There are other strong indications (reflected in the lives of other migrants) that their hunger will lead them to commit crimes to feed themselves. We invest hope in Tom, the man who says he will always be there when his people need him, but he is sober about his expectation of emerging from his experience alive: he is determined to follow in Casy's footsteps, but he knows that he has broken parole in Oklahoma. As one critic, James D. Brasch, argues, the instructive biblical parallel is found in Ecclesiastes, which states that there is nothing new under the sun. Human greed will always make people victims to those with power ("*The Grapes of Wrath* and Old Testament Skepticism" 45–56).

Various differences in interpretation of *The Grapes of Wrath* persist, but there is little doubt among serious readers that the novel has multiple psychological and philosophical dimensions that go well beyond the novel's propagandistic attempt to alleviate a social problem.

TOPICS FOR ORAL OR WRITTEN EXPLORATION

1. Write an analytical paper on the symbol of the turtle in *The Grapes of Wrath*.

2. Write an essay on the relationship of one of the Joad children to their mother.

3. The two youngest Joad children are constant presences in the novel. What do they contribute to the story's effect or ultimate meaning?

4. Write an essay on machines in the novel. Do they carry any symbolic weight? Do they have both negative and positive attributes?

5. Write an analysis of Noah Joad in which you attempt to explain why he left the family.

6. Write a paper on the theme of desertion in the novel.

7. Choose one of the ironic situations in the novel to develop into a theme.

8. What purpose does Muley Graves serve in the novel?

9. Have a class debate about whether it would have been better for the Joads to stay behind in Oklahoma or go to California.

10. Consider the critical debate about whether the novel is hopeful or hopeless. Have a classroom discussion about the issue.

11. Jim Casy might be described as developing a new religion. Discuss this idea. Would you call his stance a religion? To answer, you would have to define what you consider a religion.

12. The concept of family is central to the novel. How does the meaning of family change in the course of the novel?

13. The interpretation of nature is also central to the novel. How does Steinbeck present nature? Is nature essentially good? Essentially destructive? Consider the discussions of the land and the weather. Look at the description of the dust storms and the flooding rains.

14. Critic Peter Lisca argues that the prose style of some of the interchapters can be arranged to make free verse poems. Try making a poem from one or two of Steinbeck's paragraphs by just rearranging the line length of some of the passages.

15. Write a paper on woman as nourisher in the novel.

16. Have a class debate on the extent to which the novel shows people to be either helpless or powerful in determining the course of their own lives.

17. Using what you know about the circumstances and the personalities

presented in the novel, write an additional chapter showing what happens to some of the characters.

18. Have a debate about the way in which Steinbeck ends the novel. Does the inconclusiveness weaken the fiction in your view, or does it serve the author's purpose better than a conclusive ending might have?

SUGGESTIONS FOR FURTHER READING

Bloom, Harold, ed. *John Steinbeck's The Grapes of Wrath*. New Haven, CT: Chelsea House Publishers, 1988.

Brasch, James D. "*The Grapes of Wrath* and Old Testament Skepticism," in *John Steinbeck's The Grapes of Wrath*, ed. Harold Bloom. New Haven, CT: Chelsea House Publishers, 1988. 45–56.

Davis, Robert Murray, ed. *Steinbeck: A Collection of Critical Essays*. Englewood Cliffs, NJ: Prentice-Hall, 1972.

Ditsky, John. *Critical Essays on Steinbeck's The Grapes of Wrath*. Boston: G. K. Hall, 1989.

Hayashi, Tetsumaro. *A New Study Guide to Steinbeck's Major Works, with Critical Explications*. Metuchen, NJ: The Scarecrow Press, 1993.

Levant, Howard. *The Novels of John Steinbeck: A Critical Study*. Columbia: University of Missouri Press, 1974.

Lisca, Peter. *The Wide World of John Steinbeck*. New York: Gordian Press, 1981.

McCarthy, Paul. *John Steinbeck*. New York: Frederick Ungar Publishing Co., 1980.

Moore, Harry Thornton. *The Novels of John Steinbeck: A First Critical Study*. Port Washington, NY: Kennikat Press, 1939.

Tedlock, E. W., and C. V. Wicker, eds. *Steinbeck and His Critics, A Record of Twenty-Five Years*. Albuquerque: University of New Mexico Press, 1957.

Wyatt, David, ed. *New Essays on The Grapes of Wrath*. Cambridge: Cambridge University Press, 1990.

2

Money and the Great Depression

The story that John Steinbeck tells in *The Grapes of Wrath* is a personal account of the misery of a single family and the people with whom they associate. But at the foundation of the personal story of the Joads is a larger, colder, impersonal balance sheet. Behind the fictional book is a national account book. And to really understand these human beings and their anguish, which is so artfully told, the reader has to grapple with what has often been described as "the dismal science" of economics. For it is largely this situation on a national scale that has placed the novel's characters in their dilemma.

The Great Depression, which turned the lives of the Joads upside down, left no person in the United States unaffected. Caroline Bird, a scholar who lived through it as well as studied it, wrote that it was the single most traumatic national experience between the Civil War and the dropping of the atomic bomb. Every person who was living in the United States in the 1930s was changed in some way by the economic events that befell the country at that time. Many Americans feel the effects of the Great Depression to this day.

This chapter is intended to set a national stage—in preparation for other chapters on more specific issues—for the events that affected the Joads in particular. More than one criminal investigator has suggested that the way to understand a tragedy is to "follow the money." The same can be said for an understanding of the national tragedy that tormented the Joads. What exactly is an economic depression? What did it have to do with Wall Street? What led up to the stock market crash of 1929? What characterized that decade from an economic standpoint?

What exactly is an economic depression? It has come to apply to any length of time when the value of stocks and businesses decline and remain at very low levels, causing grief to the businessman, to the workers he fires, and to those he hires at starvation wages. With people out of work, many fewer persons are able to buy goods and services, causing businesses to suffer even more. The situation becomes a vicious cycle, or, to switch metaphors, a downhill spiral. Many who saw what was happening in the 1930s thought the situation would better be described as a crash or a crisis or a panic, but the Hoover administration encouraged the use of the word Depression as being less inflammatory, to downplay the gravity of the situation.

The economic depression that lasted throughout the 1930s was not the first depression that the United States had suffered. Various economic situations had damaged businesses and brought on unemployment as early as the nineteenth century. Crises in 1837, 1867, 1873, 1893, 1903, 1907, and 1920 had left the nation scarred. The Great Depression of the 1930s, however, was a time in our history when the economy of the United States as well as other countries reached their lowest depths. The effects of the Depression lasted for about twelve years, and created monumental hardships for vast numbers of people at every economic level. At no other time was there an extended period of such staggering hunger, unemployment, homelessness, and general business failure.

THE STOCK MARKET

The stock market, as remote as it seems from the Joad family, was absolutely central to the situation in which they found themselves. The stock market is a place where businesses that need money to operate sell shares of their business to individuals or groups who want to own a piece of the firm. The person who acts as an agent between the buyer and seller of stocks is the stockbroker. Naturally, since the investor owns a part of the business when he buys a share, he expects to take part in the profits of the business. As a particular business does well, the cost of its shares go up. If the business does not do well, the value of its shares goes down. Depending on how well the business does and when you buy or sell your shares, you either make or lose money. Sometimes the value of a share will go up or down—not from an increase or decrease in its business, but from a calculation that a situation is likely to affect it. So, for example, if you invest in a thriving business that makes mousetraps, a rumor that some other company has invented a much better, cheaper, more revolutionary mousetrap, may cause the stock you own to go down, even though at present your company is making a handsome profit. As well, the stock of any drug company that discovers a cure for cancer will shoot upward in value.

CAUSES OF THE ECONOMIC CRASH

In the 1920s, the stock market on Wall Street in New York City held out the dream of making lots of money in investments because business everywhere was booming. Eventually there were all different kinds of investors. There were men who made millions by buying stocks when they were low and selling them when they went up. And then there were whole businesses and banks that made money playing the stock market. But people who were not necessarily wealthy also got in on what was considered a glorious game of buying and selling stocks.

A number of situations combined to prepare the way for disaster. One danger sign was the great gap between the rich and the poor, even in those good times. It is true that business was booming in cities and towns, but wages paid to workers were low. To illustrate, per person income rose by only 9 percent in this so-called carefree decade, but for those in the top 1 percent, it rose by 75 percent. Wages for laborers increased by only 8 percent in the 1920s, but from 1923 to 1929, corporate profits rose by 62 percent and dividends by 65 percent. To look at it another way, most of the wealth of the country lay in the hands of about 1 percent of the population. In 1929, a year when the average income for an American was $750 a year, Henry Ford had a personal income of 14 million dollars. Farming communities were already in an economic slump, and were not sharing in the profits of the industrialized areas. So naturally while the supply of goods was healthy, the demand was very low—most people just did not have the money to buy all the goods and services that industry was producing. To make matters even worse, while wages failed to rise with increasing productivity, neither did prices go down. Still, investors were convinced that more products would be produced and that profits would rise.

One major factor contributing to the boom of the 1920s and the subsequent crash is linked with discussions in *The Grapes of Wrath*: the improvement in mechanization and electrification. Electricity had begun running machines that had once run on manual power, and a group of machines now running on electricity could make many times the number of products at a far faster rate than one person running one machine with his or her foot on a pedal. The price that human workers paid for mechanization is alluded to in *The Grapes of Wrath* when the diesel tractors drive the farmers off the land and machines for picking cotton take away their jobs. This ended up destabilizing the financial base of the country in that mechanization and electrification speeded up production in the factories, took away many jobs, and kept wages low. The situation widened the gap between production and demand. In the final analysis, there were simply not enough people with sufficient income to buy all the products that businesses were producing.

Most of the nation's production was concentrated in industries that produced what were then considered luxuries, but which only a small percentage of the population could afford. First, the producers of automobiles and materials essential to automobile manufacturing (oil, gas, and metal, for instance) were experiencing boom times. Second, was the production of radios. After a series of ups and downs, stock in Radio Corporation of America, which sold for 26⅝ per share on October 1, 1924, soared to 420 per share in December 1928. In addition, the country was producing refrigerators and stoves, packaged cigarettes, cosmetics, and motion pictures.

The failure to manage loans and credit was another key cause of the country's economic crash. Banks were lending vast amounts of money to customers so that they could invest in the stock market, often with little or no collateral. Ordinarily, you could borrow ten thousand dollars by putting up your ten-thousand-dollar house as security. Then, if for some reason you could not pay off your loan, the bank could seize your house in place of payment. Also, since banks were very loosely regulated, they could use the savings deposits of their customers to play the stock market without the knowledge or consent of their clients. And some banks did just that. Each time the Federal Reserve Board eased restrictions on lending, speculation in the stock market soared.

In 1928, businessman Herbert Hoover was nominated for president by the Republican Party, and the country's confidence that this business friendly industrialist would win the election brought about another surge of wild borrowing and buying on margin. The first day of trading after the election was one of the busiest up to that time.

What hastened the crash in 1929 was a series of foolhardy and unscrupulous practices in addition to fraud. The most harmful practice was buying shares of stock on margin. So, your broker advises you that a certain stock in a jellybean company is dynamite and will be skyrocketing soon, but you do not want to write a check for the full amount you want to buy. After all, you could just put some money into a down payment for ten shares of jellybean stock. Next week, when the price has quadrupled and you receive the dividends on all the stock you still have not paid for, you can pay for the stock at the earlier, lower price in full and still have a handsome profit. But what if the price went down? You would still owe the balance of what you had bought on margin, but in addition, you would have some worthless stock on your hands.

Rarely did anyone call attention to the fact that Wall Street often inflated the value of the stocks, that the dollar was becoming almost worthless, and that the entire economy was tied to a stock market and banks whose assets were not backed up with cold cash. Coupled with these conditions were the development of monopolies, special privileges, and exploitation.

Various tariff bills were proposed that raised the price on foreign goods in order to protect the profits of United States industry. Unfortunately, while such bills were a modicum of help to industry, they actually hurt the American farmer by favoring industry over agriculture. The most far-reaching of the tariff bills, the Hawley-Smoot Tariff Act of 1930, was highly controversial. Still, as passage seemed assured, investors rushed to buy stocks that seemed certain to escalate in value.

Various favorable conditions for the first six months in 1929 brought the stock market to its highest level on September 3. But sporadic declines occurred throughout the month, influenced in part by the disturbing news that the English stock market was on the verge of collapse.

In October 1929, stocks continued to seesaw, going up and down erratically. A few economists began to ask for caution as well as investigations into certain Wall Street practices. They observed that stocks were still easy to buy but difficult to sell. But even after key utility stocks began to fail, investors in general remained assured that the boom would continue.

By mid-October, however, investors began to see falling prices. There was little buying and much selling. Adding to the panic was the decision by key U.S. senators, influenced by the agricultural vote, to pull out of their support for the magical tariff bill. When it became evident that the bill would fail, the rush to sell stocks accelerated. On October 24, 1929, 13 million shares of stock were sold. On Tuesday, October 29, 16 million shares of stock were sold. Pandemonium broke out on the floor of the exchange and boardrooms and brokerage offices were, in their hushed horror, like scenes of recent homicides. On this, Black Tuesday, it became evident to stockbrokers and taxicab drivers alike that without a shadow of a doubt the financial system of the country had totally collapsed. In the panic that ensued, investors suffered heart attacks, strokes, and nervous collapse. Suicides were not uncommon. It would be considered bitterly ironic by many that the very, very rich—the multimillionaires—suffered little, comparatively, at least not right away.

In the following comparisons, it is possible to get an idea of just how sharply and how far stocks fell in the most respectable companies in America:

	October 30, 1929	1931
Anaconda Copper	95	12⅝
American Telephone and Telegraph	240	121⅛
Chrysler	35	11¾
Du Pont	129	53¾
General Motors	49¾	22⅛
Montgomery Ward	66	8⅝
N.Y. Central	199½	49⅝

	October 30, 1929	1931
Standard Oil, NJ	65⅝	28¼
Standard Oil, CA	63⅞	28⅛
Sears Roebuck	105	31
U.S. Steel	185	62¼
Western Union	202	83⅛

Following the collapse of the stock market, banks began to fail. Banks had loaned billions of dollars to brokers and other investors who wanted to play the stock market. Much of this money was actually in the form of certificates keyed to stock values. So when stocks plummeted, many banks found themselves holding little but worthless paper. Many banks had speculated with the savings of their depositors, and as rumors of collapse escalated, customers rushed to the banks in droves to withdraw their savings, many of them finding the banks' doors closed and their savings gone. By 1931, many small-town banks did not have enough cash on hand to give businesses the necessary cash for operating expenses. And by 1933, 300 communities were using substitutes for paper money and bartering for food, fees, and services. Many people, believing that currency would soon be worthless, demanded to be paid in gold by the banks. A total of 1,352 banks failed in 1930 and 2,294 failed in 1931. And remember that, at that time, the deposits of investors were not insured, so many people who had saved conservatively lost everything. On December 2, 1929, the National City Bank of New York City, with typical bravado, declared that there were no great failures nor would there be *any* failures, yet in the first nine months of 1929, customers in U.S. banks lost a total of $332,425,638; in 1930, a total of $473,043,174; and in 1931, $531,776,004. The plummeting confidence in the U.S. economy was apparent when Americans took $250 million in gold out of the country in Herbert Hoover's last week in office.

THE RESULTS OF THE CRASH

What did all this high finance have to do with ordinary working people? As the value of a certain stock fell and investors lost confidence in American companies, businesses no longer had the money to operate. A total of 26,355 large corporations failed in

1930 and 28,285 failed in 1931. Throughout the decade of the 1930s that we call the era of the Great Depression, over 90,000 large businesses closed down. Three years after the crash, production in factories had dropped to 50 percent of what it had reached in the 1920s. This, of course, meant that factory workers lost their livelihoods. About one-fourth of the labor force lost its jobs. Thirty-seven percent of the nonagricultural workforce was unemployed. Unemployment in the United States in the 1930s reached 15 million. Many of those who were listed as still employed were working only part-time. It has been estimated that an average of 5,000 people showed up for every 100 job openings.

Those lucky few who managed to find jobs also found that wages had dropped to sub-subsistence pay, even lower than it had been during the 1920s. Seamstresses working sixteen hours a day received ten dollars per week. Some Massachusetts factories advertised that they would pay workers four or five dollars a week. A worst case scenario, similar to that experienced by the Joads, found that a family of six, all working long hours in a Connecticut factory, made a total of five dollars a week. Men were making five cents an hour in sawmills, women seventy-five cents a week in sweatshops.

Working conditions were as notoriously inhumane in the factories as they were in the fields where the Joads worked. As the government declared that working hours had to be regulated so that men and women would not be required to work killingly long shifts, factories instituted what came to be known as the speedup or stretch-out. Since workers could not be forced to work long hours, they were forced to work twice as fast. But as bad as working conditions and wages were, complaints were minimal because workers were terrified of losing their income.

Certain urban areas like car-dependent Detroit were brutally hit because the hard fact was that no one had the money to buy cars. Some 12,000 families in Detroit simply had to hit the road. The city itself was broke, and closed many schools and fired many vital city workers like firemen and policemen.

At this time there were no safety nets like unemployment insurance to keep food on the table. There was no social security system, no welfare, no medicare. And many who had saved money in the banks found that they had no savings left. Nor did the banks have any money to lend.

To make matters worse, those who had lost jobs, income, businesses, savings, or investments could no longer meet the payments on mortgages that the banks held on their homes, businesses, or land. Mortgages were foreclosed and property seized. Evictions were commonplace, the belongings of families hauled out of their houses and onto the streets.

Dispossession resulted in massive displacement. Huge, unhealthy, shoddy camps, like the one described in *The Grapes of Wrath*, grew up on the edges of cities and small towns. They were named Hoovervilles for the president who was blamed for the crash and the onset of the Great Depression. Hobo jungles multiplied. People lived in flophouses, slept on park benches, in doorways, in automobiles, in houses made of cardboard, fabric, or old sewer pipes. In these miserable shelters, men and women slept under what they called "Hoover blankets"—old newspapers. An empty trouser pocket, turned inside out, was called a "Hoover flag," and in the Southwest, where millions of jackrabbits descended looking for food, a jackrabbit was called a "Hoover hog." Missions that had once given shelter primarily to the victims of alcohol were now overflowing with the victims of economic collapse.

Families, like the Joads, took to the road, always hoping that a different place would have work for them. A serious problem, stressed in Steinbeck's novel, was that families were torn apart during the Depression. Many men who were unable to support their families deserted them and took to the roads or the rails. Young teenagers of both sexes were forced to leave home when their parents could no longer support them. Statistics show that in a single year, 693,000 people were thrown off boxcars.

Despite protests to the contrary on the part of big business and government, starvation and malnutrition were also commonplace throughout the countryside—in the very fields where food was grown, as one sees in *The Grapes of Wrath*—as well as in small towns and in big cities. There were no federal relief programs, so that any food families received was given to them by local agencies and private charities like the Salvation Army. The New York City Welfare Council reported that 139 people, most of them children, died of starvation or malnutrition in that city in 1933. It was commonplace to see men on the streets and children in schools passing out from hunger. Hospitals complained that they were having to treat so many cases of severe malnutrition that they had little time or space to care for other ailments. Many families lived on one loaf of stale bread a day (at a cost of five cents), occasionally supplemented by dried beans. The few private relief agencies that operated were feeding individuals at a cost of four to six cents a day.

It is not surprising that suicides rose dramatically in this decade. There is a persistent legend that many stockbrokers and investors leaped out of skyscrapers on Black Tuesday. While some did die that way, what swelled the number of suicides were not millionaires who had lost their fortunes, but ordinary people who were unable to cope with daily poverty. In 1931 alone, 20,000 people took their own lives, a far greater percentage of the population than at any other time in the nation's history.

Just imagine yourself with a family in the 1930s. Perhaps you had had a white-collar job in industry in the late 1920s. Perhaps you had been carefully saving a little money every week for emergencies and your retirement. Then along comes the crash. Business in the company you work for falls off. Following this, the company has to economize. People begin losing full-time jobs and are put on half-time. You never know when the ax will fall. Finally, after various operations in the company are shut down, you are fired. There is no welfare or social security to fall back on. You are thankful that you have put a little aside in a savings account until you can find another job. But when you go to the bank to make a withdrawal, you find a long line of people waiting outside—the rumors that the bank has failed are true. Banks are not federally regulated or insured; your bank has simply gone broke and your savings have gone down the drain. Your attempts to find a desk job in other companies are futile because all of them are laying off workers. You decide to lower your expectations, but every time you show up for an opening, there are hundreds of people there applying for the same job. You look for part-time work, and are perhaps able to work at menial labor for a few hours a week at starvation wages. Meanwhile, the rent has to be paid and the family has to be fed. The time will come when you will not be able to pay the rent and you and your family will be out in the street. Perhaps the car is paid for. You can live in the car. What will you eat? After weeks of feeding the family on the cheapest food available, usually beans, you approach relief centers run by charities.

But their funds also run out long before you have a job. This was the nightmare that many families faced.

The Depression had another effect on the entire structure of society in the United States that will be explored at greater length in Chapter Six, that is, the open polarization of classes based on income, the widespread division between the two hostile camps of labor and capital, and worker and owner.

Further discussion of the crash and the Great Depression begins with excerpts from *Ten Years of Wall Street (1932)*, reminiscences of Barnie F. Winkelman, "a Wall Street man," who began his work as an explanation of the workings of the stock market but had to include the crash of 1929. Several firsthand accounts of the effects of the Great Depression follow: Louise V. Armstrong's account of bank closings; reporters' observations of the scene in the early 1930s, and letters that ordinary workers wrote to President Franklin D. Roosevelt, First Lady Eleanor Roosevelt, and Secretary of Labor Frances Perkins. A 1931 satire of big business during the Boom and Crash that ends the chapter is rendered more bitter after having read the testimony of people who went through such hardship throughout the 1930s.

RICH VERSUS POOR: WALL STREET'S ACTIONS

As has been suggested, the operations of business and Wall Street in the 1920s had a direct effect on people like the Joads, whose lives were so remote in every way from the brokers and speculators who had "made a killing" on Wall Street only to see the market crash in 1929. With the collapse of the economy, people like the Joads who, admittedly, had always been poor, found their own meager possessions and way of life usurped by the big businesses that now gobbled up smaller ones that had failed. Like so many others, the Joads found that in this economic situation, they were expendable. Barnie F. Winkelman, a Philadelphia lawyer, offers a valuable perspective of the so-called fat economic years in the 1920s and the crash of the stock market in 1929. He writes in 1932, shortly after the crash occurred, as an insider with intimate knowledge of the operations of Wall Street. The details of Wall Street in those years are fresh in his mind, but, of course, he has neither predicted how deep the Depression will get, nor how long it will last.

Winkelman knows the strategies—many of which were illegal—used by brokers to entice customers into shaky investments. The drive behind rampant speculation in the stock market is greed, pure and simple. And he knows the psychology behind the actions of far too many inexperienced speculators. He compares them to those who are addicted to betting on horses and lotteries. And, as a lawyer who has brought suit against brokers on behalf of clients who feel cheated, he knows the futility of securing any legal and economic satisfaction for the losers in the game of speculation.

Even this early in the depression, however, Winkelman, as a student of economics and the law, is sufficiently perceptive to realize that the crash has deeply affected people in all walks of life and that the fundamental reason for the economy's collapse was rampant, uncontrolled capitalism that created a widening chasm between the very rich and the very poor. Even now, Winkelman realizes that this economic situation in the United States, greatly worsened by actions in the 1920s when only the needs of the very rich were attended to, has brought the country to the very edge of revolution.

FROM BARNIE F. WINKELMAN, *TEN YEARS OF WALL STREET*
(Philadelphia: The John C. Winston Company, 1932)

. . . Long study of investments and of the needs of clients, many of whom
have suffered heavy losses, has strengthened the conviction that the law
offers little assistance in the majority of cases. An effective remedy must
precede actual financial loss. Because operative surgery is only a heroic
and final recourse, modern medicine emphasizes preventive measures.
So the real function of the lawyer who deals with investment problems
is that of investment counselor *ab initio* [in the beginning] rather than
as legal consoler after the event. Instances of financial tragedy come to
light daily. A young widow to whom over fifty thousand dollars of insurance money was paid on the death of her husband, found herself almost
destitute because of the investment of these moneys in realty bonds. In
another case an estate invested in a varied assortment of foreign and
domestic bonds, had become practically worthless. Further instances are
marked by curtailment of income because of investment in common
stocks. Another class of cases centers about the collapse of brokerage
firms and the purchase of much advertised but doubtful issues. Losses
due to overtrading, to marginal transactions, and to sheer fraud stand in
another category. But in practically all these cases, resort to legal action
is futile. Most of the losses incurred are irreparable. Even where suit can
be brought against substantial interests, the difficulty and cost of assem-
bling witnesses, of proving conspiracy, of establishing fraud or knowledge of fraud, are well-nigh insurmountable. (pp. 3–4)

• • •

During the great rise it was the continued day-after-day increase in the
prices of securities that finally galvanized the public into speculative action. Not the sudden spectacular up-rush of prices, but the steady growth
of values that after several years seemed endless, caused millions to buy
stocks. So too it was not the dramatic crash of 1929 that broke the hearts
of the nation's investors; not the collapse of banks and brokerage firms,
not the avalanche of shares in mid-1930. It was the relentless stream of
liquidation later in that year, the constant dripping of securities in 1931
and 1932; the melting of values; the seemingly infinite decline, the vision
of a deluge of stocks; of cheerless days without end, that dispelled even
the rainbow of hope and evoked the twin genii of doubt and despair. . . .
One simple truth emerges from the welter of facts, figures, and move-
ments. Twenty years ago, the complete interdependence of nation upon
nation was first given due recognition. Our experience in the past three
years makes clear the integral character of our *national* prosperity, and

that injury to one group or section brings a repercussion throughout the entire community. Few of the industrial leaders who saw the crash of investment values in 1929 realized that the losses of investors and speculators would find their way directly into their own corporate balance sheets in lessened business, curtailment of operations, and grave credit failures. The wheel of economic events has come to full circle; not a vicious circle, but a very salutary chain of inevitabilities, the realization of which will do much to hasten a constructive program. . . .

The inciting cause of a public buying movement is the urge for quick profits. A substantial gain in the remote future offers neither temptation nor attraction to the average man. The number who have excess funds for long-term investments is comparatively small, and most of the moneys of this limited group is restricted by law, custom, or tradition. Even the most alluring of common stocks attract a small number of seasoned investors in comparison with the great mass of occasional traders. Upon the latter the advice given by brokerage firms on the long-term possibilities of special stocks is entirely lost. The speculator who desires action because he is not open to long-term or even short-term commitments predominates especially in the later stages of a bull market. With this large but scattered group, stocks share interest with the race track, lotteries, and roulette. The lure is the prospect of a quick turnover, with interest rates, management, and the future prospects of stock companies far in the background.

Many are perfectly aware of the hazards of speculation—that securities are over-valued, that the market has become a simple gamble, and that a crash is inevitable and even imminent. But each man is confident of his ability to liquidate before the collapse, passing on his securities to others at a higher figure. A large number have in some form lost heavily in previous speculations or in business ventures. They have concluded that business is a ruthless game in which no quarter can be expected, and they are unwilling to enter into commitments over an extended period. A quick entry and exit from the scuffle of business is contemplated. (pp. 8–11)

• • •

By the same token, in a rampant bullish market every tipster becomes a prophet. In the general rise, one can always state that any of the regulars is headed upward, and can be quite safe in so predicting, provided he does not specify *when*. "Double the wager and *double the time*" is still good technique for the prophet of business.

But as stocks reached the lower depths in 1931, the heroes of the bull campaign of 1928–29 were revealed as sorry fellows indeed. . . .

However, it is not our purpose to gloat over those who were swept away by their own and the general fervor and saw the dawn of the golden age. They were broken even as those who scoffed at every rise in the market, put their money on the black squares of depression, and waited for the wheel of fortune to turn. (pp. 302–303)

• • •

In a normal market, much is taken for granted in the relation of broker and customer. After a severe decline, when margin accounts are wiped out, when brokerage houses fail, when investors find the shares they have bought withheld from them, there is much consultation of lawyers and an acute realization of the many technical factors involved.

Brokers themselves have fallen afoul of the law. In the crash of late 1929, hundreds of brokers sold out their clients without reasonable and proper notice. In most jurisdictions such notice means actual notice, and brokers who could not reach their clients, or who found margins obliterated before due demand could be made, were responsible for ensuing losses.

Others familiar with the rigid requirements of the law waited too long, and took staggering losses with their customers, when the accounts were finally liquidated. In such cases all customers who later appeared in Court affirmed that, had they been given proper notice, they would have furnished additional margins. The trend of prices on the Exchange proved the sole salvation of brokerage houses. Millions of clients were wiped out, and many of these, without the legal formalities. (p. 341)

• • •

More important than the fall of those in the forefront of American business was the fate of millions of the great middle and lower classes. Accountants, architects, engineers, lawyers: all who served industry directly and indirectly, merchant and manufacturer who supplied its needs, went down in the general debacle. Men of character and standing, who from youth had been pillars of the social structure, found themselves derelict. Their posts of trust and service were gone: their savings of a lifetime were lost; their investments were worthless. Craftsmen whose skilled hands had ever assured them a livelihood, wandered aimlessly in futile quest for work.

Past wealth or past glory meant nothing: men inured to leadership for generations found themselves without means and without prospects. Thousands who had given generously to others in the past became recipients of charity.

It is impossible to grasp the change in life and thought produced by the economic upheaval. Reversals of fortune as strange as those produced by the Russian Revolution are all about us. Retired bankers and business men became porters and messengers; debutantes of 1928 and 1929 became waitresses in 1932. Ladies of the highest culture and fashion peddled cosmetics, solicited subscriptions to magazines or drifted lower in the scale. A million tragedies were enacted in this interim, each more poignant than any novel ever penned. Thousands of the aged, the weak, the demoralized . . . sought a way out in suicide. . . .

More startling were the changes of thought in high places. "Even the rain wasn't wet any more," remarked a taxi driver early in 1932. Economy superseded lavish expenditure as the heroic gesture. Political creeds of a century were discarded overnight. . . .

The decade that ended late in 1929 will loom large in the pages of American business. It marked the culmination of social and political as well as business trends of long duration. Indeed the plunge of stock prices to abysmal depths in 1932 marked the end of an epoch that began immediately after the Civil War. It sounded the knell of a financial hierarchy that had been built up over a half a century: by slow and painful steps it may lift up those at the bottom of the pyramid.

There should be no regret at the passing of this era—though it witnessed the growth of the railroads, the development of the oil industry, the exploitation of inventive genius, great consolidations and vast mergers. Back of these enterprises were men who lived by the sword, and it is fitting that many shall perish by the sword. They turned back the pages of history and applied to modern commerce the traditions of the feudal lords. They were interested in power and in profits; they builded without heart and without heed to the new hopes of mankind. They made war, they controlled politics, they harnessed science, they dictated the press, only to serve the insatiable urge of commerce. . . .

There need be no requiem for the passing of such czars of finance. The disastrous crash of values was not without cleansing effects. In the first declines there was a smug satisfaction in high places as the small traders, the petty merchants and brokers . . . were thrust to the wall. A banker, early in 1931, complacently termed the depression an excellent "weeding-out" process, comparable to the "healthful reactions" of a bull market. The viewpoint was, of course, directly related to "whose ox was being gored." A few months later the bland banker was under indictment for the peculation of a cold million. Such a state of affairs was not at all uncommon, nor inconsistent with a callous indifference to the general ruin. In fact it explained much of the mental processes in high places.

Only as fear overtook the nation's leaders was there a return to human values. Only as disaster impended was there a realization that those who bait the traps for their fellowmen, who exact toll from countless thousands on the highroads of life, or play upon the heartstrings of the world, must themselves bow to Time. There must come a further understanding that all attempts to purchase security for the future are futile. For all accumulations of greed are dissipated shortly by the ravages of greed, and only in a better order does there lie hope for the future generation. (pp. 353–357)

LOUISE V. ARMSTRONG'S ACCOUNT OF BANK FAILURES

In the mid-1930s, Louise V. Armstrong was the director of a relief office in Chicago instituted by Franklin D. Roosevelt's New Deal administration. In 1929, she and her husband were middle-class, white-collar professionals who lived at different times in both a rural community in Michigan and the urban center of Chicago. Writing in 1938, well before the Depression was over, she reports on the results of the crash that could be seen on the streets of Chicago as early as 1930.

She provides the reader with a valuable personal perspective as well—a detailed account of what the perilous banking situation meant to people of modest means who once lived fairly comfortably: the fear of bank failures that led them to keep cash in bank safe-deposit boxes at first and then to remove even that from the bank; the fear of revolution in the country; the sight of runs on the bank; and the loss of all savings.

Although the Armstrongs' situation may seem far removed from that of the Joads, it is integrally connected, for the bank failures that occurred throughout the country were largely responsible for throwing small farmers off their land and concentrating land under the control of large impersonal corporations that then took advantage of the endless pool of cheap farm labor.

FROM LOUISE V. ARMSTRONG, *WE TOO ARE THE PEOPLE*
(Boston: Little, Brown and Company, 1938)

Then the crash came. We were almost, though not entirely, wiped out, like millions of other families. We saw the city at its worst. We saw Want and Despair walking the streets, and our friends, sensible, thrifty families, reduced to poverty. We saw the runs on the Big Loop banks—the Bank Holiday. One vivid, gruesome moment of those dark days we shall never forget. We saw a crowd of some fifty men fighting over a barrel of garbage which had been set outside the back door of a restaurant. American citizens fighting for scraps of food like animals! (p. 10)

• • •

By that time people in Chicago were thoroughly aroused to the situation of the country. No intelligent person, no matter how much of a Pollyanna he might wish to be, could deny any longer the perils which confronted the average citizen on every side. We did not have to read about the depression in the newspapers. We saw it right before our eyes. Even when we went for a walk in the neighborhood of our hotel, it stared us in the face at every turn. The streets were full of beggars. There were "For Rent" signs everywhere—vacant apartments, vacant houses, vacant stores. Many shops we had known and patronized in the neighborhood disappeared and went out of existence. A little tailor, who had often repaired our clothing, committed suicide on New Year's Day. He was bankrupt. As we rode downtown in the street car we passed several soup-kitchens. There were frequent demonstrations of the unemployed and also of the unpaid schoolteachers. Banks were crashing throughout the city and suburbs, and of course throughout the state and the nation. We had been fortunate in not having to meet that trouble ourselves. Our banks had survived, though one of them had a very narrow escape, and was saved only by an RFC loan of staggering proportions. However, practically all our friends now had at least a small sum of cash in their safe deposit boxes. In some cases the amounts were only fifty to a hundred dollars, but enough to take care of immediate needs in case "anything happened." We had also taken this precaution, but our small safety fund was in American Express checks instead of cash. We still had accounts in two Chicago banks, and when we left the city, we drew money from these as needed for our small account in the bank here in the county. Our circles of friends, acquaintances and business associates in Chicago were just an average group of well-educated American citizens of moderate means, and none in the group had ever been the hysterical type; but this was our plight. There were two phrases we heard constantly: "In case of trouble" and "If anything happened." If you tried to pin anyone down as to just what they meant, the answer was usually evasive. No one wanted to put the awful truth into cold, brutal words, but we all knew that those phrases meant that we feared an uprising of the great masses of underprivileged citizens—in short, that we felt the growing danger of revolution. (pp. 31–32)

• • •

The county, like the rest of the nation, was also having banking troubles. They had started a considerable time before the Presidential Election or even the Presidential Conventions. We read in the paper that several very small banks out in the county had closed. This was an old story to us, after Chicago, but we felt that these instances were unusually pathetic because of course most of the depositors were very poor people. In town there was a National Bank and a State Bank. The whole community was greatly shocked when the National Bank closed. This did not affect us personally. Our account was in the State Bank. But it was a severe blow to the Hill folks, not to mention the many less fortunate depositors, whose life savings had been entrusted to it.

. . . The crash of the National Bank had come without warning. The following day we had driven downtown to do the marketing, and, just as we stepped out of the coach, an acquaintance who was passing asked us if we knew there was a run going on at the State Bank. We walked up to the Bank, and sure enough, things did not look quite as usual. Little groups of people with serious faces stood about outside, talking earnestly. Inside we could see long lines at every window. At the entrance stood the Sergeant of State.

. . . Our account was small, but we were in no shape to lose a single nickel. However, we had confidence in that bank. We finally decided to draw just enough to see us through an emergency. I went down and stood in line with the crowd. There were probably twenty to thirty people ahead of me, and similar lines at every window. Money was pouring out. The crowd consisted mostly, though not entirely, of the working classes and the poor people. I saw many old people in the lines. They were receiving astonishing amounts of money. It was given out mostly in big stacks of small bills. Shabbily dressed people, laborers in overalls and the like, were going away with a hundred, two hundred, five hundred dollars and more. I suppose the reason that the people of this type had so much ready cash available was because their bank deposits represented all the money they had in the world. They never could save enough from their meager earnings to make investments. (pp. 44–46)

• • •

Were we helping to wreck the financial structure of the nation in trying to protect ourselves against this disaster? I suppose we were. But the small sum of money we had in those banks was all that stood between us and the bread line. We figured that it might last us a year if we counted the pennies and did not get sick. My husband had been unable to find employment. Our investments had become worthless. We could not have sold the house at any price, or rented it. (p. 49)

BRUCE BLIVEN'S 1930 ACCOUNT OF JOBLESS MEN IN NEW YORK

In March 1929, only a year before Bruce Bliven wrote this article for *The New Republic*, the country was, according to businessmen and economists, experiencing the grandest of financial times that were predicted to continue forever. Now, in March 1930, scores of men from every walk of life hover under New York City's train bridges in the cold. Few are adequately clothed against the brutal weather. Nearby, hundreds are on line to receive soup and bread, and a lodging house is crammed with homeless men seeking medical help and shelter. Bliven makes clear that these are a new class of the homeless who have only recently been forced to take charity.

FROM BRUCE BLIVEN, "ON THE BOWERY"
(The New Republic, March 19, 1930)

It seems too cold to rain; but it isn't. The drops come down in slanting lines, driven by a bitter wind, and stand in pools upon the hard-packed, icy snow along the street. A bad night to be out, even if you are well shod and warmly clothed; and most of the men lounging along the Bowery, with the L trains rumbling overhead, are neither. Their shoes are broken, their clothing is in the last stages of disrepute. Perhaps one in twenty has gloves, and perhaps two in five an overcoat of some sort, an overcoat too large or too small, or with the buttons missing so that it has to be held together with one hand, as the great ladies hold their fur wraps going into the opera. Misery does love company; these unhappy men move along the street, or stand huddled in doorways partly out of the rain, in twos and threes. Here and there you will see a born raconteur who has assembled an audience of half a dozen; they laugh noisily when he comes to the point, and that laughter is the only sound they ever make above an undertone. For most of them are frightened, and frightened men keep quiet.

You turn a corner, and here is a surprising spectacle. There is a line of men, three or sometimes four abreast, a block long, and wedged tightly together—so tightly that no passer-by can break through. For this compactness there is a reason: those at the head of this grey-black human snake will eat tonight; those farther back probably won't. Every few minutes, someone tries to break in far enough toward the front to be enumerated among the blessed; and then, from those behind him comes a chorus of hoots and jeers, the human equivalent of automobilists blowing horns in stalled traffic . . .

The Lodging House opens at four in the afternoon and by that time, the line outside the door is the better part of a block long. It will be twice as long by six. One hundred twenty-eight men are admitted about every twenty-five minutes, that being the length of time it takes for one sitting in the dining room. Every man receives a cup of coffee (in a tin cup, boiling hot), a big dish of stew (beef tonight and lamb tomorrow) and as much graham bread as he can eat. Anyone capable of consuming a second helping of stew is welcome to it. After supper, they are registered and check their valuables (nine out of ten haven't any, and if by a miracle somebody turned up with three dollars he would be refused admission). Every man hands in all his clothing, to be fumigated during the night and returned to him in the morning. Every man gets a shower bath—compulsory; a clean white nightshirt, and a medical examination. If he needs a doctor's care, he is sent over to Bellevue Hospital; otherwise; he gets a bed in a room with several hundred other men, where he sleeps about eleven hours: and so would you, if you had tramped the streets from dawn to dark and had just had a big hot meal, perhaps your first in several days. The earliest men to come in are the earliest out in the morning. Each process takes several hours, when the city's guests are running above a thousand at a time. Every man gets back his clothing and valuables, the garments fumigated in dry heat, and neither wrinkled nor given any odor by the process. Once clad, they are checked out again, are given a hot breakfast, and sent on their way. A few of the men—less than 10 per cent—are required to do a couple of hours' cleaning work to pay for their lodging; the rest make no payment except the humiliation of accepting charity. . . .

For many of them, of course, that is no payment at all. They don't mind being "pauperized"; they welcome the chance. But there are others who pay dearly. This winter differs from previous ones in the exceptionally high number of men who have never before had this sort of experience, for whom it is a personal tragedy too deep for words. (pp. 120–122)

ROBERT CRUDEN'S ACCOUNT OF DETROIT IN 1931

Robert Cruden, writing for *The New Republic*, journeyed to Detroit to have a firsthand look at what was occurring in 1931, a time when this automobile city's operations were already rapidly collapsing.

Cruden presents a picture of what it was like to pound the pavements with armies of job seekers, made desperate by the prospect that their families faced cold and hunger without relief.

Note that factories were primarily hiring children and women when they could because they could get by with paying them less.

FROM ROBERT CRUDEN, "NO HELP WANTED"
(*The New Republic* March 18, 1931)

"Nobody's buyin' autos any more."

This was the remark which greeted us as we joined the 200 men huddled together across the road from the Ford Rouge employment office. We were all former Ford workers—some of us had been laid off in October, 1929; some last summer, and some of us after New Year's when the newspapers were shrieking "Ford Hiring 75,000!" Many of the men had their badges, having never been officially "laid off." They were there with the rest of us, shivering in the cold, hoping against hope that Ford would start hiring . . .

"It ain't no use," a millwright was saying, "I went in to get a pass from my boss an' he said, 'Good God, man, we're layin' off.' "

"Yeah, that's true," added a toolmaker in a hopeless voice. "My cousin says there ain't 25,000 workers left in the whole plant."

"That means about a hundred thousand laid off," murmured another.

More and more men arrived on the line. Many of them displayed their badges, shining in the cold sunlight.

"Ah don' know what ah'm goin' t' do," spoke up a carpenter. "They done lay me off a year ago Octobah an' ah ain't worked since."

"They'll have to do something pretty damn quick," said a crankshaft worker sullenly . . .

Two and a half miles to Fisher Body. Two hours at Ford Rouge had frozen us out—we were not clad for that biting wind which numbed our feet and chilled our bodies. The Fleetwood plant of Fisher—the biggest body plant in the world—the employment office packed.

"Ever work for Fisher?" a watchman demanded.

"No."

"Then get out!"

Out in the cold again. The wind blew up from the river in icy gusts, chilling us to the marrow through our worn suits and cotton workshirts. Even those of us with overcoats were cold.

"Gawd, my feet's sore," said one. His shoes, of different makes, were cracked and cut; the soles were parting from the uppers.

Not knowing what to do next we stood talking. When would things pick up?

"Maybe in a coupla years," suggested a young machinist.

"Never," ejaculated an old die-maker. "Too many machines. They kin put out all the autos they need with the men they got."

"Things can't pick up till we get back to work," said a tinsmith. "How'd they expect us to buy autos when we can't buy food?"

"Yeah, an' it'll take us another ten years to pay our debts when we do go back to work," said a Chrysler worker with an air of finality.

On the tramp again, our heads bent in the wind, hands stuck deep in pockets, our feet sore and tired.

"I'm glad I ain't married," someone said . . .

Before it was daylight we were on the way to Chevrolet. The darkness seemed to intensify the coldness. In front of the L. A. Young plant a dozen boys were huddled together, the oldest about eighteen. Pale and cold, yet sleepy, they cowered in the wind. Some of them did not have overcoats. They stared at us as we hurried on.

The police were already on the job, waving us away from the Chevrolet employment office. "Nothin' doin'. Nothin' doin'." . . .

Scores of former Chevrolet workers were here—but they were not being hired.

Now we were tramping through falling snow, a cold and hungry line. After a half hour we reached the Hamtramck plant of Briggs Body. It was boarded up . . .

Down on one side of the street we marched, toward the Dodge plant. On the other, a steady line of men and women tramped away from it. My partner told me how he had to pawn his micrometers, costing $16, for $2.50. He had been forced to live with his brother, who had five children and who had himself been laid off just two weeks previously. "We gotta do somethin'," he growled.

Dodge employment office. A big well fed man in a heavy overcoat stood at the door saying "No, no," as we passed before him.

Women everywhere on the road to Murray Body. Native born and foreign born, young women and old women, women with whole fingers and women with hands mangled in the presses—a continuous stream of them passing and repassing, looking for jobs.

"It's come so that the women an' kids have to work now," said a Hudson worker bitterly.

Murray Body wasn't hiring. It was laying off its own workers, to whom it pays fifteen cents an hour.

On the tramp again. A young worker, married and father of two children, burst out, "A worker's got no right to have kids any more." (pp. 25–29)

FRANK G. MOORHEAD'S FIRSTHAND
ACCOUNT OF THE PAIN OF JOBLESSNESS

Frank G. Moorhead, whose story appeared in *The Nation* in 1931, writes from firsthand experience as a man who has lost his job as a newspaperman and is desperately looking for a means to survive. Moorhead illustrates that it is not just the factory worker who suffers, but also many people who had once held influential desk jobs. Before, Moorhead was the one who indifferently turned down applicants for jobs—now, he is the one who begs his friends for employment. Once, he was the one who helped his banker with advertising, and now it is the banker who demands extra guarantees that any loan will be repaid and with higher interest.

FROM FRANK G. MOORHEAD, "BROKE AT FIFTY-FIVE,"
(The Nation May 13, 1931)

I've done a good deal of thinking in the past year, largely because I haven't had anything else to do. Prior to that, for twenty-five years I wrote editorials, without thinking—sort of caught ideas out of the air, mechanically, as a riveter catches red-hot bolts.

Most of the editorials were intended to comfort the poor and downtrodden. I didn't know the poor and downtrodden personally. But they existed in large numbers, and subscribed to the paper for which I wrote. It was a farm paper, one dollar a year. A difficult kind of journal to edit, because on the one hand we must espouse the export debenture, the equalization fee, individual loans to farmers on crops, and every other panacea which offered to relieve distress and suffering on the farm; and on the other we must assure the advertisers that no better market exists anywhere in all the world than the farm market.

There was good money in it, for publisher and editor both, as well as a trip back East every little while, usually just before elections when a conference of "farm experts" was called in Washington for the purpose of helping the farmers to vote for the right candidates. It looked as though the condition and the position were permanent. It really wasn't a bad job, as jobs go, telling the farmer how poor he was, for $200 a week, with an annual bonus if advertising remained good.

I had a knack of writing things that would make folks cry, about people who had died and gone to where they were much better off. I used to look out the window and get to crying real hard myself over some person I had never seen, or cared for, or even heard of before. Good stuff, though, when one is editing a paper which is read by a million farmers who don't often get to see better sob-stuff. Some of them weren't so bad. I recall one written after the death of the mother of the man who owned the paper and signed the weekly pay checks. I sent a copy of it to a man in Washington named Hoover, who wrote back: "I had heard of the terrible accident to Mr.——'s's mother and I telegraphed him some time ago with respect to it. I have never seen a finer tribute than that which you sent me." I'm keeping the letter for two purposes: first, to use as a recommendation, if I ever find the right parties; second, to sell as an autograph as a last resort.

I remember how I used to get down to work early Monday morning, and then taper off, or peter out, a bit later each morning, until Saturday wasn't much of a day at all. On Monday morning I brought in the newspaper early, and found myself out of a job. The paper I had worked for as second in command for twenty years had been sold the day before, on Sunday.

A few weeks later a national bank in which I had invested the residue of what had seemed a small salary, until I lost it, found it advisable to merge with a larger bank. Before that, stock which had cost $250 a share went so low that it made a fellow wake up in the middle of the night, all hot and scared, and hearing every board in the house creak, he was so sure the morning mail would bring the notice of a double assessment on the poor innocent stockholders.

There's the picture: broke at fifty-five, and four hungry people still demanding three meals a day. What was the sensation?

I was greatly surprised, taking my first airplane flight, to find I had no sensation at all. I did not even know I was moving. It was somewhat the same at first when I went broke. I did not even know I had stopped moving. It should have been more dramatic. I should have paced the floor. I should have mouthed tragedy and made a pass at the chandelier with my walking stick, given me by the office force after many years of faithful service. I had written stories (fiction) about men in similar situations. I must admit they acted altogether differently, at rates varying from one to five cents a word. They said an awful lot in the higher priced articles.

A man's egoism is an anaesthetic allaying the first pains. He works fifteen, twenty, twenty-five years, no matter how many. He is either good or he becomes acclimated and the boss lets him stay on, like an old piece of furniture hardly worth carrying away. He loses his job. He says to himself, "Well, I've worked hard, and faithfully a good many years. The last three years I didn't take my regular office vacation, at full pay. Sorry now that I didn't, but a rest won't hurt me. In fact, it will do me good. I was getting in a rut. And while I'm resting other firms or plants or factories will hear that I'm out, and I'll choose from among the good offers they make me."

"Well, you're fixed all right; no need for you to worry; you'll get along fine. You can always get a good job, anywhere." So the home folks said, as they stopped me on the street and then hurried on, remembering I was no longer in the newspaper business and therefore no longer useful to them, and their children's parties, with layout, on the Sunday society page.

"It seems to me the tendency of the times; reducing overhead expenses." This from a few editors, still permanently located and pretty sure of a few years more.

As for the offers, they never came at all. It was weeks before I could figure it out. The little notice about me in the hometown paper had been hidden away between a patent-medicine advertisement and the notice of a concern passing its dividend. Maybe I'd better send out a few letters to prominent publishers and editors to let them know my address. I had opened up an office in one of the bedrooms at home and was typing, "Now is the time for all good men to come to the aid of the party" hour after hour, in order to make the neighbors think I was still writing—for a living.

I have a large number of very splendid endorsements which I shall be glad to loan to anyone prepaying the postage. The name can easily be changed. So many of those to whom I wrote giving them first chance at my service would have grabbed me off just a little while before, but "recent additions to our staff make it impossible," "we have built up a stalwart organization which we hesitate," and so on. "Surprised to hear that *you* should have been let out." No more surprised than I was, and the italics are not mine, either. You can't eat words. You can't even get credit for them at the cash-and-carry grocery stores.

The trusting hopefulness of the first few weeks turned to bitterness. "A fine fellow. A fine fellow, when he had a paper back of him; quite dumb without one." "Pretty cocky, wasn't he? Sort of held himself aloof from the gang. Oh, well, roll out another money ball and let the ancient and noble game of Kelly pool continue." I was sore for a while; then I laughed it off. No doubt I had done the same thing many a time. Nobody ever considers anything until it comes right home. I've often wondered if Longfellow wrote "There is no death" with fingers crossed. He sure slipped it over on them that day.

First indifference; next, reassuring faith; third, galling bitterness; fourth morbidity. And the last is what hurts and causes folks to fall out of ten-story windows, accidentally. "Nothing wrong with his accounts; happily married," say the newspapers. How about the rapidly dwindling bank balance; the determination that the loved ones, who were in no way to blame for the bad luck, shall go on having the things they were accustomed to having; the stiff upper lip the grand old Scotch mother used to talk about, before you ever had a penny of your own and were too young to go out in the world and work?

Around fifty a man loses nerve—I don't mean the nerve it takes to accompany Wilkins under the ice to the North Pole, or to fly with Byrd and moving-picture men to the South Pole. I mean the nerve it takes to ask a stranger for a job, when you've turned down thousands of men yourself without batting an eye; to tell a friend how good you are, and watch his face continue blank; to approach the banker whom you puffed in your paper for years and who was only too glad to lend you whatever you wanted at 6 per cent, and not even take the interest out in advance. This time he suggests that the wife sign the note, too, and makes it 7 per cent, in advance, and asks for a credit statement.

You have just as much ability as ever. You've got a book half started— whale of a plot never used before, good dialogue, nice, clean, moral sort of a book. You'll sell it soon and then you'll be all right. Maybe you'll make $10,000 out of it. But the home folks know you've lost your $200 a week, and that's ever so much bigger. And nowadays if you're counting on a $10,000 book, the home folks are right; the $200 check is much bigger—and surer.

Finally, in course of time, you begin to feel toward yourself as you imagine other folks are feeling toward you. I've never cared a rap for money. I never carried much, however far from home I went. I could always get it somehow, from somebody. There would be whole days at home when there wasn't even a penny in the pockets of any of the two suits. Now that I'm broke I always carry a few silver dollars, so I can jingle them and not feel so downcast. It has the effect on listeners, too.

Have you read Stevenson's "The Amateur Emigrant"? If you have, read it again. He tells of coming over on a steamer, second cabin, when that was different from what it is now, while the class of people with whom he was wont to associate were traveling first class. They ignored him. "In my normal circumstances," he says, "it appeared every young lady must have paid some tribute of a glance, and though I had not often detected it when it was given, I was well aware of its absence when it was withheld." He reflects a bit and concludes, "I wish someone . . . would find out exactly at what stage of toilet a man becomes invisible to the well-regulated female eye."

I have a similar problem. I should like to find out at what stage of your poverty other people realize or sense it, and pass you by as one no longer interesting or useful to them. You wear the same suit, more carefully brushed and pressed than ever before to conceal your poverty. You walk just as cockily. You know as much; you know a lot more, in fact—things you didn't suspect or believe, before. I guess, after all, it's the droop in the shoulders, the look in your eyes—furtive, expectant, resentful.

The nights are the worst; the time when all you can see is the unseen. You've done everything humanly possible to avert the inevitable. You've gone over your life-insurance policies, to be sure they are all incontestible after the first years. You've taken out additional accident insurance. You realize that for the first time in your rather carefree, indifferent life you are worth more dead than alive—a good deal more.

The boards in the house creak. You heart gives a jump. Will it be the last one? Perhaps it's a burglar. Your last chance to be a hero. To have the papers, which you pretend to scorn, use you as first-page copy. X marks the spot where the burglar was killed. Don't laugh! It's all terribly real; no make-believe. But it's a grand joke on the burglar—robbing the house of a man who is broke, at fifty-five. Poor devil!

Another board creaks. You hear Andy figuring his income tax. "Five million . . . Seven million." You go over, in your head, the dwindling bank balance. "Three hundred and two." "Two hundred and eighty." "Two hundred and forty nine."

You're wide awake now. The perspiration runs from you. It's only the ring of the window shade hitting the glass this time. The birds are beginning to sing. Pretty little things. They don't have to work on a salary. They don't take men's words, and find them salty in the mouth. A little light in the east window. Everybody else is sleeping. You've stopped all the clocks. You can't stand them any more. Every tick is one of the few remaining dollars gone.

Another day. Nobody knows, but yourself. And you're getting terribly close mouthed about things lately. (pp. 528–530)

EMILY HAHN'S ACCOUNT OF JOBLESS WOMEN

Emily Hahn, like Robert Cruden, a writer for *The New Republic*, submits her story on jobless women in 1933. Hahn gathered her information by visiting employment centers where she interviewed women seeking jobs and the social workers who tried to help them.

FROM EMILY HAHN, "WOMEN WITHOUT WORK"
(*The New Republic* May 13, 1933)

There are many women, no doubt, who struggle along until the last possible moment. Social investigators are almost of a mind that the un-employed woman of the new type is much more reluctant to apply for aid at a public charity than is her brother in similar circumstances. She tries everything else first, for the doctrine of Success has taken strong hold of the public mind, and to admit failure is still the greatest shame of all. She lives as long as possible on her savings, trying all the time to find more work and going without enough food to save money for clothes. Then she turns to her friends—private borrowing is not quite so shameful—until she becomes too much a burden. There are girls who for the past few months have risen every morning before dawn, to be first in the lines of applicants for any job that has been advertised, and when the early-morning rush is over and it is too late to hope for success, they must look for a place to sit, to wait until the day is over. That place is not easy to find, particularly in winter. The railroad-station waiting rooms grew so crowded that now they are kept clear by having the "vagrants" turned out every so often. It is not until she is reduced to actual hunger that the white-collar girl at last presents herself at the door of the relief bureaus and charity committees . . .

Homeless, friendless women are much troubled with their belongings; they cannot trudge the streets and look for work if they are burdened by their bundles and suitcases. Some solve the problem by simply deserting their possessions; they move late at night from the rooms for which they cannot pay, leaving everything they own in default of rent money . . .

Certainly at the moment there are far too many trained women for every type of work. The business colleges have gone on turning out typists, file-clerks and accountants at an increasing rate of speed, though new labor-saving office machinery is always being invented. The untrained factory worker has lost her high social position in comparison with the housemaids and cooks who used to demand enormous wages in compensation for their menial tasks. Many women are now going into jobs as cooks or maids at ridiculously low wages, for the advantage of a place to live and the certainty of regular meals. At least one college-bred woman is in New Jersey now, earning six dollars a week as a cook . . .

Half-time jobs. Temporary jobs. Free meals in restaurants that have come to the fore and offered their left-over food. Free rooms in hotels that cannot fill themselves otherwise. Failing these makeshift devices, emptiness lies before the woman who has no claim on the relief usually afforded the deserving "case," the unwed mother or the blind and decrepit. So far, the unattached woman has got the leavings, not only of charity. Even now, when it would seem they had reached rock-bottom, the greater number of these homeless drifters have not come to public attention. One by one they give up, slowly and reluctantly, or they go too far even to give up, like the fifty-year-old woman who confessed: "I had $60, but I spent it. I didn't even try to save it. I thought perhaps God would be good to me and let me die." (pp. 63–65)

LETTERS WRITTEN IN THE 1930s BY WORKING MEN AND WOMEN

The country was already deep into the Depression when Franklin Roosevelt took office as president in February 1933. His inaugural address and his periodic fireside chats broadcast over the radio were listened to by Americans in all walks of life. First Lady Eleanor Roosevelt was also a very high profile figure, well known for her compassion and dedication to the kind of social reform that would help those at the bottom of the economic ladder. Furthermore, ordinary people knew not only President and Mrs. Roosevelt, but also one of the most important people in Roosevelt's cabinet, a woman named Frances Perkins, whom he had appointed as secretary of labor because of her national reputation as a bold and smart social reformer. Working people had a sense that hers was the position that would have the greatest effect on them.

For many years, working-class Americans had regarded their presidents as aloof from the people—like President Harding who had seemed to be wrapped up in his own circle of politicians, or Roosevelt's predecessor, Herbert Hoover, who appeared to be responsive only to other wealthy businessmen like himself.

But in 1933, many people who were either without work or were working under brutal conditions, trusted that the country's leaders were going to do something to alleviate their suffering. Such people were desperate to believe that their leaders cared about them and listened to them. So they wrote to the Roosevelts and Frances Perkins to inform them about the economic situation in the country. Their letters, preserved in the National Archives, are records of how the Depression was affecting working people and their families.

Two of the letters presented here come from women who have no jobs. The first is from a woman who explains why she is out of work. Her motive in writing is not so much self-interest, but a plea to help the people who work in inhumane conditions in a factory in Massachusetts, a place where she had worked. The second letter, written to the secretary of labor, is an entreaty on behalf of young single women who find it so difficult to get work and have no husbands to help them.

A letter to Mrs. Roosevelt highlights the problem of the aging worker. It is from a sixty-one-year-old woman whose long hours and low wages have ruined her health. She writes to inform Mrs. Roosevelt about the conditions of her employment and her support for the president.

The last letter is written to the president by a woman with a husband and children. They live in Detroit, heart of the hard-hit automobile industry and one of the most economically depressed urban centers at the time. Not only does she relate the personal adversities in her own family and that of other Detroit families, she also reveals the growing resentment against those who have acquired great wealth at the expense of people who are now close to starvation. The intensity of this class consciousness and resentment, and the fact that it was becoming so widespread, was an alarming new development in American society.

These letters are included unedited.

FROM LETTERS TO PRESIDENT AND MRS. ROOSEVELT AND TO
FRANCES PERKINS, SECRETARY OF LABOR
(In *Slaves of the Depression*, Gerald Markowitz and David Rosner,
eds.; Ithaca, NY: Cornell University Press, 1987)

Boston, Massachusetts, November 20, 1936

Dear President Roosevelt:

I want ask one favor of you not for myself but for a great many other poor, honest & good citizens. There is A factory here in Roxbury Mass., The Name of it is the Graham Corp., they employe at least 75 to 100 help. There is know heat in the Building not Even to sit down & have a decent place to eat, the wages is very small the wimen get $9.12 a week the men $13.26 now when you by coal 300lb. a week, milk, for baby, food, lights, Rent $14.00 a month, will please tell if you think it is a fair living, of cause I am just asking if Graham can't fix it so the people can have a little better place to work it is a slave shop, from the Boss down they use you just like dogs it is the most unhealthiest place in U.S.A. the place was inspected about two yrs ago (but the inspector got rake off) and that was the end, it is only a trap for your death. I worked there myself & almost met my Death. The main office is 104–126 Ward St. Roxbury Mass, he also has an office in Fitchburg Mass. I am not employed there anymore as I could [not] stand the cold & exposure. But it is very hard for those who are there. I hope I have not done any harm as asking your help in regards to the poor employees there. We are all thankful to God that you were reelected because God knows you certainly are good to the people God wont let us suffer for the right man to Father our Country the ought not ever to take you from the White House until you die you are a God send to the People of America & may God Bless you & your family.

Wishing you a Happy thanksgiving.

P.S. Please excuse writing & withhold name.

M. B.

Dayton, Ohio, February 1, 1937

Frances Perkins:

I am a girl 23 years old have to make a living and can't get a job. I wonder if they don't think we got eat or if we are supposed to live off the air. We have to eat just like those who have a job.

I think our government should pass a law so that married women can not be employed in factories or stores, that would give the single girl a chance to get a job.

I think the single girl is entitled to make living more so than the married woman who has a husband to support her and mostly they work so they can buy a lot luxuries.

Furthermore we unemployed girls get very discouraged to walk every day looking for a job and then get turned down just because we haven't the experience. How in the world do they expect us to get experience when they don't give us a job. Sometimes I feel like I am at the end of my rope that's just how disgusted I get.

It's about time that our government pass 30 hour week working law and also enforced it.

VERY DISGUSTED

Atlanta, Georgia, February 19, 1937

Dear Mrs. Roosevelt:

Since Congress is in session again, and our wonderful President is also again on the job, I am begging you to help assist the women working in hotels in this country, especially in the South. I have been in the work since I was 32 years of age, and I am near 61 now, and on a hard job in one of our best hotels here in Atlanta, in the salad department.

I leave home at 10:30 A.M. to be on the job at 12 o'clock. I work like fighting fire, until 10 at night, and more than that. We have late people, and very often, it is 10:30 before I leave the department, and I must then dress for the street, get a [trolley] car, and transfer to my home car. I look over the daily paper, then to bed, and it is almost all I can do to get up and do some little things and leave for my work.

. . . I grab a cup of coffee, as I am closing up, and swallow a bite of something, as the manager is hurrying to close.

Well . . . what do I get per month for this fast hard work seven days per week and overtime and to 12:30 on Saturday nights. I get $35 per month, and 60 cents out of that on the Old Age Pension. So you see they rate me at $60. I wear some old ragged uniforms that the coffee shop girls have discarded and an average of three per week are run through their house laundry. My top aprons are brought home and put in another laundry at my expense with my caps and so on.

Yesterday . . . I had given to me for lunch a spoon of mashed potato, a little dumpling, made with something, and a spoon of collard greens. I just go ahead and eat a little ice-cream behind the backs of the managers, or I would go hungry, with $25 taken out of my salary, and me eating breakfast at home. . . .

We are not fighting for a 30 hour week, we are breaking in health under 10 to 12 hours a day of fast hard work in a hot hot kitchen (will not let cold air in during serving hours) and only beg for 8 hours in a straight watch (not a split watch) and one day to lie in bed, and rest.

. . . Give the forgotten women in Southern Hotels a chance to eat, and a day to lie in bed and rest from the hard work.

Yes I am in favor of enlarging the Supreme Court, and I know that all that President Roosevelt advocates is right, or he would not advocate it to start with, and I know you are extremely proud of such a husband for he is even greater than any that has ever been in our country. We love him, and know that he is for the working man and woman.

M. W.

Detroit, Michigan, November 27, 1939

President Roosevelt
Dear Honorable Sir:

I am living in a city that should be one of the prized possessions of these United States of America but it isn't only to a small group of chiseling money mongers.

I and my husband are and have been Americans for three generations and we are proud of what our parents did also our grandparents to help America progress. They were builders of our country not destructers as is now going on to make the rich man richer and the poor man poorer in fact try and starve them in a land of plenty. We have six growing children that are all separated each one pining for each other and our hearts nearly broken because we cannot keep them all together.

We have tried so hard these past seven years we lost our furniture twice lost our car our insurance even my engagement ring and finally the wedding ring to buy groceries pay rent and for illness. Neither one of us are lazy he worked in steel mills auto factories painting dishwashing and anything he could get. I worked at waitress janitress selling to make a few dollars now my health is slowly ebbing. I was a widow when I married my present husband my first husband died shortly after the world war having served as a submarine chaser. I received a check for $1.00 for each day he served he died leaving me two lovely children. Why should descent American people be made suffer in this manner living in an attic room paying $5.00 per week and if its not paid out you go on the streets. Welfare has never solved these problems as there are far too many inefficient social workers also too much political graft for it to survive or even help survive. We are one family out of 100,000 that are in the same position right here in Detroit where the ones we labor for and help build up vast fortunes and estates do nothing but push us down farther. They cheat the government out of taxes hire foreign labor at lower rates and if we get discouraged and take some groceries to feed our family we must serve time.

They have 40 to 100 room houses with no children to make it even like a home while we are denied a small home and enough wages to provide for them. Barbara Hutton has herself exploited that she pays $650.00 to have one tooth pulled and the girls in her dime stores slave all week for $12 or $14 and must help provide for others out of it. I'll wager to say that the poor class were lucky to have roast pork @ 13¢ per lb on Thanksgiving Day while the rich people in this country probably throwed a lot out in there garbage cans. These so called intelligent rich men including the Congressmen and the Senators better wake up and pass some laws that will aid labor to make a living as they would have never accumulated their vast fortunes had it not been from the hard sweat that honest labor men brought them.

We read with horror of the war in Europe and of the blockade to starve the people into submission and right here in Detroit we have the same kind of a blockade. Do the intelligent men of America think we are going to stand for this much longer. I alone hear a lot of viewpoints and it will be very hard to get our men to fight another war to make more wealth for men that never had to labor and never appreciated where the real source of their wealth derived from. This country was founded on Thanksgiving day to get away from the brutal treatment the British gave them and us real true Americans intend keeping it so. We need men of wealth and men of intelligence but we also need to make labor healthy and self supporting or our nation will soon crumble and it is head on to a good start. Even prisoners will balk at an injustice and we are not prisoners. God Bless all true Americans you have my permission to read this in the next session of Congress.

A true American mother & family

M. Q. L.

EDWARD ANGLY'S *OH YEAH?*

It seems appropriate to place at the end of this chapter excerpts from Edward Angly's collection of pronouncements made by many of the country's leaders about the country's economic condition and possible collapse. Their words are so wrong-headed in light of what happened from 1929 on, that they appear ludicrous. Without meaning to, they offered the world some measure of bitter comic relief. Angly, a satiric journalist and author, expects us to respond to each of these quotations with the popular skeptical phrase of the time: "Oh Yeah?"

With what we have seen of the economic devastation that lasted throughout the 1930s, the optimism of the country's business leaders was ridiculous, especially their insistence that the country was going to be fine as long as everything was done to bolster big business and nothing was done to limit it.

FROM *OH YEAH?*, COMPILED FROM NEWSPAPERS AND PUBLIC
RECORDS BY EDWARD ANGLY
(New York: The Viking Press, 1931)

STOCKS OFF 5 BILLION
IN SEVEREST BREAK OF
WALL STREET HISTORY
—*New York Herald Tribune*,
OCTOBER 24, 1929.

October 25, 1929

President Hoover
The fundamental business of the country, that is production and distribution of commodities, is on a sound and prosperous basis.
—*Statement to the Press*. (p. 11)

• • •

November, 1929
Some reassuring utterance by the President of the United States . . . would do much to restore the confidence of the public.
—WILLIAM RANDOLPH HEARST.

Any lack of confidence in the economic future or the basic
strength of business in the United States is foolish.

—PRESIDENT HOOVER.

• • •

December, 1930
Economic depression cannot be cured by legislative action
or executive pronouncement.

—PRESIDENT HOOVER,
Message to Congress. (p. 15)

• • •

January 24, 1930

TRADE RECOVERY
NOW COMPLETE,
PRESIDENT TOLD

BUSINESS SURVEY CONFERENCE
REPORTS INDUSTRY HAS PROGRESSED
BY OWN POWER

No Stimulants Needed

PROGRESS IN ALL LINES BY
THE EARLY SPRING IS FORECAST

—*New York Herald Tribune.* (p. 16)

• • •

January 21, 1930
Definite signs that business and industry have turned the
corner from the temporary period of emergency that followed deflation of the speculative market were seen today
by President Hoover. The President said the reports to the
Cabinet showed that the tide of employment had changed
in the right direction.

—*News dispatch from Washington.*

March 8, 1930
President Hoover predicted today that the worst effect of
the crash upon unemployment will have been passed during
the next sixty days.

—*Washington dispatch.*

May 1, 1930

While the crash only took place six months ago, I am convinced we have now passed the worst and with continued unity of effort we shall rapidly recover. There is one certainty of the future of a people of the resources, intelligence and character of the people of the United States—that is, prosperity.

PRESIDENT HOOVER
*—Address at annual dinner of the Chamber
of Commerce of the United States.*

October 20, 1930

President Hoover today designated Robert W. Lamont, Secretary of Commerce, as chairman of the President's special committee on unemployment.

October 21, 1930

President Hoover has summoned Colonel Arthur Woods to help place 2,500,000 persons back to work this winter.

—Washington dispatch. (p. 17)

• • •

President Hoover

JUNE 15, 1931.

I am able to propose an American plan to you. . . . We plan more leisure for men and women and better opportunities for its enjoyment. We plan not only to provide for all the new generation, but we shall, by scientific research and invention, lift the standard of living and security of life of the whole people. We plan to secure a greater diffusion of wealth, a decrease in poverty and a great reduction in crime. AND THE PLAN WILL BE CARRIED OUT IF WE JUST KEEP ON GIVING THE AMERICAN PEOPLE A CHANGE.

*—Address to Indiana Republican Editorial Association,
Indianapolis*

OCTOBER 18, 1931.

The depression has been deepened by events from abroad which are beyond the control either of our citizens or our government.

—Radio address at Fortress Monroe, Va. (p. 19)

• • •

Robert P. Lamont

MARCH 22, 1931.

There undoubtedly will be an appreciable decrease in the number of unemployed by mid-summer.

APRIL 25, 1931.

I have canvassed the principal industries, and I find no movement to reduce the rate of wages. On the contrary, there is a desire to support the situation in every way.

LAMONT PLANS CUTS
IN HIS DEPARTMENT

HE URGES DIVISION HEADS TO
REDUCE PERSONNEL IN
ECONOMY CAMPAIGN

—*New York Times*, JUNE 13, 1931

Special to the New York Times

WASHINGTON, Aug. 2 (1931)—Operating schedules in many manufacturing establishments were cut still further and the number of part time workers increased in July, the monthly employment bulletin of the Federal Employment Service reported today.

WASHINGTON, July 2 (1931)—Secretary Lamont today described as "entirely without foundations" rumors that he was planning to resign.

—*New York Times*. (p. 26)

• • •

Simeon D. Fess

THEN CHAIRMAN, REPUBLICAN NATIONAL COMMITTEE

Persons high in Republican circles are beginning to believe that there is some concerted effort on foot to utilize the stock market as a method of discrediting the administration. Every time an Administration official gives out an optimistic statement about business conditions, the market immediately, drops.

—*New York World*, OCTOBER 15, 1930.

Charles M. Schwab

CHAIRMAN OF THE BOARD, BETHLEHEM STEEL CORPORATION

MARCH 5, 1929,

I do not feel that there is any danger to the public in the present situation. Money is now being lent in Wall Street by people who never lent it before. As long as the people remain enthusiastic and interested the market will hold up. We must remember that today the United States is doing half the world's business and will continue to do so. Who can compete with us?

—*Ship news interview*

OCTOBER 25, 1929.

In my long association with the steel industry I have never known it to enjoy a greater stability or more promising outlook than it does today.

—*Address before American Iron and Steel Institute.*

DECEMBER 10, 1929.

Never before has American business been as firmly intrenched for prosperity as it is today. Steel's three biggest customers, the automobile, railroad and building industries, seem to me to justify a healthy outlook. This great speculative era in Wall Street, in which stocks have crashed, means nothing in the welfare of business. The same factories have the same wheels turning. Values are unchanged. Wealth is beyond the quotations of Wall Street. Wealth is founded in the industries of the nation, and while they are sound, stocks may go up and stocks may go down, but the nation will prosper.

—*Address before Illinois Manufacturers Association,*
Chicago

OCTOBER 16, 1930.

Looking to the future I see in the further acceleration of science continuous jobs for our workers. Science will cure unemployment.

—*Address at Dedication of Laboratory at Lehigh*
University

FEBRUARY 7, 1931.

I am not predicting anything. (pp.27–28)

$36,000,000 BONUSES
BY BETHLEHEM STEEL
ARE ATTACKED IN SUIT

—*New York Times,*
JANUARY 14, 1931.

BETHLEHEM NET
IN '30 DROPS TO
$5.25 A SHARE

LEAVES DEFICIT OF $2,356,594
AFTER DIVIDEND PAYMENTS
—*New York Herald Tribune*,
JANUARY 30, 1931.

JULY 8, 1931.
Just grin, keep on working. Stop worrying about the future
and go ahead as best we can. We always have a way of living
through the hard times.

U.S. STEEL AND
BETHLEHEM TO CUT
WAGES 10% OCT. 1
—*Headline—all papers*,
SEPTEMBER 23, 1931. (p. 29)

• • •

Henry Ford

NOVEMBER 4, 1929.
Things are better today than they were yesterday.
—*New York Evening Post*

NOVEMBER 11, 1929.
If people would stop talking about good and bad business
and concentrate on normal business, many of the evils of
hard times would vanish.
—*New York Evening Post*

CURTAILING CROPS
ERROR, SAYS FORD

ADVISES FARMER TO RAISE ALL
LAND WILL GROW

Sees Surplus as Benefit
—*New York World*,
MAY 4, 1930.

DETROIT, August 24 (1931)—Family men employed by the
Ford Motor Co. must either become home gardeners or forfeit
their positions. This edict was promulgated by Mr. Ford on an

inspection trip as a measure to alleviate temporary business depression.

—*New York Herald Tribune*
JULY 31, 1930.

Business will be all right. I am not in the least pessimistic. You notice that everybody is anxious to be at work; that is one of the healthiest signs of the times.—There is no such thing as overproduction.

—*New York Herald Tribune.*

FORD FINDS THE NATION
SAVED FROM THE EVILS
OF FALSE PROSPERITY

I, personally, am very hopeful because I think the country has ceased to be sick, is now well, and will soon be strong and active again.

—*New York World*, AUGUST 17, 1930.

OCTOBER 3, 1930.

The crash was a good thing. . . . You watch!

—*New York Times.*

MARCH 15, 1931.

These really are good times but only a few know it.

—*New York Times*

MARCH 18, 1931.

The average man won't really do a day's work unless he is caught and cannot get out of it. There is plenty of work to do, if people would do it.

—*New York World-Telegram*

NOVEMBER 19, 1929.

In the Detroit plants of the Ford Motor Co. employment has rapidly decreased during the past several weeks.

—*New York Times*

APRIL 28, 1931.

Of the Ford employees 32% now are on the full 5-day week; 18% are working four days; and 50% are still on the 3-day week.

—*Wall Street Journal*

AUGUST 12, 1931.
Henry Ford has shut down his Detroit automobile factories almost completely. At least 75,000 men have been thrown out of work.

—*The Nation* (pp. 32–33)

TOPICS FOR ORAL OR WRITTEN EXPLORATION

1. To get a feel for how the stock market works, choose two companies whose stocks are reported in the financial pages of your newspaper. Hypothetically, buy 100 shares of each. For two weeks, keep up with how much you have gained or lost each day by checking the prices of the stocks against what you paid for them. You may decide to sell some of your shares during this time and buy others, but it is important to keep up with how much you have gained or lost through selling and buying at the end of the two week period. If you intend to buy and sell stocks to make a quick profit rather than hold them as long-term investments, it will also be imperative for you to keep up with the national financial news to see whether any factors—such as rising interest rates, or the prospect of public demand for particular products, or news about European and Asian markets—might cause your shares to rise or fall. At the end of the project, submit a detailed report of what happened with your stocks and why.

2. Make a chart tracing the stock market crash of 1929 and its effect on the Joads.

3. Write a paper on big business and examine how it affected the Joads' lives. To do this, you will need to note all references, especially in the journalistic interchapters, to conditions in corporations that influenced how the Joads lived.

4. Compare the situation of the poor in urban areas in the mid-1930s, as reported in this chapter, with that of the Joads. What commonalities do you find?

5. The Declaration of Independence of the United States speaks of certain "inalienable rights." Have a debate about whether or not the Joads are being denied their rights.

6. Reasoning in part from what you have read here, stage a debate about whether it would have been better for a poverty-stricken family to be living in a rural or an urban area in the mid-1930s.

7. Many people in the 1930s, and today as well, take the position that we should be able to take care of ourselves and our families—despite social adversity—without "charity" or government assistance. Have a debate on this issue.

8. Examine the Joads' situation critically. If you were the Joads and had absolutely no foreknowledge about what was to occur, would you have made different decisions? This can be the basis of a series of class discussions.

9. Tape an interview with someone you know who lived through the Depression. Transcribe it and present it to the class.

10. Choose one month between 1931 and 1937 and peruse back issues of your local newspaper. Notice news stories, editorials, and letters to the editor having to do with the nation's economic health and its effect on individuals. You might also note advertisements and want ads. Choose your own thesis from your findings and write an essay about that one month.

SUGGESTIONS FOR FURTHER READING

Allen, Frederick Lewis. *Only Yesterday*. New York: Harper and Row, 1931.

Bird, Caroline. *The Invisible Scar*. New York: Pocket Books, 1967.

Federal Writers' Project. *These Are Our Lives*. Chapel Hill, University of North Carolina Press, 1939.

Galbraith, John K. *The Great Crash*. Boston: Houghton Mifflin, 1955.

Leonard, Jonathan Norton. *Three Years Down*. New York: Carrick and Evans, 1939.

McElvaine, Robert S. *The Great Depression*. New York: Times Books, 1984.

Meltzer, Milton. *Brother, Can You Spare a Dime? The Great Depression*. New York: Alfred A. Knopf, 1969.

Parrish, Michael E. *Anxious Decades*. New York: W. W. Norton, 1992.

Patterson, Robert T. *The Great Boom and Panic 1921–1929*. Chicago: Henry Regnery, 1965.

Rothbard, Murray N. *America's Great Depression*. Princeton: D. Van Nostrand Co., 1963.

Sternsher, Bernard. *Hitting Home*. Chicago: Ivan R. Dee, 1989.

Terkel, Studs. *Hard Times*. New York: Random House, 1970.

Watkins, T. H. *The Great Depression*. Boston: Little, Brown and Company, 1993.

Wecter, Dixon. *The Age of the Great Depression, 1929–1941*. New York: The Macmillan Company, 1948.

Wilson, Edmund. *The American Earthquake*. Garden City, NY: Doubleday and Company, 1968.

3

Farming in the Great Depression

Farmers like the Joads were hit by the Great Depression in different, and in far more harsh ways than the average urban worker. One reason for this was that the economic depression had begun for the American farmer long before the stock market crash of 1929. The crash merely worsened an already intolerable agricultural situation. The 1930s resulted in pain and suffering, especially for the owners of small farms and for farmworkers. It also widened the gap between families in these two categories and the big agribusinesses that gobbled up smaller farms and exploited farm laborers.

Still strong in numbers and political clout at the turn of the twentieth century, owners of large and small farms experienced a time of prosperity beginning in 1918 after the end of World War I. For two years after the war, farm production increased by 15 percent. In Europe, the agricultural system and the adult male population had been devastated, and the American farmer had the job of providing food for the United States and Europe. Both the farmer's land and the produce grown on the land were valuable. Throughout most of the country, the farmowner and his family did all the work, sometimes with the help of an occasional hired hand. Exceptions were found in the South where the plantation system had been replaced by a similar model of large farms worked by

Severe wind erosion made this farm uninhabitable. Cimarron City, Oklahoma, April 1936. Photograph by Arthur Rothstein. Reproduced from the collections of the Library of Congress.

hired labor, and in California and the northwest, where large spreads of fruit and vegetable farming were worked by migrant labor. Despite these regional departures, the family farm was, at this time, at its strongest in the United States.

By 1921, however, European farmers were back on their feet, growing their own food, and farm prices in the United States plummeted as a result because farmers were no longer able to find an overseas market for their goods. Contributing to the drop in prices was the farmers' loss of political power to the industrialized urban areas. Legislation that would have helped the farmer was overlooked as politicians turned their attention to smoothing the way for industry. Electrification, for example, was brought to industries in the cities, but not to rural areas where it could have made the lives of farmers easier.

So while manufacturing was thriving and many people in the cities were enjoying a booming economy in 1921, farmers saw their incomes drop precipitously. Between 1929 and 1932, the price of city-made goods dropped only 24 percent while farm prices dropped 60 percent. In 1919, total farm income in the United States was $17.7 billion. By 1921, it had declined to $10.5 billion.

The following figures illustrate just how far farm prices fell in the South:

	1919	1920	1921
Cotton	$ .35/lb.	$.16/lb.	
Sweet potatoes	1.06/bu.	.76/bu.	
Corn	1.07/bu.	.66/bu.	
Peanuts	.09/lb.	.05/lb.	$.025/lb.

Naturally, as prices fell, so did the farmers' income, which became only a fraction of what they had once realized from the sale of produce. To add to their economic woes, the value of the land they owned also declined dramatically. In the early 1920s in Georgia, for example, with the loss of the world market and production that outstripped demand, land values dropped an average of 40 percent. Land worth $150 an acre in 1919 dropped to $35 an acre in the mid-1920s; land worth $25 an acre fell to $2 an acre.

Taxes and mortgage payments, however, continued at the same rate, and thousands of farm owners were simply not able to meet the payments due on their taxes and loans. So even before the Depression officially began for the rest of the country in 1929, many small farmers and those with larger ranches lost them to the banks and to the larger corporations. The Joads were among the losers in Oklahoma, having long before lost their small piece of land, and joined the ranks of the sharecroppers and tenant farmers.

THE EFFECT OF THE STOCK MARKET CRASH ON FARMERS

With the crash of the stock market, farm life became even harder for most owners and workers. The prices farmers received for produce dropped even lower. In 1920, corn had dropped to sixty-six cents a bushel; by 1931 it was fifteen cents a bushel. Cotton, which had dropped to sixteen cents a pound in 1920, was five cents a pound by 1931. Wool was five cents a pound; hogs were three cents a pound, and beef was a little over two cents a pound. Food processors and distributors were the ones that made money on the farmers' products. In the 1930s, distributors paid farmers two cents a quart for milk, and then resold it for eight cents a quart. So, as it became more difficult for farmers to make a profit, the land found its way into the hands of agri-businesses that now owned huge stretches of farmland, as well as the canneries, and distribution centers.

Those who managed to hang onto their land desperately began producing more and more hoping to make enough money to feed their families and pay the mortgage. Excess produce, however, only brought prices down further. Farms and farm equipment fell into greater disrepair for lack of money, which further lowered the value of the farmer's property.

In the 1920s, farmowners found that the high mortgages that they had taken out on the land when prices of farm produce were higher now prevented them from producing enough to yield a profit to pay off the debt. After the crash, land values again dropped. In a fifteen-year period, beginning in the early 1920s, the average farm declined in value about 75 percent. A farmer may have borrowed $10,000 to buy a farm that was worth $10,000 in 1919, especially considering the potential for yielding farm produce at good prices. As production fell in the 1920s, the same farmer borrowed more to keep the farm going, and by 1930, he still owed the bank $10,000. Only now, his farm was worth less than $5,000 and was producing virtually no profit. During the 1920s, the bank that held the farmer's mortgage may have been enjoying the economic boom and could afford to be lenient with loans and missed payments. But after the stock market crash, banks were devastated by the collapse of their own stock investments and their negligence in collecting loans made to stock investors, and so felt compelled to acquire everything of value that they could. Since farms and houses were tangible property, unlike worthless pieces of stock, the farmer found that the bank that held his mortgage foreclosed, and put the farm up for auction. Thousands of farm families were thrown off their land, and lost their homes and livelihoods.

Farmers with large tracts of land and commercial operations owned by corporations were better able to withstand hard times, but they often survived at the expense of families with small farms and farmworkers. Legislators and farm bureaus supported those with very large farms, and money advanced to help "farmers" ended up in the control of agri-business, farm bureaus, and large wealthy insurance companies.

As more and more farmers and their families lost their land and turned to tenant farming—the only way they knew to make a living—the ranks of those looking to sharecrop increased. Former landowners were now living on another man's land and splitting the produce they grew with the owner. Yet, new technology—the diesel tractor, for example, which was widely introduced in 1920—and legislation that only benefited the large farmer, caused even more sharecroppers to be thrown out of work and out of their homes. The thousands of sharecroppers who held onto their jobs were, in 1932, making an average of $ .50 a day ($8.00 to $10.00 a month) and were reduced to having to barter in order to survive. Their average annual wage was $100 a year in 1932.

NATURAL DISASTERS

As if these economic trials were not enough, nature also seemed to conspire against the farmers of the 1920s and 1930s. At this time, the greatest, most widespread natural disaster ever to strike the American farmer—the dust storms of the 1930s—hit the farming areas head-on in the middle of the country: Texas, Oklahoma, Arkansas, Kansas, the Dakotas, Iowa, Nebraska (the plains states).

While the dust bowl could be classified as a natural disaster, it was worsened by earlier farm practices intended to turn the natural prairie into farmland. In the nineteenth century the first settlers of the plains states saw a rolling prairie of grassland and trees. It was fertile land and seemed an ideal place to farm for a population that was largely agricultural. But the pioneer farmers who first settled the plains, while able to cut down the trees, were unable to plough the rock-hard earth for planting. But by the late-nineteenth century, the means to destroy the natural plains emerged with the development of the steel plough that cut through the hard prairie soil. Furthermore, the development of winter wheat became the farmers' success as well as their downfall. While winter wheat was hardy enough to be grown perpetually and allowed the prairie to become the bread basket of the world, it also depleted the land of its natural resources.

Therefore, the steel plough winter wheat eventually caused the ruination of the land. The farmer had unintentionally prepared the soil to be blown away. In addition, after the initial boom in farming after World War I when farmers like the Joads lost their land, "suitcase" farmers intruded and took over much of the land. These long-distance farmers did not care about the land, and only wanted to plough it all up, plant one money crop—primarily wheat or cotton—and make as much money as rapidly as possible. They were not interested in crop rotation, letting the land rest, or allowing it to return to its natural state.

The disaster started as early as 1931, when unbearable heat began to settle on the plains. Farmers began trying to work in the fields at night after the sun went down. In some places, the heat turned the surface of the earth to something resembling ceramic tile. Coupled with the intense heat was a long unrelieved drought that lasted for most of the decade. Ponds and brooks dried up and the water level of lakes dropped over five feet.

The dust storms began in parts of the plains by 1931, reaching killing proportions in 1933, and lasting for five years. Dust not only blew away the topsoil that was necessary for farming, it caused thousands of people to be sick with what was called dust pneumonia. As a result of being unable to breathe, many people people died. In 1935, in Ford County, Kansas, for example, one-third of all the deaths that year, especially children, were from dust pneumonia. It was common practice to wear a damp cloth over noses and mouths to keep from inhaling the dust.

Unfortunately, the dust got into all the food and the water, so it was ingested. It got into eyes, ears, noses and mouths. The piles of dust were so great that they had to be shoveled out of the doorways, like heavy snow, so that people could get out of their houses. Farm wives hung wet sheets over the doors and windows in futile attempts to keep out the dust. For weeks at a time, the daylight hours would be dark as night.

Farmers likened the dust storms to blizzards. They never knew if they were going to survive the trip home from the fields. The dust sickened and killed farm animals by the thousands. In 1934, in response to the situation, the government destroyed herds of cattle that were already on the brink of dying from starvation. The land could not support even the most meager crops for family subsistence, so many families lived on a steady diet of beans and cornbread.

At its worst, in 1935, black rolls of dust blew across the plains, and for twenty-seven days and nights, there was no cessation of wind and dust. The force of the wind was so intense that people and animals who were caught outside suffocated.

The dust also reached urban areas like New York City and Chicago, where twelve million pounds of dust was dumped on the cities.

Even after the dust storms subsided and the government began making positive efforts to conserve the land and prevent further erosion of topsoil, the heat continued to scorch the earth. In summary, the drought, heat, and dust turned fertile farmland into a desert. In combination, these elements killed people, farm animals, and crops, and made farming all but impossible on much of the land for decades to come. Some areas, where farms once existed before the Dust Bowl, continue to be unfarmable some sixty years later.

By the time all these man-made and natural disasters were over in 1940, one-fourth of the population of the southern plains states had fled the land.

To review, many things damaged agriculture in the great farming areas of the south and midwest:

- land speculation
- the collapse of the national economy
- erosion and loss of topsoil through misuse
- technological replacement of workers
- the replacement of farm owners with farm tenants and seasonal workers
- the death of family-sized farms
- the growth of agri-businesses
- the low standard of living for small farm owners and tenants
- the growing of a single crop
- low prices caused by European competition
- the inability of farmers to control prices
- natural disasters like drought and boll weevils

FARMING IN CALIFORNIA

The Joads, and the majority of displaced farming families of the South and Midwest that hit the road, headed for California, where, it was rumored, they would not face depleted land and dust and where water, through irrigation, was plentiful. Two-thirds of inland

California, from Chico to Bakersfield, constitute the enormous growing area called the Central Valley. Within this region are the three subareas of rich farmland known as the Sacramento Valley, the San Joaquin Valley, and the Imperial Valley. Even though California had not been ravaged by the effects of the Dust Bowl, its agriculture had been affected by the economic crash that devastated the rest of the country. The farming problems in California—especially for former farm owners and farmworkers like the Joads—had developed in other directions.

Many of the problems of the family farmer in California can be traced back to the first half of the nineteenth century, when the region was still in the hands of the Spanish. Rather than deeding family-sized farms to settlers, as had happened in the northeastern and middle United States, the Spanish government deeded tracts of several hundred thousand acres to single owners. When California was subsequently taken over by Mexico, it continued this practice. Then, shortly before California was ceded to the United States in 1848, Mexico deeded further massive tracts of land to single owners. The size of a single wheat farm in the 1870s, for example, ranged from 43,266 acres to 300,000 acres. Another farm consisted of 450,000 acres enclosed in 160 miles of fence. In 1870, there were 713 farms larger than one thousand acres in California. Although laws were introduced to limit the size of farms, the many loopholes and alliances available to grantees did not significantly break the pattern of massive holdings. This meant that even from the beginning of its statehood, land in California was concentrated in comparatively few hands. Such large farms could not be worked by just the owner and a few resident hands. These farm owners needed small armies of workers.

So, from the start, the predominant pattern in California was not that of a farmer working his own family farm side by side with a resident farmworker or two, but of a large farm using migrant workers. By the turn of the twentieth century, these immense tracts depended on a multitude of seasonal labor, most of whom were Chinese, Filipino, and Mexican immigrants.

Even mechanization failed to obviate the need for manual labor in California as it had done elsewhere, because the big farmers had long before turned to the growing of vast orchards of fruit, all of which had to be harvested by hand. Fruit required little attention except at harvest time, resulting in the need for only seasonal labor.

Another situation that defined California agriculture from its inception was the need for irrigation in some of the richest growing areas. This meant that only the largest, wealthiest competitors could afford to bring water to their land. The Imperial Valley and the Central Valley, while they are fertile, required irrigation.

Even as early as the 1860s, California farming was already becoming predominantly agri-business rather than family farming. There were boom and bust periods in California agriculture, and the owners of vast stretches of land were more able to survive the bad economic times while many family-sized farms could not.

Not only did the large-scale growers control most of the land, they also amassed tremendous power. Among their most ardent and generous supporters were the industrial giants of the country. And law enforcement and politicians worked hand in glove with the growers. In many cases, growers and law officers were one and the same. One of the most influential entities in the state was the Farm Bureau Federation, later the Associated Farmers, an alliance of owners of large farms, which had the political power to control elections, newspapers, and the police. They also influenced the passage of laws designed to protect their land, to have continued access to water, to avoid taking responsibility for decent living conditions and wages for their workers, and to keep out unions.

The following excerpts document the history of problems for the family-sized farm in the 1920s and 1930s:

- an account of the defiance of big business during farm closings in Le Mars, Iowa,
- a flyer posted in a Michigan farm community to rally farmers to action,
- excerpts from interviews with three people who remember the Dust Bowl,
- excerpts from a Social Science Research Council on the character of California agriculture.

IN LE MARS, IOWA, FARMERS FOUGHT BACK

There are indications in *The Grapes of Wrath* that the Joads were once farm owners who had been expelled years before from their own land. The dispossession of land caused by the plunge of farm produce and land prices hit farmers like the Joads in the 1920s. In the 1930s, however, the loss of farms became epidemic. In 1933, for example, there were 357,000 forced sales in the United States. In 1934, there were 262,000, and in 1935, there were 193,000 forced sales. Jonathan Norton Leonard, an acute first-hand observer of the causes and effects of the Depression on a variety of people, summarizes the ills that struck agriculture. To place his generalizations in human terms, Leonard records a well-publicized instance when farmers defied the economic structure that was throwing them off their land. Instead of standing by to witness another auction in which someone in their community would be cheated, farmers in Le Mars, Iowa, took effective action and, thus, saved their unfortunate neighbor's belongings, if not his land.

FROM JONATHAN NORTON LEONARD, *THREE YEARS DOWN*
(New York: Carrick and Evans, 1939)

The impact of the depression upon the farm population can be simply expressed by a nose-diving curve and a straight, horizontal line. The curve represents the prices the farmer gets for his crops. The straight line is his fixed, irreducible overhead, mostly interest and taxes. Normally the two lines keep far apart for the distance between them stands for the farmer's operating cost, including seed, fertilizer, supplies and tools, besides what is left over for the living expenses of his family.

All during the depression the two lines drew closer together, leaving less and less money which did not have to be handed over immediately to the bank or the tax-collector. One by one the city-made luxuries were eliminated—the ice cream sodas in town, the cute clothes for the children, the gasoline for pleasant social calls. Then went the things which had grown to be necessities—rubber boots, medicine, the car itself. Finally the farm family came to spend no money at all and concentrated desperately on keeping the sheriff from turning them out on the road. (p. 283)

• • •

More dangerous to them than tax-sales were foreclosure sales of mortgaged farms. Land which had once been worth $300 an acre was now down to a third of that. In fact, in most localities it was worth nothing at all because you couldn't sell it. At a foreclosure sale the holder of the mortgage was usually the only bidder and he usually bid far below the face value of the mortgage. The difference allowed him to get a deficiency judgment. At a subsequent auction he would sell the farmer's cattle, machinery, grain and feed, even the beloved furniture brought from the East when the country was opened up. The farmer and his family would be "put out on the road" completely destitute.

On January 4 the 320-acre farm of seventy-year-old John A. Johnson was offered for sale on the stone steps of the court-house at Le Mars, Iowa. Eight hundred farmers gathered at the foot of the steps. There were no women in the crowd. One of the men went to a swing in the court-house park and cut down a length of rope, knotting it skillfully into a hangman's noose. The sheriff came through the door at the top of the steps. In legal form he announced the sale. The only bidder was the agent of the great New York Life Insurance Company, owner of the mortgage. The mortgage was $33,000. The bid was $30,000—leaving $3,000 to be covered by the sale of the farmer's personal property.

The crowd gave an angry roar. A husky farmer dashed up the steps, grabbed the agent by his collar and hauled him down like a sack of grain. He pleaded that he couldn't bid more. His instructions from New York were explicit. The farmers took him to the telegraph office where he sent a desperate message begging the company to save his neck by raising the bid to $33,000. Presently the answer came. The bid might be raised. Farmer Johnson had lost his land, but if the insurance company would not let him remain in his home as a tenant, he could move his cattle, equipment and personal possessions into some other foreclosed farm in the neighborhood.

The news of this victory flashed across the farm States. In a week all Iowa was doing it, then Nebraska, Minnesota, Illinois, Michigan. The movement spread as far east as Pennsylvania and as far south as Texas. (pp. 301–302)

FARMERS ORGANIZE TO PROTEST

The document that follows shows the extent to which owners of small farms, especially in the Midwest, had begun to organize. This was a notice posted in a small farm community in Michigan in 1933. The tone indicates that rage has inspired union and action, a theme to which Steinbeck returns repeatedly in his novel.

SIGN POSTED IN FEBRUARY 1933, IN A SMALL MICHIGAN FARM
COMMUNITY
(In Jonathan Norton Leonard, *Three Years Down*, New York:
Carrick and Evans, 1939)

Farmers and Workers! Help protect your neighbors from being driven off their property. Now is the time to act. For the past three and a half years we have waited for our masters, who are responsible for the situation, to find a way out. The result is starvation in the cities and tax sales and foreclosures on the farms. While the rich are receiving billions through the RFC, the producers of the nation are being driven into slave-like conditions such as existed previous to 1776. . . . On Friday, February 3rd, the property of ____ of ____ is to be sold at a forced auction at the Courthouse. It is typical of thousands of such cases throughout the State. Only the organized, united action of the working people on farms and in the cities will put an end to such insanity. The Farmers Committee has called a mass protest meeting to stop the above mentioned sale. Come one and all and demonstrate your protest in a manner that cannot be suppressed. (p. 300)

MELT WHITE ON THE DUST BOWL AND BLACK SUNDAY

The following interview, the first of three presented here, provides a firsthand account of what it was like to be a farmer during those disastrous times of economic collapse and natural disaster. Melt White attests to the horror of the first dust storm which, coupled with other disasters, like the falling of a meteor in Arizona, led people to think that the end of the world was at hand. For the Joads, the Dust Bowl that White describes was the straw that broke the camel's back, the catastrophe that sent them on the road to California. White is convinced that, in a sense, the Dust Bowl is God's punishment for misuse of the land, that is, ploughing up for farming what was intended as grassland. The kind of self-questioning he refers to is echoed in *The Grapes of Wrath* as various characters ask, "What did we do to deserve this?"

As a result of the Department of Agriculture's policy enacted after Franklin D. Roosevelt took office, White especially remembers the wholesale slaughter of cattle and the refusal to allow the distribution of meat to some of the many people who were starving. The practice, which the government abandoned, but which agri-businesses in California adopted in order to raise prices, is referred to in *The Grapes of Wrath*. Milk is poured out on the ground and fruit and potatoes are poisoned and allowed to rot.

In speaking of his own experience about a frightening day known in the plains states as Black Sunday, when the dust storm reached its worst, Melt White corroborates Steinbeck's own description in the early interchapters that take place in Oklahoma in about 1935.

FROM MELT WHITE, "WHAT IS IT COMIN' TO?" AN INTERVIEW
(*The American Experience* http://www.wgbh.org/pages/amex/
dustbowl/interviews/melt4.html [1998])

They was a lotta different thoughts and ideas went through people's mind. I heard a lot of 'em expressed and then in the spring of '35 there was meteor come up over Dalhart 'bout four o'clock, in the mornin'. And it lit up just like daylight and it—it really scared a lotta people. A lotta people got off their bed and got their children outta the bed and got down prayin', thought that was it. They thought that was the end of the world with all the dust storms and that meteor, which is hit over in Arizona somewheres. It's still over there. I mean I've seen pictures of it. But, naw, it was a—it was feeling that, you just wondered what—what is it comin' to, because things, just like I say, each and every day got worse and you couldn't see no end. You couldn't see anything of any improvement. And the government come in and took the cattle and killed 'em, paid $16 for a cow and $3 for a calf. When that was gone, then you didn't have anything hardly left. And you's just nearly fully dependent on the government for a job. And it was not much future.

We had two—two milk cows and one—one had a little small calf and one of the—I thought it was the prettiest and nicest Guernsey cow, they led it off and the little calf and I don't know how come they let Dad have the—the skin off the calf, but they would not let you have the meat to eat. That, I couldn't understand. People starvin' an dependin' on the government for what we called then "relief commodities." It wasn't called "welfare" then. But they'd take 'em and run 'em off in the draw somewheres and shoot a lot of 'em at a time, several head at a time, and just leave 'em for whatever. And I couldn't understand that, why they couldn't have taken 'em and had 'em butchered and give 'em back to the people for—for food. But they just didn't operate that way.

Some people thought it was an act of God and a punishment for—and possibly in a way it kindly was, because they'd more or less what you'd say raped the land. They way they had done the land, 'cause, to me, God didn't create the plains to be farmland. He created it for what He put on it, in grass and cattle. And they come in and completely changed it.

They abused it somethin' terrible. They raped it. They got everything out they could and—but there'd been cycles like that before and there'd been cycles like that since, but not that severe.

FROM MELT WHITE, "BLACK SUNDAY" AN INTERVIEW
(*The American Experience* http://www.wgbh.org/pages/amex/
dustbowl/interviews/melt3.html[1998])

It's on a Sunday afternoon about six o'clock. And we was gittin' prepared to go to church and went to church in a team and wagon. And I'd gone out to kinda tend the chickens and stuff and back in the north it was just a little bank, oh, like about eight or ten feet high. We had one of those headers out on each end, you know. And I did a few things there around the chickens and everything and went back in the house and I said, "Dad, we ain't goin' to be able to go to church tonight." And he said, "Why?" And that's how fast it's travelin'. And we was livin' in an old house that was 14 feet wide, 36 foot long, just one room, board and batten with a washed roof on it. It kept gittin' worse and worse and wind blowin' harder and harder and it kept gittin' darker and darker. And the old house was just a-vibratin' like it was gonna blow away. And I started tryin' to see my hand. And I kept bringin' my hand up closer and closer and closer and closer and closer and I finally touched the end of my nose and I still couldn't see my hand. That's how black it was. And we burned kerosene lamps and Dad lit an old kerosene lamp, set it on the kitchen table and it was just across the room from me, about—about 14 feet. And I could just barely see that lamp flame across the room. That's how dark it was and it was six o'clock in the afternoon. It was the 14th of April, 1935. The sun was still up, but it was totally black and that was [the] blackest, worst dust storm, sand storm we had durin' the whole time.

A lot of people died. A lot of children, especially, died of dust pneumonia. They'd take little kids and cover 'em with sheets and sprinkle water on the sheets to filter the dust out. But we had to haul water. We had a team and we had water barrels. We hauled stock water and household water both. And we didn't have the water to use for that, so we just had to suffer through it. And lots of mornin's we'd get up and strain our drinkin' water like people strain milk, through a cloth, to strain the debris out of it. But then, of course, a lotta grit went through and settled to the bottom of the bucket, but you had [to] have drinkin' water. And when you got you a little dipper of water, you drink it. You didn't take a sip and throw it away, because it was a very precious thing to us because we had to haul it.

J. R. DAVISON RECALLS DUST PNEUMONIA

In the late 1930s, J. R. Davison was one of the many people who grew sick with dust pneumonia, an illness that took the lives of many children. The severity of his case sent him to the hospital with fever and hallucinations. Dust was inhaled and coated the lungs, and deadly lung infections set in. This was, of course, before the use of penicillin and antibiotics as treatments for bronchial diseases. At this time, pneumonia was often a death sentence.

FROM J. R. DAVISON, "DUST PNEUMONIA" AN INTERVIEW
(*The American Experience* http://www.wgbh.org/pages/amex/
dustbowl/interviews/davidson5.html[1998])

I was pretty small when I got the dust pneumonia. I don't remember exactly getting sick, but I do remember part of my stay in the hospital. They took me to Amarillo, that was the closest good hospital, and I guess I was sicker than I ever realized, because I got, ah, [unintelligible]. I was out of my head. I can see, to this day, those merry go round horses coming out of the ceiling, you know? They'd just, like this, just like a merry go horse—round horse goes. And I'd say, "Mom?" She was always there by my bed, seemed like. I'd say, "Mom, those horses are gonna hit you," I said, "You better move your head." And she'd move her head over. Say, boy, that one like to got you. And so I don't really know how sick I was, but I was pretty sick. I think she thought a time or two I wasn't gonna make it. Ah, that's about all I can remember about it, but I can still see those horses, they were bright colored, red, green gold, just like on a merry go round. I—I really, really saw them, and you couldn't have convinced me they weren't real.

And I don't know how long this went on, but it was a—a good while there, one evening, they gave me sponge baths, I think to keep my fever down, I don't remember feeling hot, but I'm sure that I was. And they'd sponge me off every little bit there. I don't know, for a day or two. And I guess they did what I needed, I got over it. Ah, all I had really was a bronchial pneumonia.

CALIFORNIA SOCIAL SCIENCE RESEARCH COUNCIL STUDY ON AGRICULTURAL LABOR IN THE WEST

In 1938, the California Social Science Research Council did a study of the unique character of California agriculture, in an attempt to come to grips with the growing problem of migrant workers. The council explains the growth of agri-business in the state, the size of the farms, the choice of crops, and the need for water, all of which led to the need for seasonal workers and doomed many family-sized farms. Notes 1 and 2 do not appear in this document.

FROM "AGRICULTURAL LABOR IN THE PACIFIC COAST STATES"
(Sacramento, CA: *Social Science* Research Council, 1938)

INTRODUCTION

Some of the most acute and large-scale social and economic problems of the Pacific States center around the large populations of migrant farm laborers which constitute an important segment of the farm population of the area. The recognized inadequacy of dependable information concerning the economic and social aspects of this problem led to consideration of the situation by the Pacific Coast Regional Committee of the Social Science Research Council. In March, 1936, that committee set up a small sub-committee "to outline investigations that ought to be made on the seasonal agricultural labor situation of the Pacific Coast." Its report is presented in the following pages. . . .

IMPORTANCE OF THE PROBLEM

California.—For California, paid agricultural workers constituted, in 1930, 56.4 per cent of the gainful workers in agriculture (unpaid family workers omitted). Of those giving agriculture as a principal occupation, 135,270 were listed as farmers or farm managers and foremen, while 188,678 were listed as wage workers. Of the latter 106,578 were not living on farms as of January 1, 1930, while 82,100 were living on farms at that date. . . . It is evident from these figures that agricultural laborers and their families constitute a very important part of the agricultural population of California, and that the problems involving their welfare and their relation to the economy of the state are of considerable significance. . . .

HISTORICAL BACKGROUND OF THE PROBLEM

The problems arising from this large percentage of hired labor relatively unstabilized with respect to the land have been significant ones for many decades, but have not until recent years been so much complicated by large-scale migration of whole families.

IMMEDIATE OR SHORT-TERM AS COMPARED TO LONGER-TERM ASPECTS

Public agencies, itinerant workers, and farmer-employers are confronted with many immediate and acute problems. Some of these have grown out of situations that are of long standing and can change only slowly. Of such a nature, for example, is the character of the agriculture which has developed in the western states. Such development has resulted in part from a particular and rather unique set of physical conditions. In part it is a vestige left from an earlier semifeudal land-tenure situation. Because of peculiarly favorable growth conditions which do not exist in like degree elsewhere, many crops have become localized in the Pacific Coast states, particularly in California. It happens that these are, in the main, crops which require large amounts of hand labor at particular seasons of the year. Many of them also are highly perishable, high in cost per acre, and rather more speculative in character than most of the basic crops of the nation.

Along with these natural influences, leading to a special type of agricultural development, there has been an institutional situation of long standing in which it has been possible to secure large amounts of help for short periods. This has encouraged the development of the particular kinds of farming that are prevalent in this region and has made them seem to farmers a natural and logical type of agricultural organization. In addition, the problems surrounding the shipping and selling of many of the crops, with markets usually some thousands of miles distant, have tended to offer some advantages for relatively large-scale operations. The nature of the farming operations, which often can be highly standardized, and the large amounts of labor required per unit of area have likewise been conducive to relatively large-scale operations.[3]

While the number of large-scale agricultural units is higher in the Pacific Coast (p. 3) states than in the rest of the country, this should not be accepted too readily as the characteristic form of organization. There is need for further study of this problem than has thus far been given it. Even in California where large-scale operations are most prevalent, many more farmers operate small farms than large ones. A major part of the crop acreage, however, is controlled by relatively large-scale operators. Taking the 1930 Census figures, which are more complete than those for 1935, we find that 75.4 per cent of the farmers of California operated farms of less than 100 acres. Their farms in total, however accounted for only 26.6 per cent of the harvested crop acreage of the state. In other words, the larger farmers, some 24.6 per cent of all farm operators, operated 73.4 per cent of the harvested crop acreage. This situation is due in part, however, to the inclusion in the farm group of large numbers of very small farm units and to very wide variations in the intensity of operation.

Just where a size is reached above which farms might suitably be termed "industrialized" and "corporation" farms is a matter on which there is little definite information. For some intensive types of agriculture a farm of 200 or 300 acres would pretty well have lost the characteristics of the personally operated family farm. For thousands of farms growing alfalfa, and other extensive crops, especially where irrigation is not used, . . . the family-type farm persist[s] up to much large sizes, often to as high as 500 to 1,000 acres. Some 87.5 per cent of the farmers operate farms of less than 260 acres and handle 44.4 per cent of the crop land. Of the farms larger than this a considerable number are operated along high commercialized lines and under labor arrangements more or less characteristic of industrial plants. Others are in the main grain and live stock farms operated with relatively little hired help except in the harvest season.

In Oregon and Washington, as already mentioned, the family sized farm and units smaller than this are more typical except in the ranching areas and in certain special-crop sections.

While the large so-called "industrial" or "corporation" type farms present many social problems for the communities and states in which they exist, it would be a mistake to assume that the elimination of these farms would eliminate the migratory labor problem. Even small units in the intensive fruit and vegetable districts customarily hire temporary help at certain peak seasons. The nature of the work is so seasonal that operators of these farms, if they had sufficient family help to handle them at peak periods, would necessarily have idle help during much of the year and consequently, in all probability, very low incomes. The large "industrialized" farm does call for considerable study as to its place in the situation. It would seem, however, that the problems it presents should not be allowed to cloud the fact that the agricultural labor problem involves other factors besides that of large-scale farming.

. . . Since 1930, however, the general pool of agricultural laborers has been greatly augmented from two sources: one, the areas of ruthless and continuing drought which virtually drove people out whether they wished to leave or not and despite a lack of any real prospects to draw them to a particular new location; the other, the depression conditions which dislocated and cut adrift large numbers of unskilled and semiskilled laborers, many of whom tended at least temporarily to seek employment in agriculture. For many of these drifting migrant families conditions have been particularly bad. There was little in the way of housing suited to their needs, and they were easy subjects of exploitation. Often they were regarded as unwanted intruders for whose welfare the western farmers felt little sense of responsibility.

Drought immigrants have likewise been pouring into agricultural areas of Washington and Oregon in considerable numbers since 1930. They are adding to a farm labor supply that is already more than adequate during most seasons of the year. Immigrants to these states are mainly from the northern Great Plains and, unlike those from the southern Great Plains, who go in greater numbers to California, are considered preferred workers by farm employers and are therefore reducing the employment of the professional farm laborers of the coast states.

Records obtained by border check stations for California indicated for 1937 a total inflow of people seeking manual employment of 104,976. Of these 78,332 came from the drought states. In all there were 22,167 cars listed for the out-of-state migrants. This figure thus provides us with a rough indicator of the number of families. (pp. 1–4)

[3]It is possible that the survival of some large units which were originally laid out as Spanish and Mexican land grants may have influenced the present tendency to large-scale holdings somewhat. However, there appear also to be more recent and more fundamental factors working in this direction.

TOPICS FOR ORAL OR WRITTEN EXPLORATION

1. Through public courthouse records and back issues of old newspapers, write a research paper on farm closures in the 1930s in the farming area nearest your own residence.

2. As a class project, put together a volume of oral histories of people who lived on farms in the 1930s. Each student should contribute at least one history.

3. Access the Dust Bowl information at http://www.wgbh.org and/or research materials on the Dust Bowl in your library. Write a paper comparing farmers who remained in the Dust Bowl area with families, like the Joads, who left.

4. Examine the first half of the novel closely for references to banks and corporations. Analyze the novel's portrayal of the effect of big business on farming in the 1920s and 1930s and compare it with the historical record.

5. Analyze the triumph of mechanization over nature and human nature in the novel. Write an essay on how this affects mankind's relation to nature in the novel. Look especially closely at Chapter Five.

6. The farmers appear at times to prefer nature over the machine, but obviously nature can be devastating to the farmers. In light of what has been presented, especially regarding the Dust Bowl—in the novel and in the country—what view of nature emerges?

7. Formulate your own view of nature. Is it essentially good or cruel? Plan a class debate on the subject and summarize the positions presented in light of Steinbeck's novel.

8. Write an essay on the subject of greed for land as it is unveiled in the novel. How does it affect the owners of small farms in Oklahoma? Look at Chapters Eighteen and Nineteen in particular. What message about the greed for land comes across there?

9. Notice the result of government attempts to improve American agriculture. Look especially closely at Chapters Eighteen and Nineteen and relevant supporting documents.

SUGGESTIONS FOR FURTHER READING

Galarza, Ernesto. *Farm Workers and Agri-business in California*. Notre Dame, IN: University of Notre Dame Press, 1977.

London, Joan, and Henry Anderson. *So Shall Ye Reap*. New York: Thomas Y. Crowell, 1970.

Rolle, Andrew. *California: A History*. New York: Thomas Y. Crowell, 1963.
Starr, Kevin. *Endangered Dreams*. New York: Oxford University Press, 1996.
Worster, Donald. *Dust Bowl: The Southern Plains in the 1930s*. New York: Oxford University Press, 1979.

Web Site:
WGBH public television homepage: www.wgbh.org.
    Search the archives of *The American Experience* for the episode "Surviving the Dust Bowl."

4

Migrant Farmworkers

SHARECROPPING AND TENANT FARMING

Sharecroppers and tenant farmers, like the Joads in Oklahoma, were not farm owners but farmworkers. The tenant farmer rented a piece of land to farm. Housing was either rented from or provided by the landowner. The tenant farmer paid his rent from the sale of the produce he raised.

The sharecropper was technically different. He also raised crops on another man's farm, but paid for his use of the land by turning over to the farm owner one-half of the crops he raised. The share-cropper retained the other half of what he had raised and used it to feed his family and to sell on the market. In a typical case, the sharecropper or tenant farmer borrowed money from the land-owner to buy seed, fertilizer, animals, equipment, and for basic living expenses until the first food crops came in. The tenant farmer and sharecropper were always in debt to the farm owner. The entire family—even the youngest children—worked the land. An average family, with everyone working, made about $200 a year. Most of this income went to pay the family's debts to the farm owner. Farmwork was brutally hard; the workers' standard of living was low; and the death rate among workers and their families was high. The children, expected to work the same hours in the

Migrant children. Photograph by Dorothea Lange. Reproduced from the collections of the Library of Congress.

fields that the adults worked, were undernourished and uneducated. In the 1930s, there were eight and one-half million sharecroppers in the South alone.

Increasingly, the decline in prices of farm produce, mechanization, and the government-sponsored downscaling of farming resulted in the massive displacement of tenant farmers and sharecroppers. Such people, displaced from the land, joined the ranks of migrant farm laborers.

In the 1930s, as the owners of small- and medium-sized family farms lost their land, and as tenant farmers, farmworkers, and sharecroppers were driven from farms, profound chasms developed between farmers and farmworkers. Owners of large tracts of land, especially in California, tried to shed the designation of farmer, calling themselves instead growers, ranchers, or agribusinessmen. This class division was as pronounced as that between factory owner and factory worker. Moreover, the best interests of one group became diametrically opposed to the best interests of the other group.

By the 1930s, the California state government, along with the rest of the country, was suffering from acute financial pangs. The crash of 1929 had affected state budgets as well. The state and city budgets were stretched to provide services for migrant workers from Mexico, so in 1930 and 1931, the state paid Mexican workers to return to Mexico. The population of Mexican workers in the United States dropped immediately. A shortage of labor on California's farms ensued and the word went out that workers were needed.

At the same time that this labor shortage occurred, the southern and plains states were hit by economic collapse and natural disasters. Although growers' associations consistently denied issuing circulars to lure workers to California, advertisements were openly placed in Kansas and Oklahoma newspapers. Many farm families, like the Joads, claimed that they were drawn to the West because circulars and newspaper advertisements painted California as the land of milk and honey, where work was plentiful and farm ownership was a distinct possibility.

The Mexican farmworkers were soon replaced with emigrants from the South and the plains states. The year when this migration reached its peak was 1938. There were hundreds more workers than there were jobs available for them. The situation worsened when unscrupulous owners advertised for many more workers than they intended to hire. This oversupply of farm labor allowed owners to keep wages low, prices of supplies in their company-run stores high, and living conditions squalid.

There was no official network, except rumor, to inform the migrants about where jobs actually existed. Labor contractors who demanded a fee for their services were so notoriously crooked that they were eventually outlawed by the federal government.

Although California growers with huge tracts of farmland suffered minimally, even in the Depression with prices of farm products low, people like the Joads, who harvested their crops, were making only about half of what they had made ten years earlier. As a U.S. Senate investigation by Robert La Follette reveals, many farm laborers were making fifteen cents an hour in the 1930s.

Journalists from outside the state began to write about the conditions in which the migrants lived. They described unimaginable poverty, filth, and suffering. Migrants lived primarily in squalid, rotten tents along ditches, in trailer parks, and in empty fields. The only food that many of them had to eat was a piece of fruit stolen from the fields in which they worked. Sanitary facilities were non-existent, and very real hunger, malnutrition, and disease were rampant.

In the early 1930s, the growers had welcomed the migrants, but as the state filled with out-of-state farm labor, resentment mounted. The growers needed them, but resented their demands for decent wages. State and county agencies resented their demands for food and medical assistance. Other farmworkers in the state resented the outside competition for work at a time when work was scarce. Others saw the migrants as a clear health threat. Still others were frightened that the presence of so many hungry and resentful outsiders would create social chaos in the state and deepen the threat of revolution in an economically depressed country that was ripe for revolution.

Migrants were hated and reviled. They were given humiliating names, accused of degraded morals, laziness, filth, and stupidity. Vigilantes constantly harassed workers to keep them on the move and out of town, using newly devised vagrancy laws. Impromptu camps were routinely raided and torn apart. Guards posted at the state's borders attempted to keep them out. Trains were stopped and searched for migrants trying to come into California.

In 1938, the year of the greatest number of migrant workers in California, a natural disaster hit the Imperial Valley: torrential rains flooded the growing areas, ruining some crops and causing others to flourish. The effect on the migrant laborers, however, was disastrous. Observers sent to review the scene found group after group of migrant families flooded out of their quarters—as the Joads were at the end of the novel. They were starving and living out in the cold and wet under the trees.

Because there was no federal program of assistance, the only relief afforded to starving or sick families in California came from state and county coffers. But the migrants were not considered residents of California or of any particular county in the state because they were constantly on the move. So it was not until the growth of assistance programs like the government camps run by the federal government in the late 1930s that the migrants had any help at all. Even then, government agencies simply did not have the resources to help more than a fraction of the migrants.

By the middle of 1938, because of the publicity provided by the national media, the cause of the migrant worker was coming to the attention of the general population in California, and the growers were losing public sympathy.

But a growers' organization called the California Citizens' Association sprang into action with a massive antimigrant public-relations campaign supported by the growers, Chambers of Commerce, canneries, and other groups allied to California agribusinesses. In 1938, because of their influence, California demanded that Okies, as the migrants were called, be forced to return to their native states.

REMEDIES

As president, Herbert Hoover frequently voiced his opinion that farmers' complaints in the 1920s and early 1930s should not be taken seriously because farmers just naturally complained no matter what happened, that hardship was a given for anyone who chose to farm, and that the government could do nothing to help them. By contrast, when Franklin D. Roosevelt took office in 1933, he and his cabinet made it clear that they intended to rescue American agriculture. Despite their good intentions, however, it was only the owners of large tracts who benefited from various government programs like the Agricultural Adjustment Act of 1933 (AAA). Most federal programs, at best, brought relief too late and for too few, and nothing that was done significantly helped farmworkers and those who owned small farms. Until the outbreak of World War II, the lot of most tenant farmers and migrant farmworkers got worse instead of better as a result of government programs to help the owners of large farms.

One example was the New Deal's implementation of the AAA under the guidance of Secretary of Agriculture Henry A. Wallace. Wallace, a devoted friend of the American farmer, believed that one of the chief ills in agriculture was the plunge of farm produce prices. To bring up prices, he believed that the market should not be so heavily flooded with produce. So, in the interest of reducing farm produce in order to bring up prices paid by canneries and processors, the administration launched a highly resented plan to destroy food. Thousands of acres of corn, wheat, fruits, and vegetables were burned or poisoned and thousands of gallons of milk were poured onto the ground. In an act that brought on widespread outrage, six million piglets were killed and 90 percent of the meat was destroyed. The great irony was that while the policy was intended to save the American farmer, millions of people, including the owners of small, Dust Bowl farms, and migrant farmworkers and their families, were literally starving to death. The only ones who benefited from the policy, and only marginally, were the owners of large tracts, which often meant corporations. It must also be pointed out that many owners of modest-sized farms in the Midwest seized on the same strategy of destroying food as a means of protesting the low prices paid for their products by food processors, who then charged heavily for the final product.

Another AAA policy was put into action in the spring of 1934. Again in the interest of raising farm prices, the Department of Agriculture proposed paying farmers to leave fields unplanted. By growing less food, it was argued, some balance would be restored in the marketplace, and prices would rise so that farmers could make a living wage. In this case, as well, while the policy helped the top one-third of owners of large southern plantations and large western farms, it markedly damaged tenant farmers and sharecroppers who were thrown out of their jobs and off the land, because having fewer acres under cultivation left large landowners with no need for as many workers.

And while the National Labor Relations Board's Wages and Hours Bill of 1935 (and similar legislation that followed) was intended to help raise wages, lower working hours, improve working conditions, and protect children from exploitation, migrant farmworkers were excluded from the act. Thus, the first federal laws that prevented the hiring of young children did not protect children as young as five years old from going to work in the fields instead of going to school. Migrants were also excluded from the Social Security Act of 1935, which provided relief for the unemployed worker and the retired worker.

There were, however, some federal programs put in place specifically to help migrant farmworkers. These included the Federal Transient Service and Resettlement Service, part of the Federal Emergency Relief Act (1933), which began studies of the magnitude of migration and its problems in order to make corrective recommendations. In 1937, the Farm Security Administration addressed the problem of migrant farmworkers with legislation to improve housing and wages. But the big growers and the politicians in California were able to sidestep the federal laws and, while resettlement assisted some farm tenants, very little benefit accrued to the migrant farmworker.

Two programs provided some relief, but because of inadequate long-range funding and community hostility, only a small percentage of migrant workers benefited. In 1935, under the aegis of the Resettlement Administration, a few camps, like the government camp described in *The Grapes of Wrath*, were built for migrant workers, providing them with decent sanitation. But for the thousands of migrant workers in the 1930s, less than twenty-five camps in all were built in California and Arizona combined. In 1938, a federal program attempted to provide some medical care for migrants.

While many journalists and social activists, including Steinbeck, tried to draw national attention to the migrant problem throughout the 1930s, it was the publication of Steinbeck's *The Grapes of Wrath* in 1939 that elicited a national determination to alleviate the abominable situation of migrant farmworkers in California. Only then did the country listen to the voices of many people who had tried to call attention to the problem, including Senator Robert La Follette of Wisconsin, who fearlessly chaired a committee to investigate their living and working conditions and the violation of the migrants' civil rights by agri-business.

There were many other crusaders in the fight to improve the lot of migrant workers. One of the most prominent in the first decades of the twentieth century was Simon Lubin, California's first commissioner of Housing and Immigration. In the 1930s, a number of young crusaders had connections to the Monterey/Carmel, California, area. The most visible and active reformers included the novelist Lincoln Steffens, sociology professor Paul Taylor, his wife, the famous photographer Dorothea Lange, and Carey McWilliams, whose depictions of migrant workers are the most frequently cited literature on the subject.

John Steinbeck, who had worked as a farm laborer in his college days, was introduced to the enormity of the situation by Lincoln Steffens and his circle in Carmel. The details of various strikes in the 1930s came to Steinbeck's attention at this time. His own past experiences and interests, coupled with his newfound political education, resulted in two publications in 1936 on the migrant farmworker. One was a novel, *In Dubious Battle*, about agricultural-worker strikes, which will be discussed in greater detail in Chapter Five. Another was a series of articles on the plight of farmworkers that he wrote for the *San Francisco News*. It was not until the publication of *The Grapes of Wrath* in 1939, however, that Steinbeck's reputation was secured as an expert on the situation in California. Like nothing before, the novel brought widespread publicity to the plight of the migrant farmworker. Few people who read the novel were lukewarm about it, and it did provide the incentive for many to work more passionately for reforms. As a consequence, in California power circles, Steinbeck was disliked intensely.

Ironically, the event that really brought an end to the Okies' problems in California was the United States' entry into World War II in 1941. Many of the younger men joined the military, and because the war spawned a massive defense industry in California, women and those men too old for military service found jobs at plants owned by Kaiser and Lockheed. So while many migrants from the plains states returned home in the 1930s, significant numbers of families who had once been the backbone of America's agrarian society were finally rescued by industry albeit not by the agricultural industry. And as Okies left the fields for the defense industry, Mexican laborers moved back into California to take their places.

The following documents enlarge upon the problems of the migrant farmworker:

- a flyer advertising for farmworkers,
- the diary of a migrant farmworker,
- excerpt from the La Follette U.S. Senate report,
- a letter to the U.S. secretary of agriculture,
- excerpt from the autobiography of a migrant worker,
- excerpt from a Works Progress Administration (WPA) study,
- excerpt from a proposal for government camps,
- excerpt from Carey McWilliams' *Factories in the Field*,

- excerpt from a description of living conditions in camps in California in 1941,
- excerpt from a California grower-sponsored book that attempts to respond to Steinbeck's *The Grapes of Wrath*.

CIRCULAR ADVERTISING FOR WORKERS

Pa Joad speaks several times about a circular, which he pulls out of his pocket, that promises work in California. Many jobless people from Oklahoma and other states claimed to have been lured to California by circulars and newspaper ads. When they reached California, however, they found that they were unwanted and that there was not enough work to go around. The charge made against the owners of large farms was that they actively lured many more workers to the area than they needed, in order to pay the lowest possible wages. The following circular appeared in 1937 at a time when work was extremely scarce in California.

HANDBILL DISTRIBUTED BY LABOR CONTRACTOR, FEBRUARY 1938
(In Hearings before a Subcommittee of the Committee on
Education and Labor, 76th Congress, Part 53; Washington, DC: U.S.
Government Printing Office, 1940)

800 PEA PICKERS WANTED!
700 Acres of Good Peas about 20 miles West of Santa Maria, California, near Longpolk, Calif. Good Camp, Good Water and Store.

BUSY ALL SEASON
WILL START ABOUT FEBRUARY 25TH OR MARCH 1ST

L. MORT
Labor Contractor—Licensed and Bonded (p. 19750)

THE LIFE OF A MIGRANT FARMWORKER

With no future in Oklahoma, the Joads, along with many others, hit the road in search of work in the only vocation they knew— farming. The following diary of an unnamed migrant farmworker whose chronicle is used in a Works Progress Administration (WPA) study, is an invaluable look at some of the features of the migrant worker's life. Note especially the need to move with the harvests in order to have work, and the wages he was paid.

FROM "DIARY OF A MIGRANT FARM WORKER"
(In John N. Webb, *The Migratory Casual Worker*, Washington, DC: Workers Progress Administration, U.S. Government Printing Office, 1937)

June–August 1932. Jackhammer operator, railroad construction, Liberty, Mo. Wages $4.80 a day.

September 1932. Extra gang laborer, railroad, Hays, Kans. Wages $3.20 a day.

October 1932. Extra gang laborer, railroad, Cheyenne, Wyo. Wages $4.50 a day.

February–March 1933. Laborer, pipe-line construction, Topeka, Kans. Wages $3 a day.

April–October 1933. Watchman, building construction, Kansas City, Mo. Wages $1.25 a day.

February–May 1934. Extra gang laborer, railroad, Wamsutter, Wyo. Wages $2 a day.

June–September 1934. Extra gang laborer, railroad, Topeka, Kans. Wages $2.80 a day.

March–April 1933. Left for Chicago. Stayed a couple of weeks. Returned to California 2 months later.

May 1933. Odd-jobs on lawns, radios, and victrolas at Fresno. Also worked as porter and handy man.

June 1933. Returned to picking figs near Fresno. Wages, 10 cents a box. Averaged $1.50 a day, and earned $50 in 2 months.

August 1933. Cut Thompson's seedless grapes near Fresno for 7 days at 1¼ cents a tray. Earned $11. Picked cotton 1 day, 115 pounds; earned $1.

September–November 1933. Cut Malaga and muscat grapes near Fresno. Wages, 25 cents an hour. Made $30 for season.

December 1933. Picked oranges and lemons in Tulare County, Calif. (Earnings not reported.)

January 1934. Picked oranges at 5 cents per box for small jobs and 25 cents per box for large jobs, Redlands, Calif. Earned $30. Picked lemons at 25 cents an hour.

January 1934, Went to Brawley, Calif. Picked peas at 1 cent a pound. Picked 125–150 pounds a day for 15-day season.

February 1934. Picked grapefruit at 25 cents an hour, Koehler, Calif. Worked 8 hours a day on three jobs for a total of 22 days. Also hauled fertilizer at 25 cents an hour.

March 1934. Worked as helper on fertilizer truck at $2 a day for 20 days, Brawley, Calif.

June 1934. Worked as circus hand with Al G. Barnes Circus for 4 weeks at $4.60 a week and board, Seattle to Wallace, Idaho.

July 1934. Tree shaker at 25 cents an hour, averaged $2 a day for 25 days, near Fresno.

August–October 1934. Picked oranges and lemons at 25 cents an hour, working an average of 6 hours a day, for 60 days, near Fresno.

December 1934. Houseman in hotel, Fresno. Received 50 cents a day and board for 1 month, and 25 cents a day and board for 2 months. (pp. 3,4)

ROBERT LA FOLLETTE'S INTERVIEW WITH GROWER HENRY L. STROBEL

A U.S. Senate committee, chaired by Robert La Follette, investigated the living and working conditions of migrant workers between 1937 and 1941. The committee called many witnesses, including various owners of large farms who were active in the Farmer's Association that represented the owners of large farms and agri-businesses. Henry L. Strobel was an outspoken and powerful member of the association, well known for his strong-arm tactics against farmworkers and their attempts to organize. In questioning him, Senator La Follette brings to light several deplorable practices. He exposes the miserable level of wages that could not support a family during the working season, much less tide a family over during the long months of unemployment. La Follette also uncovers the fact that wages are fixed by the association that organized in its own self-interest to the detriment of migrant workers.

The point that the senator makes (and which will be pursued in greater detail in Chapter Five) is that the owners are free to organize to protect their own profits, but refuse to allow the workers to organize for better wages. Notes in the original document have been omitted.

FROM TESTIMONY OF HENRY L. STROBEL
(In Hearings before a Subcommittee of the Committee on
Education and Labor, 76th Congress, Part 53; Washington, DC: U.S.
Government Printing Office, 1940)

Senator LA FOLLETTE. At this point I would like to read into the record a copy of an excerpt from exhibit 8278, which is a letter from F. J. Palomares to Leonard E. Wood, dated July 9, 1934. The sixth paragraph reads:

For your information I quote you schedule adopted for fruit picking on an hourly basis since 1931:
1931—20 cents to 25 cents per hour.
1932—15 cents per hour.
1933—15 cents per hour until July when the picking rate was

raised to 17½ cents an hour and later from 20 cents to 25 cents an hour. (p. 19481)

• • •

Senator LA FOLLETTE. I should also like to read into the record an excerpt from the report of the special investigating committee appointed upon the request of the California State Department of Agriculture, California Farm Bureau Federation, and the Agriculture Department of the California State Chamber of Commerce. This document will be offered as an exhibit at a later point. The excerpt appearing on page 6 reads:

Wages paid on an hourly basis to field workers remained fairly constant throughout the valley during 1929, 1930, and the spring and early summer months of 1931, but by August a downward trend occurred, reduction in the prevailing scale of wages being again recorded in April, August, and November, 1932, and in April 1933. The period from April to June 1933, registered the lowest scale (viz 16⅔ cents per hour for irrigators and 15 cents for workers other than irrigators as contrasted with 35 cents and 50 cents in 1920 and 1930). Beginning in July 1933, the wage scale started to rise with increases taking place in July and November 1933. (p. 19482)

• • •

Senator LA FOLLETTE. Now, Mr. Strobel, in 1933 when wages appeared to have been at a low level, due to numerous factors, how could a seasonal laborer on a California farm which hires fifty, a hundred or more workers, negotiate with his employer about wages for his work if they were too low, except for a substandard of living?

Mr. STROBEL. How could he negotiate?

Senator LA FOLLETTE. Yes.

Mr. STROBEL. He could always come and ask for more wages. That has been done every day in the year.

Senator LA FOLLETTE. Was that effective? Did you have any such experience?

Mr. STROBEL. Well, I didn't have any such experience. We had requests for higher wages at all times, but most of our agricultural workers realized at that time that they were lucky to have a job at all. There were thousands of people who couldn't get a job, and the wages that we were paying were all we could afford. It seemed that most of them realized that. We had no more trouble then at the low wages, as you call it, than during the high wages. (p. 19482)

• • •

Mr. STROBEL . . . But there has been a tendency toward the discussion of wages with the view of being fair to everybody concerned. In my own particular territory, which is Salinas, we have a wage scale that is fairly static. Although we haven't made any money there in the last 4 or 5 years, our wages have remained practically at 35 cents an hour for our field workers. We have been paying 35 cents an hour, which is considerably higher than is paid in most other districts in California. (pp. 19484, 19485)

A LETTER FROM A FARMWORKER'S WIFE

The three documents presented here were published in 1937 when problems for the migrant workers had not yet reached their worst level, which they did in 1938. The first is a letter written to Secretary of Labor Frances Perkins, from a farmworker's wife. Although the letter is from Ohio, and this woman's family seems to be more stable than the Joads, the problem of seasonal work is much the same. Notice that her husband has no work at all in January and is not paid enough to live on from month to month. The attitude and sense of class conflict represented here was even more pronounced in California. She and her family see themselves as distinct from farmers who exploit the very people who make money for them.

FROM A LETTER TO FRANCES PERKINS, SECRETARY OF LABOR
(In *Slaves of the Depression*, Gerald Markowitz and David Rosner, eds.; Ithaca, NY: Cornell University Press, 1987)

Weston, Ohio, March 2, 1937

Dear Miss Perkins:

In hope that there is someway out of the situation in which we find ourselves, I'm sending you a letter. Please read & consider it.

There is help for men in almost every walk of life in America but the lowly farmhand. The farmer has his from the government, the shop worker, the rail-roader, in fact every working man but the farm laborer. They get nothing.

My husband works from 6 to 7 a.m. doing chores from 8 a.m. to 12 noon takes his hour then works till 6 p.m. gets $35 per mo. a very poor house to live in a garden 200 ft. sq. and 1 gal. of scimed or separated milk a day.

On this we must feed & cloth 4 children. Understand this is for 10 mo. The first of Jan. he is out of work completely.

How can this be a land of opportunity for our children if they must grow up under conditions like that? It seems to me there should be some better way for the Farm Laborer.

You see, this is only one of many cases throughout the country.

Farmers have their swell cars, their fancy meals, their nice cloths But the man who makes their money gets scarcely enough to eat.

How can we give our children a decent chance on such conditions?

Maby you, I hope you Miss Perkins sees this instead of one of your staff looking at it and tossing it in the waste basket, can see if something can be done.

Please do something for the Farm Laborers.

In hopes of better times

MRS. J. B.T .

THE AUTOBIOGRAPHY OF A MIGRANT WORKER

The second document from 1937 is a firsthand account by Tony Slotnig who was interviewed by John N. Webb, an investigator for the Works Progress Administration, an agency that was designed to put millions of people back to work, including artists, writers, and researchers. Just before the crash of 1929, Tony Slotnig was driven to the migrant worker's life by injuries he received on the job and subsequent financial problems. He returned to factory work despite his injuries only to get laid off as a result of the stock market crash. For the injured worker there was inadequate compensation and no safety net. Like so many men, mortgage and home went the way of the job, and family pressures worsened by financial woes left him no choice but to hit the road. Before the Depression, Slotnig had once made as much as twenty dollars a day. Now, on the road, he receives a total of four dollars for eight weeks of work. In one place, he leaves owing his employers money for bed and board. He tells Webb about the difficulties in securing work, the starvation wages, and the squalid conditions.

FROM "AUTOBIOGRAPHY OF TONY SLOTNIG"
(In John N. Webb, *The Migratory Casual Worker*, Washington, DC:
Works Progress Administration, U.S. Government Printing Office,
1937)

Then the papers came out all about the big wages Henry Ford was paying, and I got hungry for that. Packed up and went to Detroit. Found that everybody there was a mechanic. Worked at common labor until I could buy some tools, then worked for Ford for 13 months at $5.60 a day during the war. I quit him because there wasn't enough money in it. Went back to Detroit and worked as a machinist.

In 1924 I met my wife and got married with her. I worked at piece work in the Fisher Body Plant, getting as high as $20 a day. In 1926 I went to work for the U.S. Radio Corporation at $1.50 an hour. In 1929 I got my arm caught and tore up the muscles in it. I was sick 4 to 5 months. My wife was in the family way and we had one hell of a time. I signed a petition I was o.k. and went back to work for 2 months in 1930, then they laid me off because there wasn't enough work. I had slowed down because my hand got numb when I tried to use it and I couldn't grasp a lathe like I used to. I had the case reopened twice trying to get more damages, but the company had smarter fellows than I had.

Well, my wife went back to her folks. They forclosed the mortgage on our house. My wife's brother-in-law and sister had to move in with the old folks too, making nine of us in the little house. Her folks didn't like me and said I was a foreigner and a Catholic and didn't have any education. I packed up and left. They had me arrested for deserting my family, and made me work for the relief and report to the judge every week. I couldn't stick it, so came out west in 1933.

I hitch-hiked through the Dakotas, inquired in a pool hall for a job, and found one on a farm plowing for 50¢ a day. Worked there 8 weeks and never got but $4. Was walking around the street hungry when I met a fellow half drunk who told me about a job he was supposed to go to that I could have if I wanted it. I sure was lucky he was drunk. I harvested there, and made about $60. Then I went to Colorado to work in the sugar beets, but nothing there but Mexicans. I got a job cutting grapes for Filipino contractors. They hire more men than they need so they can collect for boarding them. We had rice three times a day and slept on the floor like hogs. I think I owed them board when I left. It was terrible there and if the government doesn't believe it, I've got the man's name here on a card and you can go see for yourself. [He produced a card with the name and address of the vineyard owner on it.]

I started to pick cotton but heard that there was a big strike on and two people killed, so I got cold feet and left the country. Had a dish-washing job for a fellow who got sick, but he was only sick a week. Then I hit the freight and got in a good job of harvesting at Colfax, Wash. I tried to pick apples, but couldn't find anything. Went to Moxie, Wash. and picked hops and sure made it good—about $25 in two weeks; slipped in lots of leaves in the bottom of the sack. I found a farm job where I have been ever since. They expected me to milk 6 cows and kept piling on more work, all for just tobacco money, so I quit. I'll do most anything I can find, though. (p. 95)

COLD STATISTICS

John N. Webb, commissioned in 1937 by the Works Progress Administration (WPA) to study migrant workers, supplies objective figures on unemployment. Several of the problems he points out are apparent in the life of the fictional Joads as well: long periods of no work at all; low employment even during the harvest season; enticing too many workers for too few jobs; and the workers' lack of any reliable information about where jobs exist. Included with Webb's study is a graph showing monthly levels of employment in two bad years—1933 and 1934.

FROM JOHN N. WEBB, *THE MIGRATORY CASUAL WORKER*
(Washington, DC: Works Progress Administration, U.S. Government
Printing Office, 1937)

EMPLOYMENT AND UNEMPLOYMENT DURING THE MIGRATORY PERIOD

Assuming that a satisfactory year for migratory-casual workers is one in which employment would cover the greater part of the migratory period, then the years 1933 and 1934 were decidedly unsuccessful years for the 500 workers included in this study. After losing an average of about 3 months each year in the off-season, many workers were also unemployed through a large part of the migratory period. Some indication of the extent of idleness during the migratory period was given when it was pointed out in the discussion of the number and duration of migratory-casual jobs, for example, that most of the workers held only one, two, or three jobs each year, and that the average duration of each of those jobs was about 2 months. In addition, it was shown that among the 500 workers, the busiest month of either year, July 1933 . . . , supplied only 1,250 man-weeks of employment out of approximately 2,160 man-weeks possible. More specifically, a distribution of the time spent in employment by the 500 workers shows that the median period was 24 weeks in 1933 and 21 weeks in 1934. . . .

It is not known precisely how the proportion of time lost during migration in depression years compares with that lost by migratory-casual workers in less stringent periods, since comparable data for earlier years are not available. Although it seems evident that the amount of unemployment during migration in 1933 and 1934 was greater than in normal

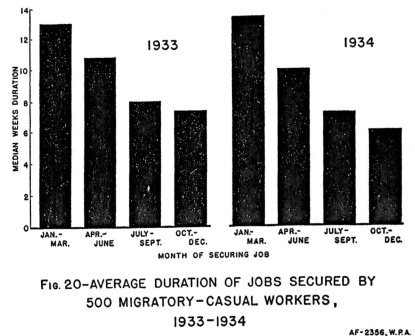

FIG. 20-AVERAGE DURATION OF JOBS SECURED BY
500 MIGRATORY-CASUAL WORKERS,
1933-1934

AF-2356, W.P.A.

times, there is little doubt that the unproductive part of the migratory period is large at any time. Necessarily, the migratory-casual worker wastes much time and motion because of the lack of proper direction into the nearest and timeliest field for labor. Even for seasonal work in which the date of the opening of jobs is known in advance, the worker often arrives at the job too late or too soon. He may be unaware of a labor shortage in a nearby community, or he may migrate in response to a rumor of a labor shortage only to find that the rumor had been spread so far that an oversupply of workers had arrived before him. In addition to the regular slack winter season there are a number of periods between jobs when, whether they wish it or not, workers are idle while waiting for new jobs to begin. Thus, the migratory-casual worker is faced not only with the imperfect adjustment of the supply of labor to the demand, but also with the difficulties resulting from the lack of direction of the workers.

During the depression this situation became acute. Even an efficient method of controlling the flow of labor in accordance with demand, which would solve many of the difficulties of normal times, would be of little use during a period when the oversupply of labor amounts to a glut in the market. (pp. 63, 64)

ROBERT LA FOLLETTE'S COMMITTEE REPORT

In 1940, the U.S. Senate Committee on Education and Labor, chaired by Senator Robert La Follette, continued bringing to light many government studies on the plight of migrant laborers. Included in the supporting exhibits of the hearings of the 76th Congress is a paper presented in 1935 at the California Conference on Housing of Migratory Agricultural Laborers. In arguing for the urgent need for government-sponsored camps, the Regional Office of Resettlement Administration draws attention to the deplorable housing in which the migrants live. Subsequently, a few government camps, like the one described in *The Grapes of Wrath*, were established, but they could only accommodate a small number of workers. Farm owners fought against the camps at every opportunity—sometimes raiding them, or refusing to hire anyone who lived in them. The farm owners believed that the camps "spoiled" the workers by providing toilets and showers. They also thought that labor unions used the government camps as places from which to organize farmworkers. The prevailing attitude of the community and farm owner is made clear in the statement by Colonel Lee A. Stone, a prominent grower.

FROM EXHIBIT 9577-E: "STATEMENT OF REGIONAL OFFICE OF
RESETTLEMENT ADMINISTRATION ON POSSIBLE
ESTABLISHMENT OF MIGRANT CAMPS," NOVEMBER 18, 1935
(In Hearings before a Subcommittee of the Committee on
Education and Labor, 76th Congress, Part 62; Washington, DC: U.S.
Government Printing Office, 1940)

The employing farmers of the state are receiving direct aid from the government in numerous ways. Among these may be enumerated the assistance of the Agricultural Adjustment Administration, the liberal extension of credit to farmers through agencies such as the Federal Land Bank, the Production Credit Association, the Bank of Cooperatives, the protection of crops through inspection and pest control, marketing assistance through the AAA and market news service, and education in the best farm practices through government experiment stations and extension services. These government benefits to the farmer have filtered down to farm laborers only indirectly and to a limited degree. It is therefore entirely just that some direct assistance from the government be extended to the farm laborers, who constitute more than 57 per cent of all persons gainfully employed in agriculture in California. Particularly it is appropriate that some direct assistance be given to the migrant laborers. The living conditions for thousands of these men, women and children are only too suggestive of China and other backward countries. In America their standard of living is intolerable. Yet upon them the crops of California depend.

A series of questions has been proposed by a committee of the California Conference on Housing of Migratory Agricultural Laborers, to which representatives of the Resettlement Administration in this region willingly make specific reply.

Question: Are growers, either actively or prospectively, taking steps with sufficient rapidity to bring about a solution to the problem of providing decent housing for migratory agricultural laborers?

Answer: No. This is the uniform judgment of those who have studied the problem. First, the California Division of Immigration and Housing has officially reported the alarming growth of squatters' camps. In its 1932 report the Division states:

> apropos of labor camps attention is called to a situation which has grown up on account of the economic stress. Groups of persons arrive at any given community and start a camp. No provision is made for sanitation, water supply or even general camp cleanliness. Such housing accommodations as they may have is eked out by wood, tin, or such cast-off material as can be obtained in the vicinity. A sorry picture is presented of a condition that threatens to be a serious menace to those communities where squatter camps exist. Moving the occupants away simply spreads the condition and local authorities are loath to act against people who came there in the hope of securing some employment. The division's attention has been called to a number of these squatter camps during the last winter, but has no legal authority to take remedial steps and must content itself with offering the best advice applicable to each individual case.

Second, Federal commissions and officials have condemned conditions in scathing language. Third, even employing interests recognize that despite all the good efforts of employers and camp inspectors, the need remains great. The Agricultural Committee of the California State Chamber of Commerce declared on November 7th that "there is real need of the establishment of migratory labor camps throughout the various districts in California for labor for the cultivation and harvesting of perishable crops." Fourth, the Division of Rural Rehabilitation of the Resettlement Administration, by extended study of the problem, has amply verified and documented the deplorable conditions which exist. Fifth, has not this conference itself, in specific statements and by its very existence, admitted the necessity for improvement?

Question: Will the establishment of such camps as are proposed by the Resettlement Administration solve, in whole or in part, the "squatter" camp problem? In this connection, it is pertinent to inquire as to what extent farm operators rely upon "squatter" or temporary camps for agricultural workers.

Answer: The camps under consideration by the Resettlement Administration will solve the squatter camp problem only in part. It is not possible to establish enough of them to meet the entire problem. In large sections of rural California farmers draw their laborers from squatters' camps. Colonel Lee A Stone, a pioneer in the movement for good housing, has made a statement which we believe unfortunately confuses the issue. He says:

The squatter is usually . . . nothing more or less than an idler and a parasite on the body politic of the people surrounding them. They are a burden on the taxpayer and on growers honestly concerned with proper housing and sanitation for the care of those laborers who will work and work efficiently. Individuals usually found in "squatters' camps" are to be classed among those types which are usually found in jungle camps here and there over the nation. These individuals go to make up that group known as hoboes or tramps.

At most, this description by Colonel Stone may apply to inhabitants of some of the "jungles." It is true that many thousands of migrant men, women and children live in squatters' camps which are no better than jungles. But California farmers are dependent upon these squatters. The issue cannot be thus dismissed by calling them "idlers" and "parasites." (pp. 22638–22639)

FARMWORKERS LIVES DOCUMENTED IN *FACTORIES IN THE FIELD*

Carey McWilliams, the most prominent historian and advocate of the farmworker (although he started out his career as an attorney in a conservative law firm), exhibited antiestablishment sentiments in his second career as a journalist. In 1934, he became even more involved in radical politics as a tireless crusader for the farm laborer. In 1939, he was appointed head of California's Division of Immigration and Housing. Through their writings, John Steinbeck and Carey McWilliams came to be regarded by California's powerful political elite as very dangerous men. Two of McWilliams' books are the most often cited references about the background of John Steinbeck's *The Grapes of Wrath*.

Factories in the Field was published in 1939, three months after *The Grapes of Wrath* appeared. McWilliams' equally important *Ill Fares the Land* appeared in 1942. When Steinbeck was continually attacked after the publication of *The Grapes of Wrath*, McWilliams became his chief defender.

In the following excerpt from *Factories in the Field*, McWilliams documents the history of farmworkers in 1917. He goes on to describe the starvation among migrants in 1937, "the indescribably wretched" housing, the malnutrition and disease, and finally, the plight of the children. The excerpt brings together, along with McWilliams' own eyewitness account, the firsthand research on migrant workers written by several other journalists who reported on what they had observed in the 1930s. Notes 1 and 2 do not appear in this document.

FROM CAREY McWILLIAMS, *FACTORIES IN THE FIELD*
(Boston: Little, Brown, 1939)

Labor conditions in the fields were so wretched during the war years that even some of the growers confessed that possibly some improvements should be made. One farmer, C. W. Kesner,[3] stated that conditions "were terrible" and that the workers on his farm—he was charging the condition to their ignorance—"did not have a blanket or a wash tub."

At a meeting of the State Council of Defense in Sacramento, May, 1917, migratory workers testified that no provision whatever was made for them on the large ranches. One man said that he had "slept in a piano box in a cow shed and a not too sweet smelling cow shed at that." One of the large growers let the cat out of the bag, at this hearing, when he said that the "Labor Hog" was responsible for conditions in the field. "The Labor Hog," he said, "is an employer who has a crop maturing and necessitating the employment of a large number of hands," so he tries to get twice as many men as he actually needs, "in order to have a surplus of men stranded on the job from whom he may draw at will, as the necessity arises." This method of employment was, of course, the established practice in California; in fact, it still obtains, only on an ever-increasing scale. . . .

Despite these occasional evidences of candor, the majority of the farm industrialists, drunk with profits, remained as impenitent as ever and alternated, in their attitude, between facetiousness and brutality. One grower stated that baths were not necessary for farm laborers. He urged his colleagues to spend five dollars and "run a pipe to the side of the tank house and cap it with a tin spray," as an improvised shower; "it will make them more efficient and they will stay longer."[4] Baths, as such, were "ridiculously inexpensive," but, even so, the pipe-shower arrangement was cheaper and one should not spoil these tramps. One grower, impressed with his benevolence, suggested that, indeed, migratory workers should be treated better. He personally, for example, favored giving them "plenty of clean hay to sleep on."

[3]*Pacific Rural Press*, June 2, 1917.
[4]*Pacific Rural Press*, June 2, 1917.

(pp. 172–173)

• • •

The first revelation to attract widespread attention had to do with 2000 pea pickers marooned in Nipomo, a small community north of Santa Barbara. For two preceding seasons, labor contractors, licensed by the State of California, had been permitted to advertise in Arizona newspapers for "thousands" of pea pickers, promising work "for the season." In response to these appeals, 2000 workers had assembled at Nipomo in the spring of 1937 only to discover, of course, that there was work for but a third of their number. To complicate matters, rain destroyed a portion of the crop and flooded the camp of the workers. Those who had any funds at all moved on; some sold what belongings they had and tried to escape. But about 2000, trapped in their miserable camp, were actually starving when a representative of the Federal Surplus Commodities Corporation discovered their plight. Local authorities admitted that there was "some distress" but tried to duck responsibility. Federal agencies rushed in supplies of food and medicine, and managed to help the workers along until the other crops matured. The pictures taken at this camp, by Federal representatives, are almost incredible in their revelation of the plight of 2000 starving, dirty, utterly dejected men, women and children. (p. 312)

• • •

In July, 1937, Californians were shocked by a sensational address by Mr. Harold Robertson, national field secretary of the Gospel Army, who charged that 70,000 transients were starving in the great valley of the San Joaquin. Speaking from personal observation, Mr. Robertson announced that "people are seeking shelter and subsistence in the fields and woods like wild animals" and that children were working in the cotton fields for 15 cents and 20 cents a day. Lured to the valley by announcements that 25,000 additional workers were required to harvest the 1937 cotton crop, a vast army of transients had assembled there to starve. Under the impetus of this forceful address, the social agencies got busy and conducted an investigation which amply confirmed the charges. The *Los Angeles Times*, taking cognizance of the crisis, sent a special correspondent into the San Joaquin areas who confirmed the findings of Mr. Robertson and added a few grim details based upon his own observations. Although everyone in California conceded that a grave crisis existed in the summer of 1937—the point of maximum employment—nothing whatever was done to guard against the obvious consequences. The transients, herded together like cattle, were permitted to eke out an existence in the fantastic hope that they would ultimately disperse, vanish into the sky or march over the mountains and into the sea or be swallowed up by the rich and fertile earth. But they did not move, and with the winter season came heavy rains and floods. Soon a major crisis was admitted to exist, with over 50,000 workers destitute and starving. The situation was tided over, for the time being, when the Farm Security Administration assumed the burden of supporting the transients. But the problem has not been solved: It has merely been shoved forward. And the army of transients continues to camp in the San Joaquin.

From an investigation conducted by the State Relief Administration in 1936, and from later investigations in 1937, supported by some excellent stories in the *San Francisco News* by Mr. John Steinbeck, Mr. Theodore Smith, and Miss Tessie Williams and a series of articles in the *San Francisco Chronicle* by Mr. Robert E. Girvin, it is possible to summarize the actual condition of migratory labor in California with reference to housing, health and sanitation, education and employment. The facts may be summarized briefly; but they are illuminating and require neither emphasis nor elaboration.

With the exception of one or two large ranches, the investigators agreed that the housing situation was indescribably wretched. One investigator reported that he had found a two-room cabin in which forty-one people from Southeastern Oklahoma were living; another described a one-room shack in which fifteen men, women and children, "festering sores of humanity," lived in "unimaginable filth." The State Immigration and Housing Commission on December 3, 1937, ordered thirty shanties near Visalia condemned as "unfit for human habitation." Most of the boasted "model camps" maintained by the growers were found to be without baths, showers or plumbing; in most districts, the workers bathed in and drank from irrigation ditches. Eighteen families were found living near Kingsburg, under a bridge. Workers in large numbers were found living in shacks built of linoleum and cardboard cartons; in tents improvised of gunny sacks on canal banks with coffee cans serving for chimneys on their makeshift stoves; in some cases a bit of carpet or sacking had been tacked against a tree for shelter. One investigator found an entire tent city consisting of "dirty, torn tents and makeshift shacks in a sea of mud." Most of the ranches, it develops, charge from $3 to $15 a month for the wretched accommodations they provide the workers and sell water at 5 cents a bucket. One ranch, taken as typical, provided a single bath house and a single shower in connection with a block of houses capable of housing 400 people. Along the way to the camps, "beside the road are sights reminiscent of Death Valley, with heaps of abandoned automobiles and farm tools, junked, rusting." "A visit to these squatter camps," wrote Mr. Ray Zeman of the *Los Angeles Times*, "leaves one aghast."

Health and sanitary conditions were found to be equally appalling. Six thousand cases of influenza broke out in one county in February, 1937, largely among migratory workers, and between 75 and 100 cases developed into pneumonia with fifteen deaths. All the local health authorities agreed that the presence of a vast army of destitute migratory workers was responsible for the outbreak of numerous epidemics. "At times we have to move them along as a health measure," was the cynical comment of one health officer. In an attempt to protect the public health, officials in one county lined up 7000 migratory workers, in the camps, and conducted a mass compulsory vaccination. Most districts in the San Joaquin Valley were afflicted with various epidemics: influenza, typhoid fever, colds, infantile paralysis, skin diseases. Fifty babies, the children of migratory workers, died of diarrhea and enteritis in one county in a single season. Children were reported dying in Tulare County at the rate of two a day, with 90 percent of the mortality being among the children of migratory workers. In one ditch camp, 27 out of 30 children examined were found to be defective through malnutritional diseases; some 25,000 families were reported in need of medical care and treatment. Inspecting eighteen camps in a four-mile radius of Kingsburg, Tessie Williams found "dozens of children with horribly sore eyes; many cases of cramps, diarrhea and dysentery; fever, colds, and sore throats." She reported the case of one woman who was taken from the county hospital, after being confined, and returned with her baby to live in the shade of a tree. Many women told her that they had lost babies for three and four successive years. Everywhere the rural hospitals were overcrowded. Dr. Omer Mills of the Farm Security Administration visited the San Joaquin area on January 25, 1937, and reported such typical cases as a man, woman and child who had lived on a diet of bread and potatoes for four weeks; and the presence of hundreds of children (165 in one camp) living "like little wild animals." Local health officers attempt to render some aid in the case of infectious diseases; but they usually remain more or less indifferent to cases of non-infectious illnesses and malnutritional diseases. Observed diets were: for a family of seven, beans and fried dough; family of six, fried oatmeal; family of eight (with six children) dandelion greens and boiled potatoes. "I'm getting mighty tired of just beans and water," said one woman, "but even that may run out any day now." In cases of childbirth, prenatal care was reported as almost unknown and the presence of a doctor at the time of delivery was described as quite exceptional. In his novel *In Dubious Battle*, John Steinbeck describes a confinement in a jungle camp, the details of which were incredible to many readers. Later investigations have revealed many similar cases. An entire volume of documentation could be supplied on the subject of health and hygiene.

The picture of the educational situation was no less distressing. Local school authorities were reported as powerless to cope with the problem. During the height of the harvest season, the schools in the rural areas are extremely crowded. When the post-season exodus begins, fifty percent of the enrollment may drop out of attendance. In one area, the investigators found a cow barn which had been converted into a schoolhouse. I quote a few lines of description (from a report of the State Board of Health): "There were no glass windows; the only openings were sections of the wall which could be propped out, and since it was winter they were closed. Some small screened openings provided all the light and ventilation. Consequently the atmosphere was dense, especially as the native effluvium of the recently washed floor mixed with other odors." A survey of the schools in Bakersfield and Taft indicated that 8515 pupils entered the rural schools of Kern County in one season and 6450 moved out, with students hailing from Oklahoma, Texas and Arkansas leading the list. Fully half of the students move twice during the school year; five, six and seven moves are not uncommon. The effect of this constant shifting is generally bad, as might be expected. Even the parents comment upon it. "There is a growing consciousness," writes Dr. Paul Taylor, "that for many of their kind the future portends, not progress from generation to generation, but retrogression." He quotes one migrant: "My children ain't raised decent like I was raised by my father. There were no rag houses then, but I can't do no better."

Most of the investigators, however, failed to realize that exactly these same conditions have existed for fifty years in California. In an article entitled "California the Golden" which appeared in *The American Child*, November, 1920, Emma Duke pointed out that thousands of children under the age of sixteen were working in the California fields; 3000 in the cotton fields alone. She noticed children five years of age picking cotton in California. She also discovered that local school board officials ignored the problem; that they seemed eager to overlook the fact that the children of migratory workers were not attending school, as they did not want to burden the schools or to detract from the educational facilities afforded their own children. Even where the local authorities were inclined to insist that migratory children attend school, the nomadic nature of the employment followed by their parents made it almost impossible to enforce the school laws. In a pamphlet on migratory child labor in California by George B. Mangold and Lillian B. Hill, issued June 28, 1929, the same conditions are described. The authors of this pamphlet state that, in 1929, there were 36,891 children reported in the school census in California who claimed no permanent residence and were migrants. A special legislative act was passed to set up some method of providing educational instruction for migratory children, but the appropriations for the department have been wholly inadequate (at one time, the appropriation was $5000 a year). Miss Hill found that migratory children were herded together in garages, school corridors and abandoned barns, with as many as 125 children for one instructor. Care was taken, also, to segregate migratory children and to discriminate against them, both as to the character and the extent of their education. Migratory children were made to attend school from 7:30 A.M. to 12 o'clock so that they might then be excused to work in the fields. The policy back of this type of discrimination was announced as an attempt to "adjust the child to the crop." Most migratory children can only attend school for a few months during the year; they are generally backward, because of lack of opportunity and fatigue, and many of them are so retarded that they fall into the second, third and fourth grades.

In two eloquent and moving articles appearing in *Hearst's International Magazine* for February and March, 1924, under the title "Little Gypsies of the Fruit," Arthur Gleason described conditions that have not changed in the intervening fourteen years, except to grow worse. Migratory existence, he wrote, unsettles the life of children. "It turns home life into a drifting gypsy existence. The family becomes wagon tramps instead of settlers and citizens. It smashes schooling into broken bits at one or two way stations each year. You can't educate a procession. Even a sailor and a drummer have somewhere to return. A street gamin has a block and a slum tenement. But these children have no fixed center. They are children of the crops. They are born in the crops. The crops condition their lives, bring them into a ranch, send them on to another county, and pull them back just one year later." Interviewing these children, he asked one of them: "Where is your home?" and received the reply: "Home? We're cotton pickers." He found one girl who was the fastest grape picker in her section, but a village doctor told him the youngster was "so keyed up that she can't sleep nights." Most of the crop children, who reported at the migratory schools, were definitely retarded; he estimated, in fact, that 50 per cent of them were "hopelessly retarded." "In the prune country," he writes, "a friend of mine went into the shack of the Meronda family at eight o'clock in the evening. The twelve-year-old boy was in bed asleep. His hands were moving ceaselessly in sleep, traveling across the sheet and picking at it. 'What is the matter?' asked my friend. And the boy's mother answered: 'He does that sometimes when he's asleep. He thinks he is picking prunes.' " (pp. 314–322)

STUDY BY THE FEDERAL SECURITY ADMINISTRATION ON MIGRANT FARM LABOR

In 1941, four years after John N. Webb's study, an investigation by the Federal Security Administration reveals that little has been done to alleviate the plight of people like the Joads. Note especially the agency's description of living conditions.

FROM "MIGRANT FARM LABOR: THE PROBLEM AND SOME
EFFORTS TO MEET IT"
(Federal Security Administration, Publication 60; Washington, DC:
U.S. Government Printing Office, 1941)

Workers with the lowest living standards in the United States pick most of the fruits and vegetables for America's tables.

They are the farm laborers who piece together a precarious living by following the crops. Mostly they travel in antiquated cars, piled high with their meagre possessions—a tent, a couple of blankets and a few pots and pans. They may find work in the vegetable fields of California, the cotton fields of Texas, in the hop fields of Oregon, the cherry orchards of Michigan, on the vegetable farms of Florida or New Jersey. They follow the road leading to any crop that still, in spite of increased farm mechanization, must be harvested by hand. Many migrants or farm laborers stay within one State from season to season; many others must cross State lines to find a living.

Today, between a million and two million workers are employed on seasonal jobs. In their problems and their way of living, there is little distinction between the habitual seasonal laborer and the migrant recently forced off the land and into seasonal crop work. Both lead mobile lives, both are cut off from ordinary community life and have little chance to educate their children. Both are limited to earnings which range from about $150 to $575 a year. For the average migrant family of four persons, these uneven and uncertain earnings must stretch to cover food, shelter, medical care and means to reach the next crop.

HOW MIGRANTS LIVE

The presence of a tide of migrants creates grave health, housing and economic problems to the community using them for a few weeks or a

few months' work. Some big farms furnish cabins for their seasonal workers, but most migrants must provide their own shelter. They pitch their
tents on the roadside, on ditchbanks, or in vacant lots. They live in abandoned chicken houses or barns, in poorly-built tourist camps where sanitation is a vanity. In such crowded and often unclean quarters, there is
constant threat of epidemics of contagious diseases.

In the summer, there is invariably a sharp rise in child deaths among
migrants as a result of eating unripe or unwholesome fruit and drinking
contaminated water. In winter, pneumonia, influenza, tuberculosis and
other pulmonary diseases take toll since few migrants have enough clothing or warm shelter.

Trained investigators surveying the living conditions of migrants in the
States where migration is heaviest found the following:

California—"In Imperial Valley in a typical ditchbank camp, dwellings
were constructed of old tents, gunny sacks, drygoods boxes, scrap tin.
All the shacks were without floors—very dirty and swarming with clouds
of flies. No sanitary facilities. Backyard used as toilet. Irrigation ditch half
filled with muddy water used for all purposes."

• • •

California—This State is the hub of the West Coast migration. Workers
come into California from New Mexico's and Arizona's cotton fields, may
go up into the small fruit regions of the Northwest, or retrace their route
back through the Southwest.

In California about 200,000 seasonal workers are needed to harvest the
200 different farm products grown for the commercial market. October
is the peak month of labor demand.

The wide variety of crops grown in California and the varying weather
conditions through the 800-mile long strip of maturing produce creates
a demand for season workers the entire year, but this demand fluctuates
widely from area to area and from season to season.

The year-to-year variations depend on the size of the major crops,
weather conditions and market prices. The Imperial Valley citrus and
truck crops need more than 50,000 workers during a harvest season hitting its peak in February.

The San Joaquin Valley's cotton, fruits and vegetables use about 75,000
seasonal workers from May through November.

The Sacramento Valley's principal crops are fruits, asparagus and peas
which require about 30,000 seasonal workers. May is the season's peak.

Around San Francisco in the central coast counties where fruits and
truck crops are grown, it takes 50,000 seasonal workers to raise and harvest the crops. (pp. 1, 5)

GRAPES OF GLADNESS, AN ANSWER TO *THE GRAPES OF WRATH*

Immediately upon publication of *The Grapes of Wrath*, the Associated Farmers and their powerful backers moved to counter Steinbeck's portrayal of the living conditions of migrant workers. *Grapes of Gladness* was one of several such volumes. The motives, assumptions, and attitudes of the powerful Associated Farmers are reflected in every word choice and detail. Look carefully at the title, the quotations used, and the statement of philosophy in the addenda. In the appendix, the author, M. V. Hartranft, takes Steinbeck to task for not knowing the geography of his home state, but never addresses the real issue at hand—treatment of the workers by the growers.

Also included is a report—inserted by Hartranft—by Thomas McManus, the secretary of the California Citizens Association, a group of landowners and their supporters who organized to counter the bad publicity they had received in 1938 and 1939. McManus denies that laborers were ever lured to California although there is tangible evidence to the contrary.

FROM M. V. HARTRANFT, *GRAPES OF GLADNESS*
(Los Angeles, CA: De Vorss & Co., 1939)

ADDENDA: ANALYZING "THE GRAPES OF WRATH"

The mood in which Mr. Steinbeck wrote his *Grapes of Wrath* and his intentions are clearly revealed on page 432 thereof, regarding the Salvation Army.

Both the United Press and the Associated Press reports published throughout the nation on November 19th, 1938, told of a plan formulated to multiply the land-banking colonies for homeless families in several parts of the state, as follows:

State Bankers to "Lend Farms" to Refugees In California

San Francisco—Nov. 19, 1938 (U.P.)—Homeless exiles from the "dust bowl"—10,000 nomadic families who came with golden hopes that turned to poverty and despair—found today their promised land.

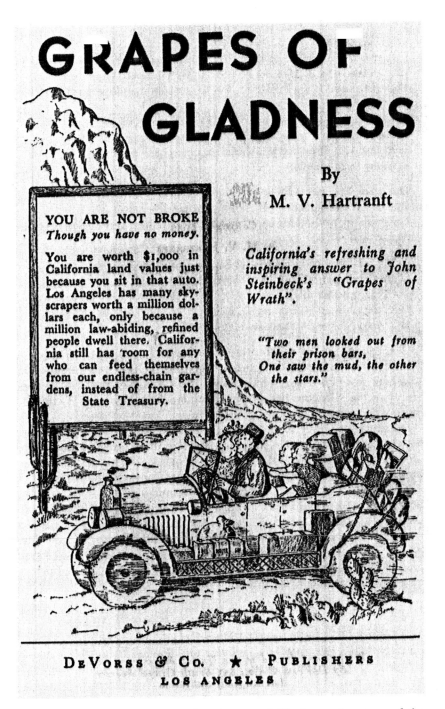

GRAPES OF GLADNESS

By

M. V. Hartranft

YOU ARE NOT BROKE
Though you have no money.

You are worth $1,000 in California land values just because you sit in that auto. Los Angeles has many skyscrapers worth a million dollars each, only because a million law-abiding, refined people dwell there. California still has room for any who can feed themselves from our endless-chain gardens, instead of from the State Treasury.

California's refreshing and inspiring answer to John Steinbeck's "Grapes of Wrath".

*"Two men looked out from their prison bars,
One saw the mud, the other the stars."*

DeVorss & Co. ★ Publishers
LOS ANGELES

Title page from M. V. Hartranft's *Grapes of Gladness.* Courtesy of the Bancroft Library, University of California, Berkeley. F855 S7 H3

It will be furnished to them for colonizing purposes by a group of California bankers, said Bert Hilborn, Salvation Army executive. First proposed homestead site, for 500 to 1000 families, was located tentatively near Riverside.

The bankers plan to lend repossessed property as they would money. The migrants will raise crops and gardens and pay six percent interest. After five years they may purchase their fields outright on easy installments.

This plan was met with scorn when presented to the organization for uplift, of which Mr. Steinbeck is a director.

He evidently revised his copy, then in preparation, and caused his characters to say:

" 'If anybody's took charity, it makes a burn that don't come out. Well, I did,' said Annie. 'Las' winter; and we was starvin'—me and Pa. Fella told us to go to the Salvation Army.' Her eyes grew fierce. 'We wuz hungry—they made us crawl for our dinner. They took our dignity. They—I hate 'em.' "

Here is one of the many private charitable organizations, collecting pennies from tambourines in the streets, to reach down and help those who have lost either their economic or moral balance; and feed the hungry. Both the state and national governments had refused to do this for those who migrated across state line!

Steinbeck says they were "hungry, starving and fed." Then, through his characters, "hates the Army" for feeding them. He denounces the inhuman treatment given the migrants on one hand and denounces the humanitarian help given, on the other. It just does not make sense.

The statement by Mr. Steinbeck that the mid-west migrants were induced to come to California through "an orange-colored circular" is ridiculous. California maintained a border patrol to keep out moneyless families. The border patrol was notoriously publicized and annulled by decree of unconstitutionality. Nations can limit and control their immigration, but states cannot. Mr. Steinbeck acknowledges the border patrol, page 163. A peculiar contradiction.

• • •

There were no "cattle company lands fenced in, lying fallow," as stated on pages 279, 280, 319. First because the demand for tillable soil and irrigable land has been so great, for over eighty years, that nothing but the mountains, and the alkali deserts and the dry upland mesas could be profitably held for grazing purposes.

The land and cattle ranches, totaling a million acres near Bakersfield were opened in 1907, as historically shown in chapter 3, hereof. The great Miller-Lux holdings have been on the market in 10 to 40 acre tracts for over twenty years. Only the deserts and oil lands remain.

The one ranch of assertedly a million acres held by a newspaper man, refers undoubtedly to the Hearst San Simeon property. These lands are principally mountains in the Santa Lucia coast range, with a few strips of dry grain land for making winter feed, to use during the long dry summers, when California has no pasture at all. The owner is putting these lands to their highest present day use, in producing steaks and chops for the open competition of the city markets.

Without such economic balance, city dwellers would have to lower their standard of eating.

California has much land that is summer fallowed. Also mountains and alkali deserts which are not land lying fallow. Following the winter rains the upper dry mesas above the irrigation ditches are disced or plowed and left to "lie fallow" over the rainless months of the summer. That is done to store up moisture for the following year and to let the open soil oxidize in the sun. It also multiplies the beneficial bacteria of the soil. Fall seeding then ensues, and with added winter rains, a grain or hay crop may be secured.

Mr. Steinbeck makes no distinction in the character of the land he describes, though he is talking about a state which enjoys the blessings of aridity; where an acre under a ditch may be worth a thousand dollars, though you can buy the adjoining dry land acre, above the ditch, for two dollars—its grazing value.

Why such vacuity and vagueness, Mr. Steinbeck?

The only agonizing sight in all California agriculture is the man and the mules and the gang-plow, dry-seeding the grain in a cloud of dust, on a September afternoon with the thermometer of interior valleys registering at 103. The most gripping stanza in California literature is in John Steven McGroarty's "Gratitude for Rain":

> *"The fallow furrow,*
> *Turned in wan despair*
> *And sown in grief;*
> *When comes the harvest*
> *Will be fair with golden sheaf."*

• • •

On Highway 99 south from Bakersfield there is for nine miles a belt of alkali-spotted soil, visible from the autos, where feeble efforts continue at farming cotton, alfalfa and alkali-resistant crops. This was known as the rich Kern River delta district, 30 years ago. Immense irrigation ditches,

injudiciously used, water-logged the land, brought the alkali to the surface and killed the beautiful fruit orchards. Aside from hot-dog stands
and tourist cabins, there has hardly been a new home built along there
in thirty years. South of that, one enters upon the 25-mile alkali desert
to the foot of Grapevine grade, which doesn't support one cow to forty
acres; excepting the one-mile-wide wild-flower strip that skirts the hills.

North of Bakersfield, the water level on those plains is three hundred
feet down and the Federal Government is spending millions on the Central Valley Project to bring those dry lands water from the Shasta Dam—
three hundred miles away.

Of this country and these conditions Mr. Steinbeck makes one of his
characters remark:

> "You git acrost the desert an' come into the country aroun' Ba-
> kersfield. An' you never seen such purty country—all orchards an'
> grapes, purtiest country you ever seen. An' you'll pass lan' flat an'
> fine with water *thirty feet* down, and the lan's layin' fallow. But you
> can't have none of that lan'. That's Lan' and Cattle Company. An' if
> they don't want ta work her, she ain't gonna git worked. You go in
> there an' plant you a little corn, an' you'll go to jail—They hate you
> 'cause they're scairt. They know a hungry fella gonna get food even
> if he got to take it. They know that fallow lan's a sin an' somebody'
> gonna take it."

Does Mr. Steinbeck offer the spotted, partly abandoned, water-logged
land, south of Bakersfield, for 'rich fallow acres' that would support families? Is this ignorance or intention to stir social strife?

The "sin of fallow land" is a Steinbeck monstrosity!

If he refers to wild mountain land or alkali desert soil it might be idle
land—but there could be no sin in that. In fact, however, sheep herders
keep the sheep hunting the loneliest blade of grass in the shadow of the
rocks for the few weeks in winter that the forage grows. Then they lease
pasture for the summer in the High Sierra forest reserves.

Mr. Steinbeck would not want to say that the diligent summer fallowing
of dry-farming is a sin, would he?

Would he want to say as a native son that he does not know what
fallow land is? He says in his own editorial words (page 319):

> "The good fields with water to be dug for. A man might look at a
> fallow field and know, and see in his mind that his own bending
> back and his own straining arms would bring the cabbages into the
> light, and the golden eating corn, the turnips, and carrots."

No land in an arid country will grow those crops without irrigation.
The lands that will produce those crops are rented by the Orientals and

other gardeners at ten to forty dollars per year, plus the labor and cost of irrigation.

There are no idle lands "where water can be dug for" at this late day. Californians have been going from 100 to 300 miles with aqueducts for their additional waters.

• • •

The communistic implication that the lands of California can be morally taken by force for the benefit of newcomers, because the original titles were acquired through chicanery, is no more true of California than it is of any other State. First the Indians. Then the Spaniards. Then the forty-niners. After one hundred years of social and legal readjustments, California land titles stand exactly as other titles do throughout the world.

• • •

Social revolution is the sinister suggestion emanating constantly from the pages of "Grapes of Wrath". Popularly it is supposed that a revolution is a sacred and noble instrument for the purpose of overthrowing injustice, and leaving men to be wise and good and just. Revolutions, however, use men for their own mysterious ends.

Revolutions tear down one tyranny only to install another. They leave behind the same relative proportion of good and evil; the same disparity between wealth and poverty plus millions of new graves and armies of crippled lives.

Can anything short of economic knowledge lift men above the level of the mule?

Even among business men, very few understand the rising and falling of the business cycle, the ebb and flow of loans and deposits. The price cycles make paupers of the well-to-do and peons of the intelligent laborers. Banks of commercial deposit, although geared fairly close to the machinery of central banking, suffer themselves in the fall of the general price-level along with the rest of society.

This civilization is based on price; the price of your labor and the cost of the goods you need. The wages paid to farm labor are geared to the price of farm products. Each individual must ride the bucking-broncho chart of the general price level, or teach a whole nation the process by which the index price level can be controlled in the interest of general welfare. Our democracy has utterly failed in that. Socialists have a better picture, but it is a picture. It has never been performed on the stage of life and put into practice.

Until evolution brings clearer economic understanding, *individuals can be helped* to help themselves.

M. V. H. (pp. 115–120)

California Citizens Association Report

Bakersfield, California, July 1, 1939 (To M. V. Hartranft)

Despite optimistic announcements of a decline in the number of migrants coming to California principally from Oklahoma, Arkansas, Texas and Missouri, the burden on the taxpayers of our state has become more acute. It is now that the local and state relief rolls are being filled with artificially created "residents", subsidized by the Farm Security Administration for the year required eligibility. It is now that we are feeling the financial pressure of building new schools for the migrants' children.

It is *now* that we are paying.

Records of the Kern County Hospital show that 44% of the patients taken care of there during the past year were non-residents, and the origin of 77% of that number was in the four states mentioned. In this period more than 110,000 cases were treated free.

These migrants are not farmers who have been dispossessed. Even the Farm Security Administration, which once claimed evidence to the contrary, now admits that they were either share-croppers or laborers in their home states. It is plain that there was no place for them here when there were already five unemployed for every available agricultural job in California.

Even in the potato fields of Kern County there were dozens of people for every job, and that is true also of the other crops. In face of this fact, most of the migrants have been living on public bounty since coming to California.

The reduction in acreage in all branches of agriculture and the necessary proration to keep the industry from disaster are such as to limit labor needs. The migration came at the time when it was utterly impossible to give employment to additional workers without destroying the established farm economic system.

The United States Employment Service is authority for the fact that no effort was made by any California farm group to bring labor here, by advertising or any other means. The farmers neither needed nor wanted additional workers, nor did they want the tax cost of supporting unneeded migrants.

California has always maintained the highest farm wages of any area in the world, but it cannot continue to be oppressed by taxes to feed these surplus workers and still uphold this standard.

The author, John Steinbeck, in his novel, *Grapes of Wrath*, did great injustice both to Californians and to the migrants themselves. These hapless people are not moral and mental degenerates as he pictures them, but victims of desperate conditions—conditions which can bring to California the same tragedy that drove them from their home states.

The recounting by Steinbeck of incidents in which violence was used upon the transients is based upon nothing more than the envisionings of an over-worked imagination. It is absolutely untrue.

A deep-set prejudice seems to be the only explanation for the involving of the American Legion in a fictionally-created harassment of these people.

The California Citizens Association, made up of various organizations, presented to the Congress petitions signed by hundreds of thousands of people, directing the attention of the Government to the fact that no further migration could be endured by the people of California. The record of the California Citizens Association has been one of sympathy for these people, but one that must now be tempered by a deep desire to maintain our standard of living and by the natural law of self-preservation.

—Thos. W. McManus, Secretary (pp. 124–125)

TOPICS FOR ORAL OR WRITTEN EXPLORATION

1. For migrant families to do farm work, a car was often a necessity. Write an essay on the role of the automobile in *The Grapes of Wrath*.

2. The documents in this chapter often speak of the plight of migrant children. Referring to the children in the novel, especially the two Joad children, and to the documents, write an essay about migrant children in the 1930s.

3. Write an essay on the subject of water in the novel, using the documents presented here and your own research. Consider, among other things, what water represents; the situation in Oklahoma; the watering places encountered on the trip; and the final chapters in the book.

4. Compare the wages offered to the Joads and their friends in *The Grapes of Wrath* with the references to wages in the introduction and documents. Does it appear that Steinbeck exaggerated in his account of wages (as his attackers frequently claimed)?

5. Using the documents and the novel, make a list of the migrants' diet. How would you evaluate Steinbeck's account? Does it make the situation worse than it is? Or, as some people have pointed out, was the real diet of the migrants worse than that of the Joads?

6. Write your own final chapter about what may have happened to the Joads two years after they find refuge in the barn.

7. The turtle in the novel, beginning in Chapter Three, has often been equated with the farmers and farm laborers described in Chapter One. Write an essay exploring this idea.

8. Why do the California natives dislike the migrants so intensely? Write about the complexity and irony of their attitudes as they unfold in the novel and in the supporting documents.

9. In the 1930s, as in the 1990s, the debate rages on about government becoming too big and too expensive, especially with regard to assistance programs and legislation. Plan a class about the debate question of whether government should have stepped in to assist the migrants.

10. Read Steinbeck's journalistic articles that are collected in a pamphlet entitled *Their Blood Is Strong* (San Francisco: Simon J. Lubin, 1938). Compare his journalistic descriptions with the novel that he wrote several years later on the same subject. It has been observed that the conditions Steinbeck and others relate in articles are worse than his fictional portrayal. Do you find this to be true? Explain. If so, for what reason do you suppose he modified his observations?

11. Do a close analysis of the words and graphics on the title page of *Grapes of Gladness*. Compare the drawing with photographs of the same traveling scene.

12. The addenda in *Grapes of Gladness* implies a particular social and economic philosophy that is in opposition to the ideas Steinbeck expresses about the relationship between society and the individual. Explore the difference.

SUGGESTIONS FOR FURTHER READING

Cletus, Daniel E. *Bitter Harvest: A History of California Farm Workers*. Berkeley: University of California Press, 1981.

Cross, William T., and Dorothy Cross. *Newcomers and Nomads in California*. Palo Alto, CA: Stanford University Press, 1937.

Gregory, James. *American Exodus: The Dust Bowl Migration and Okie Culture in California*. New York: Oxford University Press, 1989.

McConnell, Grant. *The Decline of Agrarian Democracy*. Berkeley: University of California Press, 1953.

McWilliams, Carey. *Factories in the Field*. Boston: Little, Brown, 1942.

Morgan, Dan. *Rising in the West*. New York: Alfred A. Knopf, 1992.

Parker, Carleton H. *The Casual Laborer*. New York: Harcourt, Brace and Howe, 1920.

Stein, Walter J. *California and the Dust Bowl Migration*. Westport, CT: Greenwood Press, 1973.

Taylor, Paul S. *On the Ground in the Thirties*. Salt Lake City, UT: Peregrine Smith, 1983.

Web Site:
The New Deal Network homepage: www.newdeal.feri.org.

Company housing for cotton workers near Corcoran, California. Photograph by Dorothea Lange. Reproduced from the collections of the Library of Congress.

5

Unions in the Fields

The story of the Joads is one that is largely hopeless and disheartening. After a miserable journey across the continent, they are starved, threatened, and brutalized. Their story is coming to an end as they face an even bleaker future of homelessness in a season of chilling, continuous rain with no prospect for work of any kind. The once constant center of their lives, the large supportive family, has dwindled to half its size.

Within what seems to be a story of unrelieved despair, however, there are some positive signs. Running throughout the novel is the theme of a people united in sympathy. The character who is willing to join with others in a humane and common cause is a higher order of human being, and relinquishes some part of her- or himself for the good of everyone. On an elementary level, we see this principle operating among families as the Joads unite in common cause with Jim Casy, the Wilsons, the Wainwrights, and many others.

UNIONS AND STRIKES IN *THE GRAPES OF WRATH*

On a broader scale, people joining together in a common cause results in the creation of the labor union, an idea that runs like a ray of hope through *The Grapes of Wrath*. The first explicit reference to labor unions occurs in interchapter Fourteen, just after the Joads and the Wilsons have joined forces on the road to help each other at a critical time of death and illness. Here, the narrator makes three major points about unions. First, he says that the owners fear unions and strikes and do what they can to break them. In doing so, their fears are misplaced, for what they need to dread is the day when unionizing and striking are no longer the only possible outlets for the workers' dissatisfaction. Such a situation creates just the pressure cooker in which real revolution explodes. Second, the only way to keep oppressed people from rebelling is to keep them apart. This, of course, is impossible to do. Third, the owners persistently confuse cause with result. Revolutions and labor unions are the results, not the causes of labor unrest. The cause, the narrator writes, is hunger of the body and the soul. He connects the impending labor unrest in the 1930s with the names of four revolutionaries, linking them in such a way that it identifies the American Revolution with the Communist Revolution in Russia—"Paine, Marx, Jefferson, Lenin" (194).

Although Steinbeck sought to distance himself from Communism, he seems to be acknowledging that even Communism embodies admirable ideals, as did the American Revolution. In a far different way, as Steinbeck reminds us repeatedly in the novel, the growers and their supporters denounce as a Communist anyone who wants to make changes for the good of the workingman. For example, shortly after the discussion in Chapter Fourteen, when the Joads are camping for the night, the proprietor of the campground rails against all workers who complain, calling them "trouble-making reds." When he calls Tom a troublemaker for protesting that the proprietor is greedy, Tom laughingly needles him by saying, "I'm bolshevisky," meaning a Bolsheivist or Communist (248).

The narrator again discusses the attitude of the growers toward union activity in interchapter Nineteen. This chapter, a history of California agriculture, appears just as the Joads see, from the high mountains above the plains, the fertile California valley for the first time. Here again, the narrator contends that the owners and growers have no awareness of what actually brings the masses to organize and strike. In the narrator's judgment, the growers are blind to the real causes of revolt:(1) the holding of property in too few hands; (2) widespread hunger; and (3) the kind of severe repression that tends to unite the repressed.

The Joads encounter the idea of unions daily once they begin to live in California. Beneath the surface of life in the camps, and marked by starvation wages and brutal practices, lies a desperate and forbidden hope—the idea of the labor union and the potential strike. Tom actually comes up with the idea of striking without realizing it. In the first Hooverville, when Floyd, his new aquaintance, tells him how the growers keep wages so low, Tom asks him why the workers just do not band together and refuse to pick peaches, since it is imperative to get them harvested before they become overripe. In other words, why not strike until the growers agree to pay the workers better wages? Floyd responds by telling him how growers break strikes—by offering new employees, called scabs, higher wages until the strike is broken. For all Floyd's pessimism, however, he mysteriously *implies* that something is going on: presumably some of the men are getting together to discuss their problems and unite behind a strategy. Tom easily convinces Casy to come with him, but before the mysterious meeting gets under way, violence erupts and an attempt is made to arrest Floyd for verbally challenging a labor contractor. Tom and Floyd are able to escape through the intervention of Casy who takes all the blame and goes to jail, but the Joads realize they have to leave the camp. The next day, after the Joads have left, members of the community burn the camp, which they believe to be a hotbed of "Reds."

Tom is further educated in the strategies used by owners to keep their workers quiet as he works in the fields of a small farm the day after the so-called Reds are burned out of the Hooverville. Tom asks Timothy, one of his companions in the field, what is a Red. Timothy tells him the following story: A newcomer to California once asked a question of a grower who constantly railed against Reds and warned about them taking over the country. "Just what is a Red?" the newcomer asked. The grower replied that a Red was any SOB who wants 30 cents an hour when the growers are paying 25. In other words, a Red is any unhappy worker who asks for a raise, goes on strike for better wages, or belongs to a labor union. Later, another worker defines a red as anyone who talks back to a deputy.

The subject of labor unions arises again when the Joads move to the government camp. The growers hate these camps, in part because they provide decent toilets and showers and make the growers' camps look bad because they provide neither. But their main objection to the government camps is that the workers are free to organize there. As the growers put it, the workers are free to hold red meetings in these camps, which are beyond the growers' control.

In the government camp, the workers talk freely about the development of unions in other parts of the country. One reports on the unionized rubber workers in Akron, Ohio, who made a show of strength by marching down the streets with their rifles. At the camp dance, a young man named Willie asks Tom if he has ever been in a strike before and reports on a man out on the road "organizin' for the union" (460).

A good argument can be made that a labor strike is the center of the entire novel. If the climax of a narrative is the point of high feeling and decisive action after which the story can only go in one direction, then the spontaneous strike of peach pickers led by Casy is the climax of *The Grapes of Wrath*. During this strike, Tom kills the man who killed Casy and must, therefore, from that point on, always be on the run and separated from his family. The strike also gives Tom a direction in life: he will follow in Casy's footsteps by committing himself to the cause of farmworkers.

The family's encounter with the peach strike begins as they drive up to the outskirts of the orchards. Here, the road is lined with the old cars of striking migrants picketing the orchard that lowered their wages after they had begun work. What the Joads do not realize is that they are scabs, hired to pick peaches at the higher wage in order to break the strike. Since they are the scabs, they must be escorted into the camp by deputies on motorcycles so that the strikers will not stop them. As they drive toward the camp, Tom sees men along the road yelling and shaking their fists; inside the camp they see armed guards posted everywhere.

In the evening after work, Tom is curious about what is happening outside the camp, but he finds that the growers, anxious to keep the strike from spreading, are keeping the scabs prisoners. He is not allowed to walk out the gate. The guards tell him that they are protecting him from the mob outside. As he walks away in the dark, he hears other guards planning to get and destroy the "Red" leader of the strike.

After Tom sneaks out, he heads for a tent he his spotted, hidden in the brush. Here he finds that the leader of the strike is not a red or even any outside union operative. The leader is none other than his friend, the ex-preacher, Casy. "We struck," one of the men in the tent says. "This here's a strike" (491). Casy and the others have no affiliations with a national union. Theirs is a spontaneous union and strike prompted by an immediate problem. In this case, as Casy explains to Tom, they were all hired to pick peaches for five cents a basket, but after they got on the job, their wages were lowered to two and a half cents a basket. He tries to convince Tom to tell the new arrivals in the camp that if the strike is broken, the owners will again reduce the pay from 5 to 2½ cents per basket. Casy also explains how he became committed to the idea of a union—no matter how local and informal in structure—as a way to solve the workers' awful problems.

The vigilantes hired by the growers, knowing that one way of terrorizing the workers and breaking the strike is to destroy its leader, ambush Casy's camp and kill him. In response, Tom goes wild and kills one of the vigilantes. Wounded, Tom returns to tell his family that Casy had led the strike and that the Joads, without realizing the implications, "was breakin' strike" (500). At the end of the day, after Casy is killed, they learn that the strike has indeed been broken and that their pay has been reduced from 5 to 2½ cents a basket.

Even though Casy is killed, his mission continues. The clearest evidence of this is Tom Joad's taking on Casy's calling. In telling Ma that all the workers are one, and that he is dedicating himself to the struggle as had Casy, Tom echoes one of the most famous and eloquent labor leaders in American history, Eugene V. Debs, who told the court just before he was sentenced to jail for leading a strike, "while there is a lower class I am in it. While there is a criminal element I am of it; while there is a soul in prison, I am not free." (See *The World's Great Speeches*. Garden City, NY: Garden City Publishing Co., 1942, pp. 372–374.) Tom's words are: "Wherever they's a fight so hungry people can eat, I'll be there. Wherever they's a cop beatin' up a guy, I'll be there" (537).

STEINBECK AND UNIONS IN THE 1930s

The actual events going on at the time *The Grapes of Wrath* was written are convincing evidence of the importance of labor unions to an understanding of the book itself. As a native Californian who had worked in the fields as a college student, Steinbeck was well informed about the way California agriculture operated and how migrant laborers lived. He addressed the situation often, not only in *The Grapes of Wrath*, but in short stories and a series of articles written for a San Francisco newspaper. In 1933 and 1934, when he was emerging as a writer, there were more strikes by agricultural workers in California than at any earlier time in its history. Many of the strikes occurred in Salinas, where Steinbeck had grown up and was living at the time. In September 1934, shortly after a bloody general strike in San Francisco, Steinbeck began work on a novel about labor organizing in the fields of California. Published in 1936, *In Dubious Battle* has as its central character a young man, new to labor organizing, who follows an experienced member of "the Party" to an apple-growing area where the workers are ready to organize and strike for higher wages. Of particular interest is the complexity of the situation: the psychological strategy of the organizers, the infighting among the workers themselves, the violence perpetrated by the owners and their community supporters, and the conflict between powerful growers and those who own small farms. As the strike develops, key workers in the union are threatened, beaten up, arrested, and killed. The rich growers even set fire to the barn and crops of a family farmer who sympathized with the workers.

BACKGROUND OF THE UNIONS IN THE NINETEENTH CENTURY

The 1930s was one of labor's most turbulent periods, a time when unions of national scope, embracing many different kinds of workers, experienced their growing pains. But labor organizing in the United States did not begin during the Depression, and much that occurred in labor relations in the 1930s was determined by its history in the nineteenth and early twentieth centuries. Although unions are not part of the Joads' experience until they reach California in the late 1930s, groups of skilled craftsmen had banded together to improve their wages and working conditions as early as the 1600s. By the nineteenth century, there were many specialized associations of fairly long standing: tailors, printers, carpenters, and mechanics, to name a few. From these associations grew Workingmen's Parties, which began to wield a certain amount of political clout in the late nineteenth century. As the industrial revolution flowered and more and more factories sprang up in the nineteenth century, men, women, and children worked in the system under appalling and life-threatening conditions for starvation wages. The work was exhausting, long, and dangerous, especially for the worker suffering from exhaustion. Chemicals in some industries, like the making of matches, were rapidly killing the workers. If they became sick or injured, or protested any injustice, they were summarily fired. The wealthy continued, as they always had, to regard the poor as a lower species. Unskilled workers in the cities were customarily regarded as members of "the dangerous classes." Those in power believed that unrestrained capitalism was good for the human race because it allowed the best human specimens to flourish and weeded out the weak and unfit. The first government regulation imposed on industry on behalf of labor was not until 1874, when the state of Massachusetts passed a law limiting the work of women and children to ten hours a day.

In response to unbearable conditions, union activity spread early in the nineteenth century from craftsmen to unskilled factory workers, notably in the textile mills of Lawrence and Lowell, Massachusetts. Union activity was quiet during the Civil War, but afterward, as industrial production grew enormously, so did the abuses of working people. Until the 1930s, industry was free to use workers in any way it wanted to, with only minimal regulation by local and state authorities, who were invariably sympathetic to owners. For example, wages earned from the usual ten to twelve hours a day, six or seven days a week, were judged to be 20 to 40 percent lower than the minimum needed for basic survival. Steel workers in some mills in the last decade of the nineteenth century were not allowed breaks to eat or to use the toilet during their twelve-hour days. Nor were they given one day off; they were required to work seven days a week at hard labor. For these killing hours in 1890, they were paid $10.00 a week. It is scarcely surprising that the 1870s and 1880s were some of the most violent in labor history and that the time was ripe for labor organizing on the national level. One of the first nationwide organizations formed to represent both industrial workers and farmers, rather than craftsmen alone, was the Knights of Labor, founded in 1869.

Another prominent labor organization, though small and local, was a secret, highly militant society of Irish American hard-coal miners in Pennsylvania, called the Molly Maguires. This group was active from 1862 to 1875. In 1874, hostilities mushroomed between the Molly Maguires and the mine owners. The famous Pinkertons private detectives and other lawmen along with the non-Irish fire department, all hired by the mine owners, were determined to have a showdown. To speed this along, the Pinkertons seemed to have planted evidence implicating the Maguires. An open and violent conflict with the Molly Maguires ensued, which finally crushed them. Dozens of people on both sides were killed during the secret reign of the Molly Maguires. With the hanging of ten of their number after the 1874 local war, they were crushed. But miners, whether Irish or non-Irish, continued to work under deplorable conditions and formed militant labor organizations to fight for decent wages and working conditions.

Eighteen seventy-seven was marked by an equally violent clash that is known as the Great Rail Strike. Railway workers throughout the country went out on strike when their pay was cut by 10 percent. Rail service was tied up in cities throughout the country, and riots broke out in cities in the northeast and Midwest and in San Francisco, prompting government troops to intervene to restore order.

The 1880s and 1890s brought further strikes, unemployment demonstrations, and violence. One of the most notorious events happened in 1886 in Chicago. Someone (Pinkerton agents were suspected) threw a bomb into a meeting of workers striking against the McCormick Harvester Company. The bomb and the rioting that ensued left nine people dead and at least sixty injured. Radicals of every hue were among the workers involved in what came to be labeled the Haymarket Riot or Haymarket Massacre. The presence of socialists and anarchists among the protesting laborers gave the establishment the excuse for seventy years to dismiss every labor struggle as a Communist plot. It should be understood, however, that even though Communists were in the forefront as labor movement organizers until the 1940s, they never constituted a majority of the working people who protested and participated in unions and strikes.

Two strikes in the late 1890s are especially important in the annals of U.S. labor history. One was an 1892 strike by Andrew Carnegie's steel workers in Homestead, Pennsylvania. Once the strike got under way, Carnegie hired 300 Pinkerton detectives to break the strike. In the course of the conflict that followed, the strikers and the Pinkerton agents began firing on one another. Hundreds of people on both sides were injured and ten were killed before the National Guard was called on to intervene. The strike was broken, union members locked out, and nonunion workers hired. Not until 1937 were union members allowed back into Carnegie's steel mill.

Another bitter conflict came two years later in 1894, when the American Railway Union struck against the Pullman company near Chicago. The immediate cause was a cut in the workers' wages. The initial effect of the strike was to tie up the nation's railway system. Soon, however, the government sent in 3,000 deputies to keep the rails open. The rioting provoked by this move caused President Grover Cleveland to send in more federal troops. The end result was that the strike was broken and Eugene V. Debs, who led the strike, was arrested along with 200 workers, and sent to prison.

UNIONISM FROM 1900 TO 1940

At the turn of the century, divisions developed in the labor movement itself, between skilled and unskilled workers, and between conservative and aggressive unions. Of the conservative unions, one that exists today is the American Federation of Labor (AFL), first organized under the leadership of Samuel Gompers in 1886. The AFL was interested in working within the existing industrial structure to solve immediate practical problems like low wages, brutal working hours, and unsafe working conditions.

More radical unions, however, were convinced that the only way to bring about meaningful improvement in workers' lives was to change the whole economic structure, to modify capitalism by placing limits on the ways in which wealth and land could be accumulated. More power would be given to the government to legislate protections for working people, and to transfer more power and ownership to laborers. Many unions for unskilled workers fell into this category, who, nevertheless, remained in mainstream politics. The workers were usually members of the Democratic Party. In the 1920s, the more aggressive unions included electricians, and those who worked in the steel, rubber, and mining industries.

As Samuel Gompers and his successor, William Green, are associated with the establishment of the nationwide conservative AFL, Eugene V. Debs, a leader of the Socialist Party, and, later, John L. Lewis, founder of the Congress of Industrial Organization, (CIO), are well-known figures associated with the early development of the more aggressive unions.

The government and owners organized a concerted campaign to suppress unions in the 1920s. In 1919, the California legislature was one of the first to pass a Criminal Syndicalism Act that was used for two decades to destroy unions by making it illegal to teach, advocate, or abet acts of violence to effect political change. In effect, however, the act made it a crime, subject to imprisonment, to teach or advocate changes of any kind in elected offices or individual businesses. One of the tactics used by companies to combat unions was to establish company unions. These consisted of groups of workers who were required to join and take their grievances to a pseudo-union sponsored by the owner/managers, as a substitute for an independent union that could use strikes as weapons. In this way, companies were able to control unhappy workers. By 1930, there were 593 company unions operating in the United States.

Labor unions had other setbacks in the 1920s, and the improvements in the lives of working people, which earlier unions had hoped to achieve, were never realized. Owners, for example, were free to insist on what were called "yellow dog" contracts. In signing such a contract, the workers promised not to join a union; this was a condition of employment. A further blow was delivered to unions and working people in 1923, when the United States Supreme Court struck down many reforms for which unions had worked. Most notably, the Court declared child labor laws to be unconstitutional in the District of Columbia, and ruled against the setting of a minimum wage for women and children.

Union activity grew enormously in the early 1930s when Franklin D. Roosevelt became president. One of the many measures his administration enacted to help the workingman was the National Industrial Recovery Act. Passed in 1933, it had an immediate impact on working people and labor union leaders throughout the country. Section Seven A of the NIRA decreed that "employees shall have the right to organize and bargain collectively through representatives of their own choosing." Furthermore, the NIRA set forth minimum wages, maximum working hours, and child labor laws.

Unfortunately, the NIRA was immediately declared unconstitutional by the United States Supreme Court in May 1935, but not before it gave unions and working people (even farmworkers who were excluded from the act) the impetus to organize more aggressively and to make more demands of employers.

In the 1930s, unions tried to organize in every trade and industry, with varying degrees of success. The AFL, which earlier had been restricted to skilled craftsmen, began organizing unskilled workers in the auto, steel, and trucking industries. Supported by numerous national and local unions, strikes for decent wages and working conditions were only somewhat successful. Still, despite failures in some areas, unions grew in the 1930s. In 1933 alone, 1,056 labor stoppages were documented, involving 1,470,000 workers. In 1933, three times as many workers went out on strike as in 1932. One of the largest and most traumatic was a strike of 100,000 laborers across the workforce in San Francisco, California. In 1937, 75,000 steel workers walked out in one strike, and 100,000 auto workers participated in a single walkout. John L. Lewis' CIO had a membership of 3,700 by 1937. By 1937, membership in both unions was over ten million workers.

UNIONS AND AGRICULTURAL WORKERS: THE WOBBLIES

The organization that first stepped in to organize farm laborers in the West was one of the most radical groups in the history of labor. The Industrial Workers of the World (IWW), usually called the Wobblies, was formed in Chicago, Illinois, in 1905 to challenge capitalism and the wage system. The Wobblies were extremely militant and largely Communist in sympathy. Initially, the strongest element in the IWW were miners in the western states. But the Wobblies soon turned their attention to lumberjacks, textile workers, and then to a group that had been ignored by the national unions—the agricultural workers. The growing strength of the Wobblies, an estimated 50,000 members by 1917, or about 8 percent of the workforce, was frightening to employers and the government. Though they had comparatively few recruits among agricultural workers, they were a visible presence, sending organizers onto ranches that were about to explode into strikes.

The Wobblies were central to one of the most notorious incidents in agricultural history. This conflict, which occurred on Ralph Durst's Wheatland Ranch in California in 1913, is historically important because it gave the agricultural labor movement its first martyrs, and forced the government to investigate conditions in the fields, though little was actually accomplished in the way of remedies.

The conflict began when Durst advertised widely for workers to pick hops on his ranch, giving the impression that he could hire around 2,700 people, even though, as he admitted later, he had only 1,500 jobs. About 3,000 workers showed up. This, of course, gave Durst the advantage of being able to offer the lowest possible wages because there was always a man who was so desperate and had traveled so far that he had to work for any price. Many workers and their families left, but others felt that they had no choice but to stay. About 2,800 remained, camped on a hillside near the ranch, some working and some stranded without work.

Working on the Durst ranch was more nightmare than privilege. An average day's wages at Wheatland ranged from 78 cents to $1.90. Durst withheld 10 percent of their wages, to be paid only if they worked for the entire season. Then he deliberately made working and living conditions so abominable that many workers left and forfeited the 10 percent.

Durst rented rotten tents to the families for seventy-five cents a week. Many families had no choice but to sleep out in the open. To sleep on, they were given a pitchfork's worth of straw instead of beds or bedding. For over 2,800 people who were working or waiting to be hired, Durst provided nine latrines. Most of them were open holes in the ground, but the few with seats were soon covered in filth. The stench of the latrines was so intense that workers were seen vomiting near the area. Because no latrines were provided near any of the work areas across the road—well away from the camp—workers began relieving themselves in or near the fields. Women who left the fields to relieve themselves in the bushes were yelled at and scolded for leaving their work. Two to three hundred children were taken into the fields at 4 A.M. to work. By noon, temperatures had reached 105 degrees, yet no drinking water was provided in the fields. The only drink available was lemonade—a brew later found to be made entirely of citric acid—which Durst's cousin sold to workers for five cents a glass. Merchants from the nearby town of Wheatland were forbidden to truck food in for the workers to buy at the going rate. This forced the workers to pay exorbitant prices at Durst's company store.

Of these workers, about 100 were card-carrying Wobblies, which eventually included two Wobbly leaders, Blackie Ford and Herman Suhr. Outrage at the living conditions immediately united the workers—whatever their affiliation—under the direction of Ford and Suhr. The many families camped outside the ranch lined the roads and sang songs as part of entirely peaceful and, reportedly, quiet demonstrations. The songs they sang, identifiable as tunes made famous by the Wobblies, as well as the defiant words from their meetings, naturally reached Durst's ears. He became anxious about their effect on the workers who continued picking, and he was afraid that the mob would charge into his ranch. Most of all, he was angered over their disruptive behavior along the road next to his property. For two days he was unable to convince law-enforcement officers to forcibly remove the demonstrators. Finally, during an emotional meeting of the protestors led by Blackie Ford, a cooperative sheriff and the district attorney arrived on the scene with a posse, intent upon arresting Ford. But as the sheriff moved toward Ford, one of his deputies fired a gun into the air. The shot set off a massive fight that left the district attorney, a deputy, and two workers dead and hundreds injured. Meanwhile, the posse fled. The national guard and local law-enforcement officers arrived on the scene soon after to arrest 100 workers, some of the few remaining at the camp. In *Factories in the Field* (1939), Carey McWilliams called what followed a reign of terror. As a result of the Wheatland Massacre, over one hundred Wobblies were arrested in California and held for months without trial. They were moved from county to county so that their lawyers could not find them. Both Wobbly leaders were tried and sentenced to life in prison for murder.

The Wobblies played a significant part in improving the lot of nonfactory, skilled workers in the West, but in 1917, another concerted, brutal effort was waged by owners and the government to track down and arrest Wobbly leaders as violaters of the Criminal Syndicalism Act, to destroy their meeting halls, and generally to terrorize their membership. The campaign against them was effective; by 1918 the Wobblies had been destroyed and no longer posed any threat to California agriculture.

With the demise of the Wobblies, agricultural workers were largely ignored by national unions as well as the federal government for about two decades. Farmworkers were specifically excluded from the protections first extended to workers through the NIRA of 1933 and subsequent similar legislation, while national unions lost all interest in organizing farmworkers for a number of reasons. First, the growers had ironclad control over their workers, sometimes (as in the camp for fruit pickers in *The Grapes of Wrath*) imprisoning the workers as if they were in concentration camps. Before the mid-1930s, growers could also threaten most migrants who complained or tried to unionize, with deportation, since the majority did not have United States citizenship. Second, the workers' need to move around constantly from place to place made organization difficult. In addition, the large unions usually charged higher dues than a migrant could pay. Third, in the 1920s and early 1930s, organizing was also impeded because the migrant workers came from so many national backgrounds. There was no common language and no small degree of racial tension and segregation in the fields. Most unions were wary of a situation that defied organization, believing that their difficulties in trying to organize agricultural workers would hurt their hard-won gains in industry. Nevertheless, appalling conditions in the early 1930s led to the informal creation of independent local unions and spontaneous strikes (like the one led by Casy) to address particular complaints.

Still, in 1930, a union called the Trade Union Unity League (TUUL) did some organizing and attempted to form a single union of workers involved in different areas of agriculture. Another union, the Cannery and Agricultural Workers' Industrial Union (CAWIU), like the TUUL that it supplanted, was also led by Communists. It was the only large organization to step into the breach in 1932, when agricultural workers desperately needed the assistance that only a union could provide. At its convention in August 1933, the CAWIU identified the following goals for agricultural and cannery workers. To us today, these measures seem modest and minimal, but in 1933 they were radical:

- seventy-five cents an hour for skilled labor,
- time and a half for overtime,
- decent housing and sanitary conditions,
- abolition of child labor,
- equal pay for men and women,
- pay by the hour.

AGRICULTURAL STRIKES IN 1933 AND 1934

The agony caused by the Depression was worsened by plummeting wages in the fields, higher prices charged by owners in their company stores, and deteriorating living and working conditions. In 1930 and 1931, some wages for backbreaking "stoop" labor had dropped to 10 cents an hour. An independent commission found that the average wage of striking pea pickers was 56 cents a day. A family of ten, all of whom worked in the fields, could make no more than one dollar a day. These inadequate wages were all the more outrageous because it was obvious that the growers were making handsome profits.

Low wages were not the workers' only complaints. On many ranches, no water was provided in the fields and workers had to drink from irrigation ditches filled with silt and solid waste. Far too few latrines were provided for the number of workers hired—and none at all in the fields, which were far from the camps. Drinking water in the camps was polluted by the latrines. The food provided by the growers or labor contractors was too often spoiled, and the cost of even rotten food was invariably deducted from the workers' meager wages. When they dared to protest, their civil rights were usually violated, and they were often fired, blacklisted, driven out of the camps, arrested, or beaten.

These were some of the major conditions that led to the strikes in the 1930s. And several things gave the agricultural worker hope that conditions would improve through unionization. After all, the first federal legislation, the National Industrial Recovery Act, addressing the grievances of laborers, had passed in 1933. And even though it was soon overturned and had never included agricultural workers in the first place, it was an encouraging sign to workers and unions that eventually something positive would happen. Moreover, farmworkers were encouraged by the high degree of union activity in factories.

Nineteen thirty-three and 1934 constituted one of the most active periods in agricultural labor history. Ninety-nine strikes of farmworkers were recorded in this period, some 200 altogether during the entire time of the Great Depression. Most labor historians agree that there were also many spontaneous strikes that were undocumented. During the two years 1933 and 1934, some 87,364 workers throughout the country were involved in agricultural strikes of record. Of the ninety-nine strikes in the fields, forty-nine occurred in California, involving 67,887 workers. Three strikes in 1933 involved over 5,000 workers each. In Santa Clara and Alameda Counties, a general strike of pea pickers in April 1933, brought out 3,000 workers who wanted their wages raised from 12 cents an hour or 10 cents a hamper. The strike ended with a raise to 20 cents a hamper. There were also strikes at Mountain View, Sunnyvale, Merced, Sacramento, El Monte, Kern City, Pixley, Brawley, San Diego, Oxnard, Tulare, San Jose, Chico, Fresno, and Gridley, among other places. The CAWIU led two-dozen strikes in 1933 and in all but four the union won wage increases for the workers. As low as wages were, the costs of making modest gains in wages were still very high.

Strikes occurred all during the summer of 1933, but the longest, and involving the most workers, came in October 1933, when the time neared for picking cotton. Pickers had seen a drastic fall in their wages in 1932—from $1.00 per hundred weight of cotton picked in 1930 to 40 cents in 1932. In 1933, the rate fixed by cotton growers was 60 cents. Any grower who tried to offer more than the agreed-upon rate was harassed by the community and run out of business. And pickers, no matter where they looked, could not find work for more than 60 cents. The workers, who had asked for the 1930 rate of 90 cents to $1.00 per hundred weight, were so angry over the predetermined price that they refused to even begin picking cotton. Instead, they formed some nineteen new local unions to ask the growers for the higher wage, to put an end to the contract labor system and discrimination in hiring. In this they were assisted by the CAWIU, headquartered in Tulare, California, in the heart of the cotton-growing region. On October 4,

1933, the workers voted to strike. The strike began with around 5,000 strikers, who assembled in Corcoran, California, where they soon set up headquarters on the edge of town.

The protest soon spread, with 18,000 workers joining the strike. The Associated Farmers immediately fired up the communities, alerting them to the presence of an army of "Red" outside agitators. In reality, the army was made up of four organizers from the CAWIU, including Pat Chambers, a laborer/organizer who was arrested for leading a strike parade through the streets of Tulare.

The growers immediately began a reign of terror throughout the region with arrests, raids, and beatings. The families of all the striking workers were evicted from camps run by growers.

Around noon, a week after the strike began, many workers were assembled in a union hall in Pixley. During the meeting, a group of vigilantes, made up of growers and their private police force, drove up carrying rifles. When they were safely crouched behind their cars, they began firing repeatedly into the hall. Two workers in the hall were killed and about twenty were seriously wounded. On the same day, a striker was killed by police in Arvin, California.

On October 17, five more strikers were arrested. On October 19, a grand jury indicted eight ranchers for murder and sixteen strikers on a variety of charges. At the hearing, police and growers were found to have planned the Pixley "riot," as the newspapers called it. Despite positive identification of the growers as murderers, the jury found them innocent. Because of labor shortages, area schools were closed on October 19, and school children were bused into the fields to pick the cotton.

The terror continued with more and more arrests, eventually totaling about 200, including the strike leaders. Police officers confiscated all the strikers' automobiles on October 24, so that the picketers had to walk. So-called night riders continually raided the camps and took the families of strikers to stockades. To keep the scabs from being swayed by the striking workers, hundreds of strikers were rounded up on October 25, and placed under heavy guard in a stockade on the Tulare City fairgrounds. In a Corcoran, California, camp, 3,700 men, women, and children were kept prisoner by armed highway patrolmen and guards in a ten-acre field, with only four shallow latrines.

Finally the strike was broken. Those who participated in it were blacklisted, that is, prospective employers were warned that they were troublemakers. Many were deported. As in other strikes, the gains were modest—a 15-cent raise—and the cost in human life was high.

In January 1934, strikes of vegetable pickers broke out in the Imperial Valley. Lettuce workers, who were making from 15 to 22½ cents an hour, struck for an increase to 35 cents an hour. Like other strikers, their demands included more than higher wages: they wanted clean drinking water in the fields, transportation to the fields from the camps, the end of the contract labor system whereby a middleman drained their wages in return for finding them jobs, and, for the first time in agriculture, union recognition. Five thousand lettuce pickers went on strike at the height of the lettuce-picking season. The strike was broken, however, and the workers returned to work on the growers' terms with only modest gains. Another strike in February, by 3,500 pea pickers, attracted the attention of the government even though it lasted only a week without any change in wages. The independent board appointed by the California state government found that the average daily wage for picking peas was 56 cents.

During the Imperial Valley strikes, growers continued to terrorize the strikers as they had in October 1933. Vigilantes raided union halls, made eighty-seven arrests, raided the camps of striking workers, burned their shacks, drove them away with tear gas bombs (killing one infant), and evicted 2,000 people. "Concentration camps" were established in many areas of California. One camp set up on the Tagus Ranch was surrounded by a water-filled moat in addition to barbed wire. Armed guards were stationed at the entrance, some of them manning a huge machine gun. At night guards and spies reported any suspicious worker to the owner.

Growers began to organize in 1934 as the Associated Farmers of California, Inc. They proved effective at preventing labor organizing, breaking strikes, alarming the public about the dangers of "outside communist agitators," and improving the image of agribusiness.

Trying to assess the value of the the Communist agricultural organizers like the Wobblies (IWW), the Trade Union Unity League (TUUL), and the Cannery and Agricultural Workers' Industrial Union (CAWIU) to the workers is somewhat complex. Without a doubt, the laborers themselves had appalling grievances against their employers. Little had changed since the days of the 1913 riot at Wheatland ranch. Conditions were so dehumanizing that workers were forced to attempt small strikes on their own to feed their families. The Communists were the only large, well-organized group that lent any assistance in 1933 and 1934. In addition, the Communist organizers were courageous supporters of field workers and for a long time stood up to beatings and imprisonment. There is little doubt, as well, that the workers would have made even the modest gains they achieved without the help of Communist organizers. Still, many reformers, like Steinbeck, while they acknowledged their value, disliked their commitment to an overarching political agenda and their tactics, which often stemmed from their ideological commitment. Making a final determination of the value of Communist organizers to the cause of agricultural labor is also complicated by the fact that their presence in these early years gave credence to the growers' insistence that every worker who complained was a "Red," whose ultimate goal was to take over the world and therefore needed to be stamped out. By continuing to testify that Communist agitators were the cause of the strikes, rather than the starvation wages and squalid conditions imposed on workers, growers continued to deflect the problems away from themselves, all the while increasing their own profits.

Despite the CAWIU's far-reaching vision and their successes (or perhaps because of them), the CAWIU fell victim, as did the Wobblies, to arrests, raids, and general intimidation. The union lasted only six years, from 1929 to 1935. On July 20, 1934, as Carey McWilliams describes it, "Raiding parties, armed with sawed-off shotguns, handcuffs, blackjacks, rubber hoses, billies, riot clubs, gas bombs" tore into CAWIU headquarters in Sacramento and arrested eighteen people who went to jail on charges of criminal syndicalism. This was the end of the CAWIU.

UNIONS AND FARMWORKERS: 1935–1940

Primarily because so many Mexican and Filipino workers were involved in the 1933 and 1934 strikes, foreign labor was deported en masse in 1935. As labor shortages resulted, the growers courted displaced U.S. citizens like the Joads, believing (which was largely true) that the ex-farmers were independent by nature, inexperienced in the ways of labor unions, and suspicious of socialists and Communists. Compared with the 42,000 workers who went out on strike in 1933 and 1934, only 4,000 struck in 1937 and 4,800 in 1938. Trade union leaders continued to neglect the farm laborer (now coming from the South and plains states), on many occasions even siding with the big growers, claiming that the Okies were taking California jobs at a time when unemployment was rampant. There were instances in which the AFL, for example, took the side of the growers against their workers. However, the CIO, historically more interested in unskilled workers, sponsored a new splinter union to work with agricultural and allied workers. The new organization, however, called the United Cannery, Agricultural, Packing and Allied Workers of America (UCAPAWA), was not Communistic, as its predecessors had been.

In 1935, the UCAPAWA met with continual violence perpetrated by the militant and now well-organized growers. On June 10, the growers decided to put down any opposition before it began. On the night before the apricot harvest was set to begin, on a hillside overlooking the camp, they erected three crosses and set them on fire to frighten the workers. On August 23, five union leaders were seized and dragged through the streets of Santa Rosa. Three of them were released after being forced to kiss the American flag and promise to leave the country. The two others were kicked, beaten, and then tarred and feathered, before being put on display at the courthouse and then dumped over the county line. The leaders of the mob who committed this act were the mayor, a member of the state legislature, the president of a bank, the president of the Chamber of Commerce, some motorcycle policemen, and some members of the American Legion.

The grower-sponsored shootings, beatings, arson, and tear gas bombings continued throughout the 1930s. In some quarters their acts had driven away so many workers that it was feared that there would be insufficient laborers to harvest the crops. But despite the opposition, the UCAPAWA was a strong organization by 1937, and by 1938, had gained the support of active private organizations, including one named for John Steinbeck.

Because field-workers never felt welcomed by the AFL—which finally showed an interest in organizing cannery and field workers in 1936—farmworkers interested in union representation tended to form CIO affiliations. The general pattern, however, was for so-called Okies to organize themselves on the spot in protest of a specific problem rather than joining in the long-range planning and negotiations typically practiced by unions. These spontaneous strikes sprang up in a number of places in the last years of the 1930s—in Marysville, Winters, Westley, and Nipomo, for instance.

Despite diminished union activity after 1935, even in the face of serious grievances, one major union-sponsored strike was set in motion in October 1939, again by cotton pickers in the San Joaquin Valley. The grievances of the cotton pickers were substantial and of long standing. In 1938, they were paid 13 cents for a pound of picked cotton. The federal government had paid cotton growers to cut the acreage planted in order to raise the price of farm produce. So, with fewer jobs and a glut of laborers, many growers were paying cotton pickers only 50 cents per hundred pounds of cotton picked. The union asked for $1.25 per hundred pounds of cotton picked, but the growers would agree to only 75 or 80 cents per hundred pounds. When negotiations fell through, the strike began, and spread to other cotton-growing areas, as it had in 1933. As in the earlier strike, this one also ended in violence.

The California state government, sympathetic to the union for the first time, tried to intercede, and recommended that growers pay a fair wage of $1.25 per hundred pounds of cotton picked, or at least 27½ cents an hour. The strike lasted for two weeks, the longest and largest strike since the cotton strike of 1933. During this time, strikers' families had no salary and no relief of any kind, and were thrown out of the camps. On October 21, 1939, after many beatings and arrests, three hundred of the growers' deputies moved against the assembled strikers with a variety of weapons. After two weeks, the cotton fields were filled with pickers who came to work on the growers' terms of 20 cents an hour. Later, at the urging of the state government, growers finally agreed to pay $1.00 per hundred weight of cotton picked.

The growers and local Chambers of Commerce in California revived charges of a Communist conspiracy with every breath, even though UCAPAWA was not Communist and did not have Communist leadership. Laws long in place to impede organization—against picketing, obstructing roadways, making noise, vagrancy, and trespassing—continued to be enforced with a vengeance. Anyone suspected of striking could be jailed on any one of these charges. Leaders who urged organizing and strikes were sent to prison on the old, but more serious charge, of criminal syndicalism. Furthermore, the Associated Farmers kept records of troublesome workers. Any person suspected of being a union supporter or who had been on strike was known to all members of the association, and was refused work. They were also thrown out of all but the government-sponsored camps.

On April 12, 1937, workers across the country had reason to celebrate the passage of the National Labor Relations Board's (NLRB) recommendation that gave labor the right to organize, an act reinforced by a new Supreme Court decision. But these protections still were not available to agricultural workers.

In the final analysis, unions were never able to improve the shameful conditions suffered by people like the Joads, not just because the workers were suspicious and ignorant of unions, but because they were demoralized and terrorized. Beginning in 1937, and continuing into the 1940s, the U.S. Congress began an investigation into the wrongful attempts by owners and management in all areas of industry and agriculture to destroy the unions and break strikes. Transcripts of the formal hearings, which began in 1939 and continued through 1940, were later published. The great sympathy for agricultural workers after the publication of Steinbeck's novel in 1939, and the horrors uncovered in the Congressional hearings seemed to make the times right in 1941 for Senator La Follette to push through Congress a recommendation that the Wagner Act (concerned with labor rights) and the NIRA (concerned with working conditions) be extended to farmworkers. But World War II intervened, and the proposal failed in a Congress that claimed it was too busy with pressing war matters to fight the giant agricultural growers of California. It would be decades before unions rose again in the agricultural fields of California to fight for improved working conditions.

The documents included below begin with a speech by President Roosevelt's secretary of the interior, Harold L. Ickes, about the socioeconomic conditions that lead to class warfare between workers and the very rich. Thereafter, the documents are arranged in chronological order. They include union pronouncements and postings, statistics, labor songs of the period, testimony before a Senate Committee, and affidavits of activists.

WOBBLY SONG ABOUT THE WHEATLAND

The Wobblies were famous for creating rousing songs—often set to well-known tunes—to express their philosophy and spread the word about the union. Their most famous songwriter was Joe Hill, a Wobbly activist who was executed for a murder that he denied committing. Among his songs is one called "Pie in the Sky," which shows the unrealistic attitude of the gullible worker who expects a good life but who will never be allowed to make a decent living in the system.

The other great chronicler of the farmworker emerged two decades later in the 1930s. Woody Guthrie was a genuine Okie who migrated from Oklahoma to California. His songs include "This Land is Your Land" and "Ballad of Pretty B. Floyd."

The Wobbly song about the Wheatlands Riot in 1913 is unsigned. The men named Blackie Ford and Herman Suhr in the song were the two Wobbly leaders sent to prison after the riot. Ralph Durst was the hop grower against whom the workers struck. In the song, "vag" means to be arrested for vagrancy.

FROM "OVERALLS AND SNUFF"
(Unsigned Verses in Line *Solidarity* August 1, 1914)

(Tune: "Wearing of the Green")

One day as I was walking along the railroad track
I met a man in Wheatland with his blankets on his back,
He was an old-time hop picker, I'd seen his face before
I knew he was a wobbly, by the button that he wore.
By the button that he wore, by the button that he wore.
I knew he was a wobbly, by the button that he wore.

He took his blankets off his back and sat down on the rail
And told us some sad stories 'bout the workers down in jail.
He said the way they treat them there, he never saw the like.
For they're putting men in prison just for going out on strike.
Just for going out on strike, just for going out on strike,
They're putting men in prison, just for going out on strike.

They have sentenced Ford and Suhr, and they've got them in
    the pen,
If they catch a wobbly in their burg, they vag him there and then,
There is one thing I can tell you, and it makes the bosses sore,
As fast as they can pinch us, we can always get some more
We can always get some more, we can always get some more,
As fast as they can pinch us, we can always get some more.

Oh, Horst and Durst are mad as hell, they don't know what to do.
And the rest of those hop barons are all feeling mighty blue.
Oh, we've tied up all their hop fields, and the scabs refuse to
    come,
And we're going to keep on striking till we put them on the bum.
Till we put them on the bum, till we put them on the bum.
We're going to keep on striking till we put them on the bum.

We've got to stick together, boys, and strive with all our might,
Just free Ford and Suhr, boys, we've got to win this fight.
These scissorbill hop barons we are taking no more bluff,
We'll pick no more damned hops for them, for overalls and snuff.
For overalls and snuff, for our overalls and snuff
We'll pick no more damned hops for them, for overalls and snuff.

THE BEGINNINGS OF AGRICULTURE UNIONISM

The following document, which introduced a statement of intent by the Industrial Workers of the World (IWW), indicates their radical position with regard to labor and management. The IWW, or Wobblies, took the position that fair wages alone would not solve labor's problems; what was needed was a radical reorganization of society, specifically the abolition of capitalism and the wage system. In the place of a profit-based society, divided into owners and employee-workers, the IWW envisioned a system whereby land and industry were owned in common by all the workers. Workers and owners would be one and the same.

Radical they may have been, but the IWW was the first union of national scope to show an interest in organizing agricultural workers. The Wobblies' open admission of their radical position and their sympathy with Communism led most Californians to label all labor unions Red for two decades.

FROM PREAMBLE OF THE INDUSTRIAL WORKERS OF THE
WORLD POSITION PAPERS (1905)
(In Porter M. Chaffee, *A History of the Cannery and Agricultural Workers Industrial Union*; A Federal Writers' Project, typescript, Bancroft Library, The University of California, 193–)

Instead of the conservative motto, "A fair day's wage for a fair day's work," we must inscribe on our banner the revolutionary watchword, "Abolition of the wage system."

It is the historic mission of the working class to do away with capitalism. The army of production must be organized, not only for the everyday struggle with capitalists, but also to carry on production when capitalism shall have been overthrown. By organizing industrially we are forming the structure of the new society within the shell of the old.

GENERAL OFFICE
2422 N. Halsted Street, Chicago, Ill.
W. H. Westman, General Secretary.

(Appendix, p. xvii)

THE DIVISION BETWEEN WORKERS AND OWNERS

The following newspaper article, dated October 21, 1938, describes an address by President Roosevelt's secretary of the interior, Harold L. Ickes, to the Commonwealth Club, an organization of civic leaders warned of the trouble that comes with the concentration of wealth in such few hands, pointing out that the urge for economic control by a few wealthy families clashed with the desire for democracy on the part of the great masses of people who were suffering economically. The total income of one group of 178,000 families in the United States equaled the total income of another group of 12,500,000 families. Such a gap between the few very wealthy families and the rest of the population was bound, he said, to create open warfare between the two groups—warfare that had already erupted many times in the 1930s.

Although this article reports on a speech delivered in California in 1938, the situation about which Ickes warned had been developing since the 1929 stock market crash. Nowhere was this so much in evidence as in California, where land and wealth had become concentrated in comparatively few hands.

The landscape had become a battlefield between growers who wanted maximum profits and agricultural and cannery workers who joined together to seek better wages and decent living conditions.

FROM "CONCENTRATION OF U.S. RICHES ALARMS ICKES"
(Oakland Tribune, October 19, 1938)

POLITICAL DEMOCRACY FACES FIGHT FOR LIFE,
SAYS CABINET MEMBER
By the Associated Press

Harold L. Ickes, Secretary of the Interior, called "over-concentration of economic power" the Nation's "public enemy No.1" today in a speech before the Commonwealth Club, San Francisco.

He dug up his famous "sixty families" bone of contention, subject of

Nation-wide comment following his radio speech last December on that subject.

Ickes attributed "economic indecision" to the clash between growing "economic autocracy and a growing political democracy."

Each tries to curb the other, he said, and "so long as that struggle goes on we shall never have a clear-cut direction in our economic life."

$250 a Year

Citing various statistics on division of the National income—one group to show 178,000 families got as much as 12½ million other families, another to balance the income of 327 families against more than two million getting less than $250 a year—Ickes asserted concentration of wealth is "aggravated by concentrated economic power."

Turning to the American Telephone and Telegraph Company, he said 43 large stockholders have almost as much stock and voting rights as 250,000 small stockholders. The right of stockholders of large corporations to vote, he asserted, "is only a paper right; not an effective right."

Asserting this must be corrected, he left the club to figure out its own solution. He swung into a discussion of class consciousness:

"In a recent speech, Mr. Herbert Hoover said: 'Class hate is the rock upon which every republic has been wrecked.'

Class Consciousness

"This speech indicated Mr. Hoover's expedient of dealing with class hate would be the simple one of not recognizing it.

"Class consciousness in this country has never begun with the people at the bottom. It has always been created by the very fear of it on the part of the privileged few. You can always tell which side is really class conscious by taking note of which side talks about the dangers of class war."

The only way to get rid of the feeling, Ickes asserted, is by getting rid of the basis for it. It arises from "inequality of opportunity amid excessive inequality in wealth and economic power."

"Either our democracy will solve this problem in the next few years or the problem will dissolve our democracy.

"Private collectivism fights against the public collectivism which it breeds.

Economic Insecurity

"No economic system can function during such a war. Unemployment and insecurity are the results.

"If political democracy is to survive it is obvious that the conflict between economic and political power must be resolved. If it is not resolved democracies will not be able to withstand either the pressure from the left for the State to take to itself all the economic power or the pressure from the right for economic power to take to itself the State."

In defense of New Deal concentration of economic power—public power vs. private—he said:

"I'll wager that the portion contributed by ambitionless Government servants in RFC, WPA, PWA, Rural Electrification, FHA, CCC, the Army engineers, the Navy, Interior and Agriculture—compare favorably in immediate financial economy and in ultimate social benefit with the contributions made by the great financial promoters at the cost of loss to at least half their investors to say nothing of the tremendous cost to the country as a whole from the looting of the public domain.

Private Investors

"The whole public debt of today does not aggregate the losses of private investors over a generation.

"The grandest things you have in San Francisco, those breathtaking bridges across your bay, were built by the organizing genius of Government servants. And whenever, as far back as I can remember, a job has been too big, too difficult and too expensive for private industry to handle, the supposedly so inefficient Government has had to step in and do it.

"Our fathers had to fight to achieve democracy. We must bestir ourselves if we are to retain it." (p. 1)

LABOR STATISTICS NATIONWIDE

In 1929, the Trade Union Unity League (TUUL), a large national union, was formed and unlike the American Federation of Labor (AFL), the league was interested in both industrial and agricultural labor problems. The following article describes the growth of unions nationwide in the early years when the TUUL flourished. Notice the TUUL's need to defend itself against charges of Communism.

The Labor Fact Book II goes on to comment on the rise of company unions in 1937 and 1938 and on strike statistics of 1937.

FROM *LABOR FACT BOOK II*, PREPARED BY THE LABOR
RESEARCH ASSOCIATION
(New York: International Publishers, 1934)

TRADE UNION UNITY LEAGUE

The Trade Union Unity League, which was formed in 1929, is now the acknowledged leader of the revolutionary trade union movement in the United States (for a full discussion of T.U.U.L. see *Labor Fact Book*, Vol. I, p. 135). It describes itself as "a center of trade unions standing on the policy of the class struggle. . . . The T.U.U.L. and its affiliated unions are based on control by the rank and file and stand for the united action of all workers, irrespective of their trade union affiliation."

To the charge that the T.U.U.L. unions are "Communist unions," the T.U.U.L. replies: "The T.U.U.L. and its affiliated organizations are not political parties. They are trade unions based on the struggle of the workers against the bosses. They embrace workers of all opinions including Republicans, Democrats, Socialists, Communists and others." Communists are of course among the most active workers in these unions as in many A. F. of L. and other unions.

The T.U.U.L. stands definitely for both the building of new industrial unions among the unorganized and at the same time for work within the existing A. F. of L. unions and independent unions. It supports the program of the rank and file opposition in the A. F. of L.

The T.U.U.L. has grown considerably since 1931, especially in the needle trades and among food, agricultural, steel and metal, and furniture workers. At the beginning of 1934, the T.U.U.L. claimed about 125,000 members, the largest union being the Needle Trades Workers Industrial Union with about 30,000 members.

T.U.U.L. led unions have directed important strikes during the last two years. Strikes led or participated in by these unions have increased in number, especially since the T.U.U.L. has been foremost in the struggle against the NRA codes and the conditions which these codes have in-

SOME IMPORTANT STRIKES LED BY UNIONS UNDER LEADERSHIP OF TRADE
UNION UNITY LEAGUE SINCE 1931

Month and Year	Location	Trade and Number Involved
1931		
June	Pa.-Ohio	Coal miners, 40,000
Nov.	Ybor City, Fla.	Tobacco, 10,000
1932		
Jan.	Eastern Ky. & Tenn.	Coal miners, 6,000
Feb.	N. Y. City	Needle trades, 5,000[1]
May	Colorado	Beet, 18,000
Aug.	South River, N. J.	Needle trades, 2,160
1933		
Jan.–Feb.	Detroit, Mich.	Auto, 16,000[2]
April	San Jose & vicinity, Cal.	Pea pickers, 2,200
"	Pennsylvania	Coal miners, 3,000
May	St. Louis, Mo.	Nut pickers, 1,500
Aug.	Gallup, N. M.	Coal miners, 2,000
"	Utah	Coal miners, 1,500
"	N. Y. City	Shoe, 12,000
"	N. Y. City	Tobacco, 2,000
"	N. Y. City & vicinity	Metal, 5,000
Sept.	Paterson, N. J. & vicinity	Silk, 15,000[1]
"	Lodi, Cal.	Grape pickers, 3,000
Oct.	Ambridge, Pa.	Steel, 5–6,000
"	San Joaquin Valley, Cal.	Cotton pickers, 18,000
Nov.	St. Paul, Minn.	Meat packers, 1,200
"	Pittsburgh, Pa.	Meat packers, 2,700

[1]This includes only the member *directly* led by the T.U.U.L. union. Many more were involved in the strike.
[2]In four strikes of auto workers.

flicted. Here are a few of the strikes and struggles that attest the increasing importance of the T.U.U.L. in the labor movement.

. . .

Belligerent employers' associations, such as the National Association of Manufacturers, have advocated establishment of such "independent" unions to replace the company union as a more subtle technique in anti-labor campaigns. And professional "patriotic" organizations, such as The Neutral Thousands, in California, have openly sponsored such unions in the campaigns to break strikes and destroy real trade unions. They have been played up in hysterical propaganda drives against the A. F. of L., the CIO and the National Labor Relations Board.

Federations of "Independents": The sponsors of these so-called "independent" unions have recently begun to realize that they stand a better chance of survival if they are linked at least loosely with other groups of the same sort. This does not mean that the "independent" in one factory of a given company is getting together with a similar group in another factory of the same company. That might resemble real unionism. It simply means that a group of this type in a chocolate factory, a textile mill, a steel plant, or what not, are in a "federation" which may be used by reactionary interests for national lobbying and other such purposes.

Several more or less abortive efforts to set up such national unions of "loyal employees" were made in 1937 and 1938. One resulted in the *National Federated Independent Union.* This outfit grew out of a combination of company unions like the one at Hershey Chocolate Corp., Hershey, Pa. (which, however, is since reported abandoned) and the ones used to break the strike at plants of the Remington Rand Co. This "national" union is being used to fight both the A. F. of L. and the CIO. It is against all sit-down strikes as "un-American." After a convention at Buffalo, N. Y., in February, 1938, it was reported as issuing "charters" to 38 local "independents," mostly in the eastern part of the country. Pres. F. S. Galloway claimed at the time that this new group represented approximately 250,000 employees.

STRIKE STATISTICS

1937 Strikes: More strikes took place in 1937 than in any previous year in American history, according to the report of the Industrial Relations Division of the U. S. Department of Labor (*Monthly Labor Review*, May, 1938). Less than half as many workers, however, were involved in 1937 strikes as in 1919, the peak year. Of the 1937 strikes, 46.4%, involving 903,965 workers, resulted in substantial gains to the workers, and another 31.8%, affecting 605,823 workers, resulted in partial gains or compromises. Thus 78.2% of the 1937 strikes, affecting 77.5% of all workers involved, won at least some gains for the strikers.

A. F. of L. unions were involved in 48.7% of the 1937 strikes, and CIO unions in 38.7%. Strikes of the CIO, however, affected twice as many as those of the A. F. of L., "due to their organization drives in the mass production industries," as the *Monthly Labor Review* put it. CIO strikes in 1937 affected 1,163,515, or 59.8% of all workers involved in strikes, and A. F. of L.-led strikes 583,063, or 30% of all affected.

Here are U.S. Department of Labor figures for 1937, compared with those for 1936. (Figures in parentheses indicate percentage of the total in that category.)

	1936	1937
Number of strikes	2,172	4,740
Number of workers involved	788,648	1,860,621
Man-days idle	13,901,956	28,425,000
Results:		
Substantial gains to workers		
Number of strikes	991 (45.9%)	2,191 (46.4%)
Number of workers involved	288,952 (40.7%)	903,965 (46.4%)
Partial gains or compromises		
Number of strikes	508 (23.6%)	1,503 (31.8%)
Number of workers involved	254,751 (35.9%)	605,823 (31.1%)
Major issues:		
Wages and hours		
Number of strikes	756 (35.1%)	1,410 (29.9%)
Number of workers involved	250,672 (35.3%)	435,568 (22.4%)
Union organization[a]		
Number of strikes	1,083 (50.2%)	2,728 (57.8%)
Number of workers involved	365,019 (51.4%)	1,163,197 (59.8%)

	1936	1937
Industries (by largest number of workers involved)[b]		
Transportation equipment[c]	54,049 (6)	372,399 (1)
Textiles	128,578 (1)	213,455 (2)
Iron and steel		186,017 (3)
Extraction of minerals	56,063 (5)	162,645 (4)
Rubber products	76,699 (3)	
Transportation and communication	83,231 (2)	135,489 (5)
Domestic and personal service	72,246 (4)	

[a]Involves recognition, or recognition and wages and hours, closed shop, discrimination against unionists.

[b]Figure in parentheses here indicates rank of industry by number involved in the year.

[c]Mostly automobile manufacturing.

DOCUMENTED LABOR STRIKES BETWEEN 1930 AND 1936

The following list of strikes compiled by Porter Chaffee, a labor activist in California in the 1930s, shows only those strikes that he could document. Most historians agree that there were many more independent strikes that were never officially recorded. The following table shows the county in which the strike occurred; the crop the strikers were expected to pick (where the information was available to Chaffee); the day, month, and year of the walk out; union demands; and the resolution of the strike. In some cases, the same strike reached a number of areas.

The list, while incomplete, gives some idea of the scope of strike activity between 1930 and 1936. We also get some idea of how low wages were and how modest were the union's demands. Finally, there is an inkling of the extent of the violence on the part of the growers to end the strikes and union activity.

FROM PORTER CHAFFEE, *A HISTORY OF THE CANNERY AND AGRICULTURAL WORKERS INDUSTRIAL UNION*
(Federal Writers' Project, typescript,
Bancroft Library, The University of California, 193–)

County	Kind	Demands	Remarks
Imperial	lettuce 2/11/30	.04 a crate	some demands met
Imperial	cantaloupe 3/4/30		103 arrested, 9 sentenced
Solano	pruners 11/12/32	1.50 a day	no gains
San Mateo	peas 5/32	.60 a sack	strike lost
Alameda, Santa Clara	peas 4/33	raise from .90 day	arrests, deportation, no gains
San Luis Obispo	peas 4/33	.30 hr	
Los Angeles	berries 6/33	.25 hr	.20 hr won, arrests
Santa Clara	cherries	.30 hr	riots, 24 arrests, 2 injuries
Ventura	beets 8/33	.35 hr	violence, no gains
Tulare	peaches 6/33	.35 hr	.25 granted

County	Kind	Demands	Remarks
Fresno	peaches 8/33	.27 hr	.02 gain
Kings	same strike	.30 hr	
Kern	same strike		
Butte	same strike	.35 hr	.30 granted
Stanislaus	same strike	.30 hr	.25 granted, injuries, arrests
Yuba	same strike 8/33		
Sutter	strike threat 8/33		12 arrests, no gains
Kern	grapes	raise from .17 hr	.25 granted
Santa Cruz	lettuce 8/33	.30 hr	
Santa Clara	pears 8/33	.30 hr	won .25 hr
Sacramento	hops 8/33		
Sonoma	apples 8/33	.25 hr	won .25 hr
Fresno	grapes 9/33	.40 hr	some gains
Tulare	grapes 9/33	.40 hr	arrests, deaths, free strikers deportations
San Joaquin	same strike		
San Joaquin	hundred 10/33	1.00 per hundred-weight (cwt)	
Tulare	same		evictions, deportation, 3 killed, wounded
Stanislaus	same		
Fresno	same		
Merced	same		
Kings	same		
Kern	same		
Madera	same		
Imperial	same		
Santa Cruz	artichokes 9/33	9 hr day	got 10 hr day
Los Angeles	walnuts 9/33		4 arrested
Tulare	citrus 10/33	.12 to .16 box	
Imperial	cantaloupe	pay raise	some gains
Tulare	olives 11/33	pay raise	some gains
San Mateo	spinach 1/34	.25 hr	
Imperial	peas 2/34	no contractors	

County	Kind	Demands	Remarks
San Bernardino	oranges 2/34	raise from .04 box	gained raise of 1½ cents
Los Angeles	same		
Fresno	citrus 3/34	raise from .06 a box	no results
Sacramento	asparagus 3/34	.12 a crate	
Sacramento	berries 4/34	.25 hr	no raise, tear gassed
Alameda	peas 9/34	.30 hr	some gains
Imperial	pickers 3/34	right to bargain	reported kidnaped
Monterey	peas 4/34	.35 hr	some gains
San Mateo	peas 5/34		
Contra Costa	apricots 7/34	.35 hr	lost and reduced wages, paid .15 hr
Alameda	same		
Santa Barbara	pickers 8/34		
San Joaquin	cotton 5/34	1.00 cwt	granted
San Joaquin	peas 4/36	.33 a hamper	got .30
Los Angeles	celery 4/36	.30 hr min.	gained raise, violence
Monterey	lettuce 5/36	no nonunion workers	demands met
Los Angeles	beans 5/36	.30 an hour union rights	no gain, violence
Los Angeles	same; berries		
Kern	potato 6/36	.50 an hr	given .25, violence
Los Angeles	farmworkers 6/36	same	
Santa Clara	pears 7/36	.07 a box	won .065 box
Orange	citrus 6/36	.40 hr	won .35 hr, violence
El Dorado	pears 6/36	raise .01 box	won raise, 20 fired
Lake Monterey	lettuce 9/36	contract renewal	violence
Santa Cruz	same		
Santa Cruz	sprouts 10/36	.35 hr	some gains
San Joaquin	celery 11/36	raise	lost, arrests

County	Kind	Demands	Remarks
Santa Barbara	agricultural workers 11/34		
San Diego	celery 1/35	.30 hr	given .30 hr
San Luis Obispo	peas 1/35	.30 hr	failed
Orange	peas 1/35	.35 hr	given .25 hr
Orange	peas 2/35	.25 hr	given .225 hr
San Joaquin	cotton 2/35	1.00 cwt	given .75 cwt
Butte	field workers		
San Diego	oranges 6/35	.06 per 38 lb. box	
San Joaquin	cherries 6/35	no cut to .20 hr	successful
Sonoma	apples 6/35	higher wage	raids and violence
Santa Barbara	potato 8.35		
Kern	grapes 9/35		firings and arrests
Orange	oranges 11/35		
San Diego	farm workers 2/36	.30 hr	strike broken
Yolo	peas 4/36	higher wages	given .25 hr

(Appendix, ii–xv)

CIRCULAR ANNOUNCING A STRIKE OF PEA PICKERS

A circular, distributed in 1933 by the Cannery and Agricultural Workers Industrial Union (CAWIU), shows just how low wages were for the pea pickers the union was leading out on strike. Their demands are very modest. They are striking because the growers have refused to raise their wages to one cent per pound of peas picked.

Note also the foresight with which the union has planned, organizing carefully to anticipate the strategy of the growers to break the strike and the tendency of workers to settle with the growers on any terms just to be allowed back to work.

A CIRCULAR ANNOUNCING A STRIKE OF PEA PICKERS
(San Jose, CA: CAWIU, 1933)

PEA PICKERS

Strike!   Strike!   Strike!

The conference of Pea-Pickers called by the Cannery and Agricultural Workers Industrial Union on Wednesday night, April 12, 1933, voted unanimously for a general strike in all Pea Fields, starting Friday morning, April 14, 1933. We call on all workers to join.

Demands

1. 30¢ a hamper; 30¢ a sack; 35¢ an hour or 1¢ a lb.

2. All workers to be hired through Union Committees in each town, and not through contractors.

Notice

1. Every camp elect a Strike Committee of 13 members. Send a representative to General Strike Committee, 81 Post Street, San Jose, California, for help.

2. Don't settle with owners, contractors, charities, police, or any other officials without a representative of the General Strike Committee present. This is for your own protection, as experience has taught us that the bosses use many tricks to fool us.

3. Notify Union Hall, 81 Post St., San Jose, California, and a representative of the General Strike Committee will be immediately sent.

Issued by the Cannery and Agricultural Workers Industrial Union. District Office, 81 Post St., San Jose, California.

INDEPENDENT COMMISSION REPORT ON THE SITUATION IN THE IMPERIAL VALLEY IN 1933

In 1933, the Imperial Valley was wracked by strike after strike by agricultural workers, like the previously mentioned pea pickers. Such was the violence (usually on the part of the growers) and the general disruption, that an independent commission was appointed to investigate the situation. This report, included in the La Follette Senate committee's records, stands as evidence that conditions were sufficiently deplorable to cause strikes, even without the interference of established unions.

FROM EXHIBIT 8766: "CONDITIONS WHICH PROVOKED UNION
ACTIVITY AND STRIKES," FROM A REPORT BY A COMMISSION
NAMED BY THE NATIONAL LABOR BOARD TO INVESTIGATE
DISTURBANCES IN THE IMPERIAL VALLEY IN 1933
(In Hearings before a Subcommittee of the Committee/ and on
Education Labor, 76th Congress, Part 54; Washington, DC: U.S.
Government Printing Office, 1941)

. . . There is legitimate complaint about the water that is taken from irrigation ditches. It is muddy in appearance, liable to contamination from the people who temporarily reside on the banks of the streams, and is not purified by chemical treatment, as in the cities. This is not only a serious health problem for those who use the water, but there is a distinct menace to all the people of Imperial County. Typhoid fever is not unknown. The diseases that follow the use of impure water are prevalent.

. . . The rectification of the water complaints is a duty that belongs to those public officials who are responsible for the protection of the health of all the people. . . .

Living and sanitary conditions are a serious and irritating factor in the unrest we find in the Imperial Valley. We visited the quarters of the cities where live Mexicans, Negroes, and others. We inspected the camps of the pea-pickers, and know that they are similar to the camps that will serve as places of abode for workers in the field when melons are gathered. This report must state that we found filth, squalor, and entire absence of sanitation, and a crowding of human beings into totally inadequate tents or crude structures built of boards, weeds, and anything that was found at hand to give a pitiful semblance of a home at its worst. Words cannot describe some of the conditions we saw. During the warm weather when the temperature rises considerably above 100 degrees, the flies and insects become a pest, the children are fretful, the attitude of some of the parents can be imagined and innumerable inconveniences add to the general discomfort. In this environment there is bred a social sullenness that is to be deplored, but which can be understood by those who have viewed the scenes that violate all the recognized standards of living. Even in the section of cities that house Mexicans and people of other nationalities, we found shacks that are disgraceful, and a lack of sanitation in all its aspects, even though these folks are permanent residents, and, in some instances, taxpayers. Here again there is danger to the general public health in permitting such harmful conditions to prevail. (p. 20047)

ASSOCIATED FARMERS' MINUTES REVEAL
PLANS AGAINST LABOR

By the spring of 1934, the growers' campaign to unite against labor unions had intensified. Their sophisticated strategic planning is revealed in the following proposal presented for approval to a statewide association of growers. Note how each item will be used to thwart union organizing, strikes, and workers' demands. There is also clear evidence that the growers sought the collaboration of other segments of established society in attempting to improve their rapidly tarnishing image.

FROM EXHIBIT 8859: MINUTES OF A STATEWIDE FARM LABOR
MEETING OF THE ASSOCIATED FARMERS
(In Hearings before a Subcommittee of the Committee on
Education and Labor, 76th Congress, Part 55; Washington, DC: U.S.
Government Printing Office, 1940)

As a basis for discussing the purpose of the statewide organization, the Chairman submitted a tentative list of activities as follows:

Secretary:

Promote country units; keep them informed and active.

Keep affected industries advised of developments.

Keep in touch with agricultural fact sources, such as College of Agriculture, State Department of Agriculture, etc.

Keep in touch with official peace agencies, such as Division of Criminal Identification, red squad of Los Angeles police department, district attorney of Alameda County, etc.

Carry out desires of organization relating to mediation.

Carry out desires of organization relating to public relief funds.

Contact organizations and groups best able to combat menace, including Legion, women's clubs, schools, etc.

Organize opposition to repeal of the Criminal Syndicalism Law.

Urge passage of national legislation.

Expedite deportations.

Attorney:

Clarify laws and ordinances for local authorities.

Prepare proper laws and ordinances for localities needing these.

Assist district attorneys with prosecutions.

Publicity man:

Expose red organizations and affiliates.

Publicize purposes of communistic organizations.

Quote red propaganda, its source and distribution.

Publicize agricultural wage data and the status of agriculture.

Print human interest stories regarding the difficulties of farmers and their families.

Detail instances of intimidation, trespass, bodily harm to workers, employers, or officers.

Develop losses to willing workers through unemployment due to strikes.

Publicize police records of agitators.

Write articles for magazines and trade papers. (p. 20253)

UNION FLYER POSTED FOR FARMWORKERS IN MARCH 1934

Lettuce pickers gained no increase in wages or other benefits from their strike in 1934. After the strike had been broken and declared a failure, the CAWIU issued a circular asking workers to act as a group and to believe that things would eventually get better if they joined together. The circular echoes the sentiments of Jim Casy as he pleaded with Tom on the night he was killed: if we act together, we will not lose in the end. Notice in the flyer the implication about the tendency of farmworkers to act spontaneously when grievances arise, rather than join the union. Many workers joined union members in a strike, but they resisted setting up long-standing mechanisms for negotiations and well-considered actions. The union, however, is practical and does not stand on principle Their message is to accept that the lettuce strike has been broken, go back to work, try to remain optimistic, and plan together for the future.

FROM EXHIBIT 8921: UNION FLYER POSTED FOR FARM
WORKERS IN MARCH 1934
(In Hearings before a Subcommittee of the Committee on
Education and Labor 76th Congress, Part 55; Washington, DC: U.S.
Government Printing Office, 1940)

FELLOW WORKERS IN IMPERIAL VALLEY WE ARE NOT
DEFEATED!

Even if we did not win higher wages in the lettuce strike, we are much stronger today than we were before the strike. We have gained much valuable experience and in the future will not repeat the same mistakes. THE BIGGEST MISTAKE WAS THAT WE WERE NOT ALL ORGANIZED IN THE CAN-NERY & AGRICULTURAL WORKERS INDUSTRIAL UNION.

Willingness to strike is not enough. We must be strongly organized in our militant union with good connections with all parts of the strike area. We are now starting to organize ALL the workers in Imperial Valley into the Cannery & Agricultural Workers Industrial Union so we can win higher wages we fought for in the lettuce strike.

We *can* and *will* win higher wages for ourselves. But we must organize all the workers in Brawley, El Centro, Calexico, Calipatria, Holtville and all other towns in the valley—NOT JUST BRAWLEY ALONE. We must organize all the workers regardless of race and nationality. The bosses try to defeat us both by terror and by splitting us on nationalistic lines. DON'T LISTEN TO THE LIES IN THE BOSS OWNED NEWSPAPERS, OR ANY OTHER TOOL OF THE BOSSES ESPECIALLY THE MEXICAN CONSUL.

MANY OF THE WORKERS HAVE gone back to work because of hunger, but they are not scabs. Many others are refusing to go back to work. Workers should always act together. Therefore, since the lettuce strike is over, all workers should go back to work BUT WHILE ON THE JOB THEY SHOULD JOIN AND BUILD THE C. & A. W. I. U.

We are not defeated! We will go back to work and when we are all organized we will strike again and the next time, by good organization and not repeating mistakes, *we will win*.

Issued by: CENTRAL STRIKE COMMITTEE, CANNERY & AGRICULTURAL WORKERS INDUSTRIAL UNION AFFILIATED WITH THE TRADE UNION UNITY LEAGUE. (p. 20314)

TESTIMONY BEFORE SENATE SUBCOMMITTEE ON WORKING CONDITIONS OF AGRICULTURE WORKERS

In the late 1930s John Steinbeck's *The Grapes of Wrath* added fuel to Senator Robert La Follette's hearings on the plight of agricultural workers. The following excerpts include testimony from two witnesses, Henry Strobel, a wealthy grower who had held a high position in the Associated Farmers and was known for his intractability with regard to his workers and John Miller, a member of the Chamber of Commerce who had cooperated with the growers in fighting unions. Senator La Follette tries to establish that strikes are primarily caused by poor wages and abominable working and living conditions. The growers and their supporters attempt to absolve themselves from blame by consistently arguing that there would be no union activity were it not for outside agitators. Grievances, they contend, had nothing to do with strikes. Reference is made to the 1933 strikes of lettuce workers in Salinas (John Steinbeck's home) and to earlier strikes in 1913 led by the Wobblies at Wheatland. The senator suggests that the deplorable, subhuman conditions that existed in 1913 have scarcely improved over the years.

FROM TESTIMONY OF GROWERS
(In Hearings before a Subcommittee of the Committee on
Education and Labor 76th Congress, Part 53; Washington, DC: U.S.
Government Printing Office, 1940)

Senator LA FOLLETTE. Now, the foregoing would seem to indicate, would it not, Mr. Miller, that the strike began as a wage dispute over the 15- and 20-cent-an-hour scale for the third and fourth picking of berries?

Mr. MILLER. Yes; I would say that was the case.

Senator La FOLLETTE. On or about this time a man by the name of Armando Flores, who was, as I understand, an undercover politician in Mexico and the United States, and who has a print shop on East First Street printing communist literature entered the picture as the leader of the Pro-Strike Committee.

Now, this memorandum would also seem to indicate, would it not, that a person described as a "Communist" by Mr. Gast [an employee of the Chamber of Commerce] began to encourage the strike some considerable time after it had been under way?(p. 9491)

. . .

Mr. STROBEL. It has been an outside influence that has been injected there that has created the trouble that we have had at all times.

. . .

Senator La FOLLETTE. Now, in order that I might get your view of the situation, Mr. Miller, would you say the strike in 1933 was a step taken by seasonal laborers in agriculture, Mexicans and Americans alike, against their working conditions, and would you say that was due to the outside agitation which Mr. Strobel has mentioned in connection with the lettuce situation in Salinas?

Mr. MILLER. I would say that the original difficulty—just basing my opinion on a review of Mr. Gast's memorandum—was because of dissatisfaction of the employees there with some of their conditions and the difficulty of arriving at an amicable settlement, which resulted from the interjection of outside influences there, as Mr. Gast has indicated.

. . .

Senator La FOLLETTE. Now, do you recall whether or not the chamber took note of some of the conditions with regard to wages, and so forth, in the early part of 1933? [No response.]

To refresh your recollection, I will offer for the record an excerpt from minutes of the meeting of the board of directors of the Los Angeles Chamber of Commerce on September 14, 1933.

It may be given an exhibit number.

(The document was marked "Exhibit 8758.")

Senator La FOLLETTE. It reads as follows:

Agricultural Labor Situation. A report was rendered from the Agricultural Committee in connection with the labor difficulties being experienced by the agricultural industries throughout California, pointing out that labor agitators have encouraged itinerant laborers engaged in harvesting work to demand wages out of line with the ability of the farmer to pay.

The Board was also of the opinion that possibly some of the labor disputes were brought about by the fact that in some agricultural sections ridiculously low prices were quoted for agricultural labor which resulted in these prices being brought up under the threat of strikes or actual strikes which lent encouragement to similar operations in other sections.

Would you say that it was a fact that wages for agricultural labor rose in 1933 coincidental with the wave of strikes which took place in the middle and latter part of the year?

• • •

Senator La FOLLETTE. Would you agree or not agree that improvement, from whatever source or by whatever means, in the living conditions of the migratory or seasonal workers would tend to prevent disturbances or not?

Mr. STROBEL. I believe that it would tend to prevent them, to a certain extent, that it would lessen them, but whenever you find a group of migratory workers, it is not hard for any dissatisfied person, or some agitator, to get into that group and stir up an imaginary grievance in many instances. I don't believe that just a mere improvement in housing conditions and in living standards is going to do away with the trouble. As long as we have these people who haven't the best interests of the worker at heart, nor of the farmer, we are going to have trouble, and it doesn't make any difference what we do. Those boys are going to come into the picture, they are going to stay in the picture, and they are going to create disturbances between the farmer and his workers, having no regard for the welfare of either one.

Senator La FOLLETTE. Let's assume for the moment the correctness of the statement that you have just made, that these agricultural strikes are going to continue because of radical agitators, I would like to get your reaction to a statement quoted from an eminent I.W.W. leader in the report of the 1913 troubles, which has just been made an exhibit in the record. He is quoted as saying:

We can't agitate in the country unless things are rotten enough to bring the crowd along.

Do you agree or disagree with that?

Mr. STROBEL. Well, I would say that perhaps at that time that might have been true—conditions have changed—but I would say that there is a certain amount of justification for that statement.

However, that is not the sole reason for agitation, and they have improved their methods. As these people's conditions have improved, the methods and technique of these boys have improved, too. They find other ways to create disturbances. It doesn't have to be a rotten condition. They can make the condition seem rotten that is satisfactory to the farmer and his workers. These boys will come in and, in a very short time, create in their minds and in the minds of workers a rotten conditions. (pp. 19501–19502)

REVISIONS TO FEDERAL WAGE-HOUR LAW
CONSIDERED IN 1938

In the fall of 1938, the U.S. Congress, prodded by the Executive Branch, considered revisions of federal labor regulations that would address problems of the minimum wage, maximum working hours, and child labor. The following article appeared in the *Oakland Tribune*, one of the leading newspapers of the northern California agricultural area. Note the disappointing exemptions created by the law.

FROM "WAGE-HOUR LAW PROVISIONS TOLD IN QUERIES, ANSWERS"
(Oakland Tribune, October 19, 1938)

MILLIONS OF WORKERS TO BE AFFECTED BY NEW MEASURE EFFECTIVE THROUGH U.S. MONDAY

WASHINGTON, Oct. 19—Millions of workers will be affected when the new wage-hour law goes into operation next Monday.

Here are questions and answers on most important features of the act:

What is the purpose of the law?

To place a floor under wages and a ceiling over hours and to improve certain working conditions.

How is this to be achieved?

Over a period of years, the minimum wage permitted to be paid will be raised to 40 cents an hour and the work week will be shortened to 40 hours.

What are the wage provisions?

In the first year the law establishes a 25-cent minimum; for the next six years a 30-cent minimum, and thereafter, 40 cents.

Maximum Week Set

What are the hour provisions?

A maximum work week of 44 hours the first year, 42 the second and 40 thereafter.

To whom will the law apply?

With a few exceptions, it covers all workers whose employer is in interstate commerce or who themselves produce goods for such commerce.

What is meant by interstate commerce?

The act defines the term as trade, commerce, transportation, transmission or communication among States and territories and possessions, or from one State to a point outside.

How many workers will be affected by the law at the start?

It is estimated officially that pay of more than 750,000 will be raised and the hours of more than 2,000,000 will be shortened.

Some Jobs Exempt

What types of worker are exempt from the wage and hour provisions?

Federal, State and local employees: agricultural workers, seamen, and employees of air lines, streetcar, motorbus, interurban railways and of weekly or semiweekly newspapers with a circulation of less than 3000: executives, professionals, outside salesmen or persons engaged in a local retailing capacity: persons in a retail or service establishment and in the fishing industry and in the area of production of dairy products.

Who determines whether an industry is in interstate commerce?

The legal staff of Elmer F. Andrews, administrator of the act, whose decisions may be reviewed by the courts.

Can a minimum higher than 25 cents an hour be established during the first year?

May Order Minimum

Yes. Upon recommendation of industry committees, the wage-hour administration may order employers to pay a minimum wage as high as 40 cents an hour, providing it doesn't curtail employment.

Who are members of industry committees?

Persons selected by the administrator to represent, in equal numbers, a certain industry, its labor forces and the public.

Will a minimum wage below 25 cents be permitted?

In cases of apprentices, learners, handicapped workers and messengers, the administrator may, upon request, approve a lower scale.

Is the recommendation of an industry committee final?

The administrator must accept the recommendation if it is in accordance with the law.

Differentials Barred

Can the committee recommend geographical differentials?

The act prohibits such differentials but the committee can consider competitive conditions affected by transportation, living and production costs.

May the committee recommend different rates for men and women?

The law prohibits classification by age or sex.

What does an employer or worker do if he is not sure whether the act applies to him?

Pending issuance of complete definitions of the scant terms in the act, wage-hour officials advise full compliance.

Are there penalties for violating the act, or for an assumption, subsequently proved erroneous, that a person is not covered by it?

Penalties Fixed

Employees can recover twice the amount of unpaid minimum or overtime wages and the employer may be fined up to $10,000 or imprisoned for not more than six months.

If overtime is permitted, what is the rate of pay?

Overtime is authorized if the employer makes compensation at the rate of time and a half the regular rate.

Must this be in cash?

Presumably, officials say, cash must be paid but the administration has not ruled officially on that point.

What are the act's provisions relating to employment of children?

Congress prohibited use of "oppressive child labor," described as employment of children under 16 unless the Labor Department finds the work not to interfere with their schooling, health or well-being; and as employment of children between 16 and 18 in an occupation the department finds particularly hazardous or detrimental to health and well being.

Exemptions Listed

What are the exemptions to these provisions?

Child actors, children under 16 employed by their parents in nonmanufacturing and nonmining occupations and children employed in agriculture while they are not legally required to go to school.

What effect does the law have on union contracts in existence in industry?

Employees are exempt from the hour provisions who work under a collective bargaining agreement sanctioned by the National labor board which calls for a maximum of 1000 hours in 26 weeks or 2000 hours in 52 weeks. But, for work over 12 hours a day or 56 hours a week, they must be paid for overtime. (p. 5)

AFFIDAVIT OF GEORGE BELL ABOUT SETTLING COTTON PICKERS STRIKE, 1939

In October 1939, cotton pickers asked for a raise to $1.25 for a hundred pounds of cotton picked. George Bell, owner of a small farm, was unsympathetic to the Associated Farmers in this as in all their other activities. On his own initiative, Bell attempted to ne-gotiate an agreement to put an end to the strike. In so doing, he got assurance from the strike leaders who were willing to talk to the growers about settling for $1.00 per one hundred pounds. But, as Bell reports, the growers refused to talk to the strikers, and ugly fights ensued.

FROM EXHIBIT 13070: AFFIDAVIT OF GEORGE BELL TAKEN ON
NOVEMBER 16, 1939
(In Hearings before a Subcommittee of the Committee on
Education and Labor, 76th Congress, Part 71; Washington, DC: U.S.
Government Printing Office, 1940)

STATE OF CALIFORNIA,
   County of Madera, ss:
George Bell, a Madera County, California farmer, being first duly sworn, deposes and says:
Some time the evening of Monday, October 16, 1939, about a week after a strike of cotton pickers in Madera County had been called, I went to Memorial Hall in Madera to attend a meeting of growers. I don't recall just how I was solicited to attend, but I believe it was by word of mouth.
As I approached the door leading into the auditorium, my name and cotton acreage was entered in a book by Jim Buffington, a grower, who was standing at the door. At the same time, this man asked me for a dollar to join the Associated Farmers. Personally, I don't believe the As-sociated Farmers has the actual interest of the farmers at heart, so I flatly refused to join. This refusal caused an argument between several of the farmers there and me, during which they threatened to throw me out of the hall. I told them they were perfectly welcome to throw me out if they could, and this stopped the argument.
By this time I was pretty angry and rather than let the farmers think they were chasing me out of the hall, I went into the auditorium. As I entered, Stuart Strathman, State Secretary of the Associated Farmers, was

addressing the meeting and telling the audience "how it was done in Imperial Valley in 1934." I just happened to catch this phrase as I walked in, but didn't pay much attention to the rest of his speech because I left a few minutes later.

One or two nights after this meeting I was in the Madera County Park during a union meeting. I sent for Carl Patterson, one of the strike leaders, to come off the stand, and asked him whether the union would settle the strike on the basis of a dollar per hundred pounds of cotton. The union was then demanding a dollar and a quarter. Patterson replied, "We will be glad to discuss the matter." I took this reply to mean that the union would probably settle for a dollar. Some time before this I met Ollie Baker, another Madera County farmer, and a member of the Grower's Emergency Committee that was formed at the Monday night meeting in Memorial Hall, mentioned above, and suggested that the growers get together with the union and negotiate. Baker's only answer was that negotiations would bring the CIO into Madera County and that the growers didn't want this to happen. I made several approaches to other farmers about negotiating with strikers but got the same answer from them all.

I honestly believe that if the growers had negotiated with the union on the basis of a dollar a hundred pounds of cotton, there would never have been any trouble in Madera County, as there was in the Park on Saturday, October 21, 1939. With the Federal Government paying us three cents a pound for cotton, plus the market price of around nine cents, we can well afford to pay a dollar.

/s/ GEO. P. BELL.

Personally appeared before me this 16th day of November, 1939, George Bell, a Madera County, California farmer, who swears that the above statement is true and correct to the best of his knowledge and belief.

/s/ CHARLES F. PRECIADO,
Notary Public.

My commission expires June 21, 1943. (p. 26278)

TOPICS FOR ORAL AND WRITTEN EXPLORATION

1. Collect as many of Joe Hill's Wobbly songs as possible. Produce a musical/historical performance that includes a substantial historical background of each song before it is performed. The performance can be as simple or as elaborate as you like—period dress, single singer, or chorus.

2. Produce a musical/historical performance using Woody Guthrie's songs.

3. Do some research on labor history in your own area of the country. Use old newspapers and perhaps some interviews to develop your history. Some suggestions to help locate what you need, in case you run into problems: for the South, look especially for textile mills, mines and tenant farmers' unions; for the North, also look for textile mills and garment factories. In the Midwest, look for steel mills and railroads. In the far and southwest, look for agriculture, longshoremen, and lumbermen.

4. Stage a debate in which students take the roles of growers and union organizers and argue the causes of agricultural strikes.

5. Write an article on one of the early union leaders, using a biography or other primary sources. You may want to choose one of the following: Eugene V. Debs, Samuel Gompers, Big Bill Haywood, Harry Bridges, Pat Chambers, John L. Lewis.

SUGGESTIONS FOR FURTHER READING

Bernstein, Irving. *Turbulent Years: A History of the American Worker, 1933–1941*. Boston: Houghton Mifflin, 1970.

Dyson, Lowell K. *Red Harvest: The Communist Party and American Farmers*. Lincoln: University of Nebraska Press, 1982.

Goldbloom, Maurice. *Strikes Under the New Deal*. New York: League for Industrial Democracy, 1935.

Jamieson, Stuart. *Labor Unionism in American Agriculture*. Bulletin no. 326. Washington, DC: United States Labor Statistics, 1945.

Loftis, Anne. *Witnesses to the Struggle: Imagining the 1930s California Labor Movement*. Reno: University of Nevada Press, 1998.

Loftis, Anne, and Dick Meister. *A Long Time Coming: The Struggle to Unionize America's Farm Workers*. New York: Macmillan Publishing Co., 1977.

London, Joan, and Henry Anderson. *So Shall Ye Reap*. New York: Thomas Y. Crowell, 1970.

Stein, Walter. *California and the Dust Bowl Migration*. Westport, CT: Greenwood Press, 1973.

Steinbeck, John. *In Dubious Battle*. New York: Penguin Books, 1936.

Web Sites:

"Eugene V. Debs: An American Paradox," an abstract by J. Robert Constantines: http://stats.bls.gov/opub/mlr/1991/08/art4abs.htm.

Industrial Workers of the World homepage: www.iww.org.

Industrial Workers of the World (Wobblies) site: www.nothingness.org. iww.

6

Law and Lawlessness in the Joads' World

The Grapes of Wrath proceeds on the assumption that lawlessness is at the very foundation of capitalism in 1930s America, in that large corporations and agri-businesses fail to pay fair wages while they rake in huge profits and thrive by stealing from their workers. Note the conversation on page 305 in Chapter Nineteen, in which one worker shows how the owner of a huge ranch obtained his land by cheating the government and exploiting street people. "Would you say that was stealin'?" he asks. The narrator suggests that stealing is at the heart of any kind of business:

> Fella in business got to lie an' cheat, but he calls it somepin else. You go steal a tire an' you're a thief, but he [a business man] tried to steal your four dollars for a busted tire. They call that sound business. (155)

In the unrestricted pursuit of capital and power, the law itself has been twisted. For example, the state of California, at the insistence of growers, had passed mandates that were clearly unconstitutional—they violated the civil rights of citizens. The old Criminal Syndicalism Act that made it illegal to criticize anyone in power was most often applied to union leaders, but violated their constitutional right to free speech. There were laws against trespassing, picketing, and unlawful assembly. They were used to keep strikers far away from other workers whom they might want to influence, and made it possible for sheriffs and their posses, often called vigilantes, to prevent union meetings. In effect, these laws were used to violate the right to free assembly.

Several laws were interpreted so broadly that they came to be applied in a lawless way. The police, invariably controlled by the growers, found the antivagrancy law to be a particularly convenient one because any individual, especially a striker who had walked off the job, was subject to arrest for vagrancy. As far as the migrant farmworkers was concerned, California had turned into a police state where policemen operated outside the spirit of the law.

Officers of the law, usually privately deputized guards who were paid for every prisoner they brought in, were an integral part of the Joads' world. They stopped workers at state borders and tore apart their vehicles; they guarded private ranches to keep agitators out and workers imprisoned within; they raided and burned down private migrant camps; they patrolled camps and stood with loaded firearms in the fields. In the novel, on the occasion of the dance in the government camp, they conspired to start a brawl in order to move in and make arrests. As Casy reminds Tom just before they are attacked, the law causes more trouble than it prevents.

The police are always patrolling the periphery of the Joads' life, and are central to several important scenes in the novel. In one incident, which occurs in Chapter Eighteen as the Joads are making their way to their first destination, an armed private guard goes to each tent that is occupied for the night to harass the occupants, telling them in no uncertain terms that "their kind" is not wanted in the community and that he will arrest them if they remain the next day. His confrontation with Ma, who picks up an iron skillet to run him out, sets forth a pattern of conflict between the Joads and those who purport to uphold the law. A second important scene occurs in Chapter Twenty when a labor contractor enters the Hooverville with a sheriff. During this conflict, when the young man Floyd challenges the intentions of the labor contractor, the sheriff is called over to arrest him as a suspicious person. Floyd and Tom attack the sheriff to prevent the arrest, and as Floyd escapes, the sheriff begins firing from the ground, shooting off a woman's fingers in the process. To stop the shooting, Casy kicks the sheriff in the neck and is subsequently arrested.

The Joads' final confrontation with the law occurs when a law officer kills Casy after a full force of troopers and private guards have been called out to put down his strike, and Tom retaliates by killing one of them. The troopers and guards line the road and escort workers into the camp; they patrol and stand guard at the site where the migrants work; they police the fields; they keep the migrants from leaving the camp; and they eventually track down and shoot Casy.

THE LAW IN THE HISTORICAL ACCOUNT

The lawless violence perpetrated and condoned by lawmen in the California agricultural fields in the 1930s was well documented in many eyewitness accounts and brought to the public's attention by the Senate committee chaired by Senator Robert La Follette. Violence deemed legal against striking migrant workers took the form of arrests, beatings, shootings, raids, tear gassings, kidnappings, and intimidation, like burning crosses. While such actions were regarded as legal by the California court system, they were clear violations of civil rights and the Constitution of the United States.

As discussed in Chapter Five, unconstitutional violence by law officers had a long history in California agriculture, most prominently at the notorious Wheatland Ranch in 1913. During the 1930s, as subhuman conditions provoked strikes, growers routinely used the law to break strikes. In 1936, writers for the League of Industrial Democracy described the situation nationwide:

Legal and extra-legal violence was widely used in efforts to crush the revolts of labor. In 1934 more than forty workers were killed on picket lines, and the number of injured ran into many hundreds. In the first year and a half under the NIRA, upward of 40 injunctions were issued against labor and in 16 states the troops were called out against strikers. Especially in California, lawless bands of vigilantes, organized by employers, with the full support of the authorities, violently suppressed labor's rights. (29)

Violence either perpetuated or abetted by police against agricultural workers and their families was rampant. The following instances of behavior that were widespread throughout California in the 1930s were later labeled lawless by the United States Senate:

In Vacaville in 1932, six labor leaders were taken from jail to an area twenty miles outside of town where they were beaten with leather straps, their hair was cut off with animal clippers, red paint was poured over them, and they were abandoned.

In the Imperial Valley and San Joaquin Valley in 1933 and 1934, three strikers were killed; eighty-seven were arrested; a meeting hall, workers' shacks and tents, and peaceful pickets were teargassed (killing one infant); automobiles were seized for no reason; five labor lawyers and American Civil Liberties Union delegates were beaten, and another delegate was kidnapped, taken to the desert, beaten, and abandoned without his shoes.

In Salinas in 1934, workers' shacks were torched, workers were shot at, and labor leaders arrested. In the Imperial Valley in 1935, two lettuce workers on strike were killed and four were wounded. In San Jose in 1934, workers were abducted and severely beaten. In Santa Rosa in 1935, two labor leaders were seized, kicked, severely beaten, tarred and feathered, and dumped outside the county line.

In the spring of 1936, in Los Angeles county, the strike headquarters of celery workers was tear-gassed and fleeing workers shot at, beaten, and arrested. In Orange County in the same year, 200 workers were arrested; camps were bombed and raided; families were threatened with machine guns pointed into the camps; and scores were seriously injured and unable to get medical help.

THE OUTLAW IN THE 1930s

A society in which law and justice are no more than thin veneers laid over a foundation of greed-engendered lawlessness will inevitably be more inclined to inspire admiration—especially on the part of the common people—for the person who is perceived as robbing the rich and giving to the poor. It is not surprising that America produced numerous outlaws of this kind following the Civil War, when a type of greedy, unbridled industrialism soared in the United States. Two institutions came to be identified with cold-blooded greed. The first were the railroads, which were built and run with little more than slave labor. Huge tracts of land were confiscated for right-of-ways and destroyed many farmers in the process. The railroads received political favors from corrupt local governments that helped them to become a law unto themselves. They were brutal in putting down challenges to their authority, whether it was the farmers whose land they confiscated, or railroad workers who struck for decent wages. The result was that a handful of men made immense fortunes from ruining and exploiting thousands and thousands of people. So in the late nineteenth century, outlaws like Butch Cassidy and Jesse James, who robbed railroads, were admired by much of the general public. Our glorification of gangsters, wrote James Truslow Adams in 1932, arises not only from our admiration for their fearlessness and self-reliance, but from our disgust at the dishonesty and incompetence of the whole system of government—from big business and government at the top, to policemen at the bottom. When ordinary citizens are successful in punishing these "authorized" criminals like big business and the police, then, perhaps, they will be less inclined to glorify the outlaw who outwits the police.

The other bitterly resented institutions in the 1930s were the banks. They foreclosed on more and more properties and held thousands of public auctions of farms, homes, and businesses. The banks refused to grant loans, and often closed down, leaving their customers with heavy losses. They became the symbols of the oppressive forces that had caused the Great Depression.

At the same time, officers of the law were seen as unjust tools of the rich. The ordinary person's encounter with the police was scarcely pleasant: He was jolted by the experience of the police arriving on his land to order his family out of their home; he saw the police overseeing the public auction of his property; he was thrown off the railroad by the police when he tried to ride a boxcar to find work; he was arrested by police when he tried to sleep in a public place; and he was beaten, tear-gassed, and shot at when he joined a strike for a living wage.

It is little wonder, then, that the 1930s produced men and women who became legends, if not heroes, by robbing the rich and outwitting the law. Many among the law-abiding unemployed also fantasized about robbing a bank when they hit rock bottom. They were not outraged when a bank that had robbed them, was robbed by an outlaw. Nor were they displeased to read that law officers, like ones who had bullied them, had been outwitted.

There were a number of gangster heroes, but the two who were most admired were John Dillinger and, especially pertinent to *The Grapes of Wrath*, Pretty Boy Floyd. Dillinger fit the Robin Hood pattern earlier Americanized by Jesse James. He was an Indiana farm boy from a poor, hard-working family. He had grown up in a time when people were desperate and exploited. He got into trouble as a youth and was given an excessively severe prison sentence, after which he was hounded by the police wherever he went. He was easy to like and admire in that he was physically attractive, athletic, charming, witty, and intelligent. The public grew to enjoy the ways in which he exposed the incompetence of the police and the FBI. Once, he broke out of prison with a gun whittled out of wood and stained with black shoe polish. Another of his jokes was leaving a booklet about how to be a good detective on the doorstep of a highly placed law officer.

Dillinger's reputation as a Robin Hood figure was enhanced by his avowed distaste for violence and his reluctance to harm individuals, as opposed to his antipathy toward banks. In a typical move during one bank robbery, Dillinger called to a customer, who had come to cash a check, to pick up the money owed to him, saying that he had no interest in an individual's funds, only the bank's.

That he had the admiration of many people is shown by the actions of the people in his hometown of Mooresville, Indiana, who presented the governor with a petition in 1933 asking that Dillinger be pardoned on the grounds that he had only robbed the banks that had robbed them—he had not robbed the people.

The manner of Dillinger's death, on July 22, 1934, like that of Jesse James, Billy the Kid, and Butch Cassidy, contributed to his legend—and as many felt, martyrdom. Like his predecessors, officers of the law shot him down. There was no attempt to capture Public Enemy Number One and bring him to trial. Thousands of Chicagoans flocked to the Biograph Theatre when they heard that Dillinger had been shot. As if he were a saint, men dipped their handkerchiefs, women the hems of their dresses, in his blood. Several thousand people forced the police to allow them to file past his body in the morgue, and five thousand people paid tribute to him at his funeral in Indiana.

THE OUTLAW IN *THE GRAPES OF WRATH*

Looking at Steinbeck's novel from the perspective of the law and lawlessness, we see that the novel's chief protagonist, Tom Joad, is an outlaw. At the beginning of the Joads' story, he has served time in the penitentiary for manslaughter. As soon as he leaves the state of Oklahoma, he is an outlaw who has broken parole. By the end of the novel, he is a hunted man—an outlaw who has killed again—this time, the man who has killed his friend Casy. Much of Tom Joad's trouble with the law comes not only from his hot-headedness, but from his refusal to stand by and let the police push powerless people around. The trouble he gets into, for example, when he trips a sheriff at his family's first Hooverville camp, comes not from greed or self-interest, but from his instinct to help others like Floyd.

Floyd and Casy both become outlaws when they speak out against the exploitation of the migrants and then physically attack a sheriff. Yet, both men are among the most admirable characters in the novel.

PRETTY BOY FLOYD IN *THE GRAPES OF WRATH*

We explored the implications of Jim Casy's name and his actions in Chapter One. Floyd's name is an allusion to another outlaw mentioned several times in the novel: Charles Floyd, also known as Pretty Boy Floyd, an Oklahoma native who became one of the FBI's most wanted criminals in the 1930s.

Ma Joad, who has known Pretty Boy Floyd, repeatedly links the famous outlaw with her own son, Tom. When Tom returns to his family near Sallisaw, Oklahoma (also the hometown of Pretty Boy Floyd), Ma wants to know if his stay in the penitentiary has destroyed him the same way it had Floyd. In her opinion, Floyd had been "a good boy," driven to being "mean-mad" and self-destructive by the authorities (98). Much later, as the Joads approach the peach fields where they will inadvertently help in breaking the strike, Tom begins to talk about some of his experiences in prison that made him despise cops. Tom's revelations again remind his mother of Pretty Boy Floyd: "He wan't a bad boy. Jus' got drove in a corner" (471). Finally, as Ma says goodbye to

Charles "Pretty Boy" Floyd.
Reproduced courtesy of AP/
WIDE WORLD PHOTOS.

Tom, she worries that he will be hounded and killed like "young Floyd" (537).

Ma is not the only one on whom the story of Pretty Boy Floyd has made an impression. Pa Joad also thinks of Pretty Boy Floyd as the Joad family, on their way to California, plans to break the law by burying Grampa without securing the proper papers and fees. Pa observes that he and other members of Floyd's community had broken the law by refusing to help the FBI track him down. The passage indicates several sentiments: the sympathy with which ordinary working people viewed Floyd and the conviction that sometimes it is "indecent" to follow the law. "Sometimes the law can't be foller'd no way. . . . Not in decency, anyways" (179).

PRETTY BOY FLOYD AS HEROIC OUTLAW

The legend of Pretty Boy Floyd as a folk hero surpassed even that of John Dillinger, from whom Floyd inherited the FBI's designation as America's Most Wanted Criminal. Floyd was born and reared near Sallisaw, Oklahoma, and spent time in the Cookson Hills, which for decades had been an outlaws' hideout, so notorious that even J. Edgar Hoover had mentioned it in a book on crime. The famous Younger gang—often allied with Jesse James—was from the area and, with others, including the Kimes gang and Wilbur Underhill (known as the "Tri-State Terror"), found refuge from the law in the Cookson Hills, not only because of a terrain conducive to eluding the law, but because their families and friends in the area hid them and refused to cooperate with the law, as Pa Joad suggests.

As a legend and folk hero, Floyd's life closely paralleled Dillinger's. Like Dillinger, Floyd was physically attractive, athletic, brazen, and quick-witted. Like Dillinger, he had "style." Both men were from a group that felt misused by the law—farmers in the rural, middle United States. When he was still in his teens, Floyd traveled from place to place seeking work, unsuccessfully. For his first crime, robbing a payroll, he was given an excessively severe prison sentence, an experience that gave him the bitterness and the expertise for a life of crime. His first murders were excused by his people in Oklahoma, if not by the law: he returned home from prison to find that his father had just been murdered and the legal system had acquitted his killer. Floyd supposedly followed the murderer into the Cookson Hills, and the man was never seen again. The first murder he acknowledged was the shooting of a sheriff who had insulted his wife in some way. Shortly afterward, having eluded arrest, Floyd began one of the most spectacular bank-robbing careers, seeming to be everywhere at once throughout the Midwest, and especially Oklahoma, where citizens believed that the real robbers were the banks themselves.

Floyd's brazen style endeared him to many people. It was widely rumored that he, like Dillinger, would even notify some banks before he robbed them. Probably his most bizarre robbery occurred in his hometown, on November 11, 1932. He notified his friends and family in the area of his intention to rob the Sallisaw bank, as if the circus were in town and not to be missed. He parked his car on the main street and strolled toward the bank with his machine gun under his arm, waving and greeting friends, showing them his gun and announcing that he was on his way to rob the bank. His grandfather was sitting on a bench across the street, at ringside, to see the show. No one took the trouble to alert the chief of police, who was parked around the corner. Floyd took the bank manager hostage in his car and drove a couple of miles out of town where he let him out, gave him some money to get back home, and told him to take care of himself. It was reported that all who watched Floyd's actions got a vicarious thrill from seeing the bank getting robbed so brazenly.

Floyd's reputation as a Robin Hood figure surpassed that of any outlaw in the 1930s. Some of his extraordinary generosity to the poor is well documented. He was known for paying off the mortgages of a number of poor farmers who had been kind to him. He even went so far as to linger in the banks he was robbing to seek out and tear up mortgages that might not yet have been recorded. He provided a year's worth of groceries for scores of families and routinely left $1,000 for families who gave him meals.

Like Dillinger, Floyd firmly believed in stealing only from the rich. In a letter to Acting Governor Burns of Oklahoma, he wrote that he had robbed no one but rich men. And to Vivian Brown, a reporter for the *Muskogee Daily Phoenix* to whom he gave an interview, he said, "I guess I've done more bank hold-ups than anything else . . . and no one ever lost anything except the big boys." In her account of the interview published on January 4, 1932, she said, "There is much to support the picture of Floyd as a modern Robin Hood. Like the famed marauder of the English forests, he took money from those who had it—the banks—and divided the proceeds of his raids with the poor" (quoted in Jeffery S. King, 278).

The actions of the FBI and the police in dealing with Floyd further contributed to the reputations of law-enforcement officers as bunglers and killers. Convinced that Floyd was involved in a massacre in Kansas on June 17, 1933 in which six officers died, the FBI began hunting him down—"dead or alive." However, to the last, Floyd and his partner, Adam Richetti, adamantly denied that they were involved in any way, and criminologists have since come to the conclusion that Floyd could not have been involved in the Kansas City massacre. Nevertheless, on October 23, 1934, he was finally hunted down on a farm in Ohio, and one of the officers who was there later testified that Melvin Purvis—the famous FBI agent who had caught Dillinger outside the Biograph Theatre— had Floyd killed in cold blood while the outlaw sat wounded and unarmed on the ground. As in the case of Dillinger, no serious attempt was made to capture and bring him to trial.

Pretty Boy Floyd's death elevated him to the status of martyr, as had happened with Dillinger. In Ohio, 10,000 people stormed the funeral home where he lay, tearing up the lawn and breaking the porch in a frenzy to get inside. His body was sent to Oklahoma for burial, where 20,000 people from twenty states came to the funeral. Six thousand automobiles carrying mourners clogged the country roads.

Poems and biographies honoring Floyd appeared in newspapers throughout the country. The famous Oklahoma minstrel, Woody Guthrie, wrote a song about the Robin Hood of the Cookson Hills: some people (the banks) rob with a fountain pen, but outlaws like Floyd never drive families from their homes. In further tribute, it is said that for fifty years after Floyd's death, Oklahomans named their children after him.

The documents that follow show the way in which the law became unjust and lawless men became heroes. The first one is an examination of the reasons why the police turned lawless. The next three describe the extralegal violence perpetrated by law officers during farm labor strikes in California. The final group of newspaper articles documents the controversial death and burial of Pretty Boy Floyd.

JONATHAN NORTON LEONARD: THE POLICTICS OF WEALTH AND THE FEAR OF THE UNEMPLOYED

In 1939, Jonathan Norton Leonard wrote about the developing political crisis he had been observing from as early as 1932. Because of the desperate circumstances of so many people in serious economic trouble, those with financial and political power had become frightened, with some justification, that revolution would break out and that they would lose everything. In order to retain their positions of power and wealth, they used oppressive law enforcement to secure their primacy. In these turbulent times, ordinary citizens often could not depend upon the police for either protection or justice. Instead, especially for those who were down-and-out, the police became the enemy.

Leonard notes the police violence used against "hunger marchers" in Washington in 1932, and the hostility displayed toward the unemployed by police departments in other cities. The petty stealing of bits of food by starving people does not even come close to being as reprehensible as the misbehavior of the law.

FROM JONATHAN NORTON LEONARD, *THREE YEARS DOWN*
(New York: Carrick and Evans. 1939)

Another sign of the change in the public state of mind was the new popularity of comparative economics as a subject of conversation. During the boom economics had meant how to make big money by speculation, high-pressure selling, corporate jiu-jitsu and allied arts. In 1932 it meant criticism or at least investigation of the current system of financial government. Formerly trusting people began to poke and pry, ask questions, get answers. For the first time they learned how bankers collect interest by lending money which does not exist and how the money they thus accumulate gives them control of industry. . . .

During the Great Boom the word "capitalism" had shone with self-generated radiance. Where capitalism ruled there was joy and hope; there was leisure and ease; there was limitless opportunity for every man. . . .

Now, in 1932, the above eternal truth did not seem quite as sharp and clear. Capitalism was all very well, but perhaps there were different varieties. Certainly the prevailing type was not the best. Anybody could see with his own eyes that it wasn't working very well. Perhaps we ought to change it some. But how? Endlessly the talk went on, in cross-roads stores, in offices, on street-corners, around the box-board fires of Hooverville. There was starvation in a land of overflowing plenty. There were homeless men sleeping on dumps surrounded by empty houses. What in hell was the matter? No one had very clear ideas, but resentfully like a cat which has fallen into a garbage can, America was trying to cleanse itself of boom-time mental swill. (pp. 216, 217)

• • •

Nor had Hoover gotten over his fear of *them*. On November 24 a great crowd of hopeful spectators crowded the streets near the White House. They knew the signs. Outside the high iron fence were a hundred police with tear-gas and deadlier weapons in readiness. Reporters thought these preparations rather premature. A Communist "hunger march" was scheduled to arrive in a couple of weeks, but it hadn't even left New York. There were practically no resident Communists in Washington.

The mystery was finally cleared up when two taxi-cabs stopped in front of the White House gate. Whistles blew. Cops concentrated. Out stepped the Reds—one man, one white woman, one Negro woman and six small Red children. They were arrested at once and stuffed into a patrol wagon—all except the colored woman who somehow escaped in the confusion.

When the main body of the "hunger marchers" arrived on December 4 they were treated with studied cruelty. General Glassford had resigned to devote himself to the homeless boys, so there was no one in Washington to protect petitioners from "the highest authority." In all there were less than 2,500 unarmed Reds—a third of them women or children—but they were met by 1,500 police who herded them into a short section of New York Avenue between a railroad yard and an embankment. There they were kept surrounded, guarded by machine-guns and $10,000 worth of tear-gas and nausea-producing D. N. gas. Sympathetic people in the city had offered them various sorts of shelter, but they were not permitted to leave their outdoor concentration-camp and had to spend the freezing December night in their trucks or on the pavement.

Until the following night they were allowed no food or water. The next day the police made a deliberate attempt to incite them to riot. They jeered at the men and insulted the women. They "tested" D. N. bombs on a bonfire and let the sickening fumes drift across the camp. They slashed the tires of seventeen trucks. For an entire day the Reds were refused permission to construct an improvised toilet, and when the women tried to find some private spot they were followed around by crowds of hooting cops. Many were sick or suffering from exposure, but they were not allowed medical attendance until they were actually unable to walk.

At last they were rescued by members of Congress who were not in sympathy with Communism but were outraged by the treatment the petitioners had received. They even got permission to parade. Only a little more than half of them were able to march by this time and this small group was escorted all along the way by 1,200 police and 700 deputized firemen armed with shotguns, rifles, submachine-guns and gas, who hid them almost completely from the eyes of the public. They did not attempt to approach the White House, but the "highest authority" had his hundred cops outside the iron fence, just in case they made a dash his way. (pp. 299–300)

• • •

. . . The city police departments were adding to their riot squads, laying in stocks of tear-gas. The auto factories of Detroit were enlisting private armies. Henry Ford with characteristic hypocrisy called his the "Service Department." . . . Wives of wealthy commercialists pictured themselves as romantic aristocrats about to flee an eruption from the lower depths . . . Most of the "help" were sore about having their pay-checks caponized, so there wasn't much hope there.

"What's the matter with the unemployed? Why don't they help themselves?" . . . What if the cities can't pay the police to hold them down? What if the federal government can't pay the troops? What if our paper empire tears to bits? What if money no longer can shout its commands? Then the twisted, loathsome creatures of the bottom will boil to the top like things raised up by a submarine earthquake. They will burn our houses, kill our men, rape our women, trample our flower-beds. How much nicer it would be for all concerned if the 13,000,000 unemployed and their dependents—a third of the people—were to take themselves quietly off somewhere and leave us to dominate in peace the half-empty shell of the nation."

As a matter of fact, the unemployed were doing to the best of their ability exactly what the tremblers wanted them to. . . . Their battles with the police made old ladies quake their foundations loose when they read about them over the morning orange juice, but they were hardly battles at all. No deadly weapons were used. The casualties were never among the police.

Nor were there looting and pillage. In some of the most distressed cities—notably Detroit—there was a certain amount of food stealing. Children would snatch groceries off counters and run. Two or three men would walk into a chain-store, order as much as they could carry and calmly walk out without paying. . . . In the smaller cities near fertile sections of farming country the unemployed would hike out at night and forage for vegetables and fruit, but the amount they took was insignificant. (pp. 270, 271)

ATTITUDE OF CALIFORNIA LAW ENFORCEMENT TOWARD FARMWORKERS REVEALED TO SENATE SUBCOMMITTEE

In 1933, California state peace officers met to discuss the threat of striking agricultural workers. Their aims were, above all, to get the crops harvested before they rotted in the fields, and do this without being forced to pay higher wages. To this end, they used the law to arrest picketers on the road and anyone else they chose to accuse of disturbing the peace.

Note the unabashed tone of these conversations: Sheriff Driver of Alameda County talks of "cleaning up very nicely," and Sheriff Overholt of Fresno is disappointed that the strikers are not breaking the law, giving the police little excuse to "[get] them by the neck."

The attitude and organization of the police was revealed in the late 1930s, when the La Follette committee subpoenaed the minutes of the association.

FROM EXHIBIT 14289: MINUTES FROM THE CALIFORNIA STATE
PEACE OFFICERS' ASSOCIATION
(In Hearings before a Subcommittee of the Committee on
Education and Labor, 76th Congress, Part 75; Washington, DC: U.S.
Government Printing Office, 1941)

STATE PEACE OFFICERS AND LABOR DISPUTES

EXCERPTS FROM ANNUAL CONVENTIONS OF PEACE OFFICERS' ASSOCIATIONS
A. YEAR 1933
(1) CALIFORNIA PEACE OFFICERS' ASSOCIATION
EXHIBIT 14289
[Extracts copied from Convention Proceedings of "California Peace
Officers' Association," August 1933]

GEORGE F. OVERHOLT (Sheriff, Fresno). Gentlemen of the Convention . . .

Down in San Joaquin Valley we have, right now, quite a problem facing us. I have talked with a good many of the different sheriffs here concerning it. There doesn't seem to be anything in the way of suggestions that would be effective in handling the situation. I was just in touch with my office a few minutes ago, and we have quite a formidable grape harvest down there, and also a cotton harvest, and the Reds or Communists are raising quite a disturbance with the labor. About the only thing we have got that we can handle those fellows with, that are probably disturbing us is "disturbance of the peace" or something like that that is very effective, and I don't know what is going to become of us down there if that thing gets started in a big way with us, because when our harvest naturally commences it must be taken care of because that stuff is very perishable. . . .

I would like to hear from some of the men here some time this morning—not intending to butt in on this particular subject—on what their labor situation is in the different counties, and how it is handled. I wish someone would speak on this after the present subject is disposed of. It is kind of a nightmare to us down there.

President HARBER. Thank you, Sheriff. Is there anyone else wishes to offer anything else on organization? If not, is there anyone here than [*sic*] can answer the sheriff's question?

Chief DAVIS (Los Angeles). I may say that probably the situation as laid out by the sheriff is true of many other sections of the State, and the reds are trying apparently to get control of labor in the State of California. There is much activity on the part of the reds in the City of Los Angeles. And it doesn't matter whether they are supplied by the County Charities or Social Service or any other public charity, they are still agitating and quite active. So that is one of the things that can be accomplished by the organization, suggested by Chief Quinn: the peace officers of the state will have the strength by going out and working under their organization to put over the laws necessary to control that type of agitator. We haven't controlled the roads as effectively as they should be controlled. The sentimentalist shows that he somehow doesn't support the police, or, I should say, that because of the active opposition of the sentimentalist in their support of the reds, it has been difficult for the police to take the action necessary to effectively put the red agitator away, or the communist leaders in those areas where the communists are organized.

So you are simply suffering from what we are all suffering from. And with all that you now have, I would suggest that you use it through your local judges to give every agitator the limit for disturbing the peace or inciting riot or destruction of property or any other charge you can put against them. That at least, is going to be our policy in Los Angeles. (Applause.) . . .

Sheriff DRIVER (Alumeda County). Speaking of sheriff's difficulty, if it is in order, Sheriff Overholt, I would be very glad to relate our experience, which came in the pea harvest of this year. That harvest's work, as you all know, is done by the itinerant, mostly Mexicans and some other foreign peoples that live where they are and move from place to place wherever there is work to be done.

In that pea harvest in our section, which is not a large section, they used about 3,000 harvesters or pickers. The agitators gave us quite a little trouble and we met them rather promptly. Some of you know that our force for that kind of work is very small. We only have a small organization, and after we take care of the Superior Courts and the jail and the civil work, we only have a very small force to do the outside policing in the unincorporated area and in the county.

We found it necessary to put on twenty-five additional men for a period of about two weeks, but we only had one skirmish that you could call a riot. We were fortunate in that instance in cleaning up very nicely. There were quite a number of sore heads after the riot. We only made one arrest. One or two of our men were slightly injured, but it was a proposition on our side of using these brake-sticks used to brake cars with. They are a very useful instrument in a matter of that kind. There were some 300 of this group of strikers that undertook to put on a march down the road. There were about half a dozen of our men in the vicinity at the time, and they met them and contested the march and stopped it. But the fight that followed might have proved disastrous for us if it had not been for the prompt arrival of another half dozen men. From that time on it was just a very short time until they were all in our power. And from that time on there has been no trouble in our county.

As to the fruit, which spreads over quite an area, as other fruits do in other sections, there hasn't been any trouble there at all. Up until the time we left home the other day we hadn't had any trouble at all of that kind after the pea harvest. I don't know whether we shall continue to be free from it or not, but I thought it wouldn't hurt to relate that experience here at this time. Thank you. (Applause.) . . .

Sheriff OVERHOLT (Fresno). Our situation down there hasn't become acute at all. We haven't serious trouble, a lot of annoyances at all, but my idea of talking about it here was due to anticipating the possibilities of trouble in the future, and to equip myself with possible information, so that if it does get serious I will be better able to handle it.

So far we have had no riots. We are well equipped to handle riots. We are not afraid of any overt act they might commit. In fact, that is the thing that troubles us; they don't commit any overt act, don't give us a chance to help ourselves by legally getting out and getting them by the neck. They just agitate and agitate and keep the farmers unsettled. Of course, the farmer always looks to the sheriff to do this, that and the other, and they will go through this course and in the winter they will go back to the cities and make demands upon the Welfare Boards and so forth. (pp. 27601–27603)

REPORT BY TAYLOR AND KERR ON THE 1933 COTTON PICKERS' STRIKE

In a lengthy independent report about the 1933 cotton pickers' strike, Paul S. Taylor, sociology professor and Steinbeck's friend, and Clark Kerr, later President of the University of California, show the open collusion in California between law officers and cotton growers, who were supported by the press in their endeavors to suppress strikes. To keep workers terrorized, policemen admit— even boast, about—using tear gas and armed vigilantes.

Taylor and Kerr also discuss the controversial use of picketing— the key to a successful strike, but the pretext used by police to make arrests. Their report was included in the La Follette committee hearings.

FROM EXHIBIT 1864: PAUL S. TAYLOR AND CLARK KERR,
"REPORT OF POLICE AND COTTON STRIKE OF 1933"
(In Hearings before a Subcommittee of the Committee on
Education and Labor, 76th Congress, Part 75; Washington, DC:
U.S. Government Printing Office, 1941)

LAW ENFORCEMENT

The problem of maintaining the peace and at the same time protecting all parties to a labor conflict in the exercise of their legal rights has generally proved difficult for American officers. Even when authorities wish to preserve an equal balance between the parties to the dispute, they are confronted with vagueness and uncertainty in the law, and with heavy pressure from interested parties. The problem proved particularly difficult during the cotton strike in communities inexperienced in labor conflict.

The sheriffs and their deputies concentrated their efforts on the following program: (1) suppression of violence, but not including the disarming of growers; (2) prevention of anything but "peaceful" picketing, variously interpreted, with primary consideration for pickers working in the fields; (3) arrest of strike leaders as violators of the law. Also, growers were assisted in eviction of strikers from their temporary camps. . . .

The program was based on the "axiom" stated by the District Attorney of Tulare County, "The crops must be harvested." (Chronicle, Oct. 29). The attitude to which this led is suggested by the statements and actions of some of the officers. Sheriff Hill, for example, wished to handle the strike in his own way, declaring:

I know I can handle the situation, but I don't know whether it would meet with the approval of the growers or the public at large. (Times-Delta, Oct. 19.)

He warned the strikers:

We're going to try to force them to obey the law . . . if they won't obey, we're going to have a scrap, that's all. (Times-Delta, Oct. 24.)

Hill's son, a deputy sheriff, is reported to have told University of California students when they objected to interference with picketing on the grounds that strikers had a legal right to picket:

We had a meeting last night and changed all that. We make the law in Tulare County. (Testimony before Fact Finding Committee.)

The sheriff of only one of the three counties made active preparation for the strike. According to an under-sheriff in Kern County the officers—

knew the strike was coming and we were well prepared. We had two machine guns. We bought one thousand dollars of tear gas. We swore in forty five deputies during the strike and secured fast cars to cover the county. Cars were better than motorcycles on the rough roads and the men could protect themselves better. We tried to prevent trouble in every way. As a result there was fifty per cent picking all during the strike because we protected our farmers. The strikers didn't dare do nothing here. We had them covered and they knew it. They were afraid. (Interview.)

The sheriff of Tulare County was reluctant to create new deputies, not wishing to assume responsibility for their actions. He had but two deputies at the time of the Pixley shooting and created more only as the strike progressed and the seriousness of the situation appeared to demand them.

The board of supervisors . . . vested Sheriff R. L. Hill with full power to take all steps necessary to hold the strike situation under control, authorizing him to swear in as many deputies as he wants and purchase all needed equipment. . . .

Shortly after receiving authorization of the board of supervisors, Hill sent in an order for some gas shells to be used in 12-gauge shotguns.

Hill has had no special deputies on duty during the strike, and his only help has been that of his regular deputies assisted by the

California Highway patrol and the Constables of the County. (Times-Delta, Oct. 12)

However, eighteen special deputies were sworn on October 13, and fifty-one were on duty by the 24th. (Times-Delta) Sheriff Buckner of Kings County created four special deputies to take care of the situation.

The special deputies which numbered more than a hundred in the three counties, were even more inexperienced in handling strikes than the sheriffs and their judgment was continually in danger of being warped by their prejudices. Many of the deputies were ranchers, ranch managers, and gin employees. There is no report that any of them were from the ranks of the strikers.

The focus of clashes between employers and strikers is commonly the picket line, and so it proved during the cotton strike. This device is one of the most conspicuous and tangible of the efforts of the strikers to increase their adherents, and its defeat is a major aim of employers endeavoring to maintain active operations. Definition of permissible conduct, during picketing, therefore, is of high importance to the parties to a labor dispute, and to officers who must enforce the law. In California the law on picketing was in somewhat the same condition of confusion as elsewhere in the country, the legality or illegality depending upon such vague criteria as the circumstances surrounding each case, and the conduct of the pickets themselves. Since the guiding decisions of California, as elsewhere, refer principally to conditions obtaining around factories or places of business on crowded city streets, their discussions of specific situations are not very helpful to officers confronted with rural conditions. Some have thought that California courts, notably liberal in holding that all strikes are legal, were not equally liberal in holding that "Picketing always amounts to intimidation." (Commons and Andrews, Principles of labor legislation (1927) 108, 110.) However, less than two months before the cotton pickers' strike a California appellate court specifically denied that California law holds "there could be no such thing as peaceful picketing." In a concurring opinion, one judge stated even more broadly:

> That picketing, peaceable in fact, if not violative of a statute or ordinance, is not unlawful—and that the word intimidate—refers only to fear caused by threats, abuse or violence and not to the natural effect of picketing. . . . (Lisse v. Cooks, Waiters and Waitresses. 74 Cal. App. 518, 523–525)

Without discussing in detail the law on picketing, it is sufficient to stress that although peaceful picketing was lawful, it was left largely on the shoulders of local officers to determine in the light of "circumstances" and the "conduct of the pickets," the line between "persuasion" and "intimidation." . . .

Statements and demonstrations of force behind the law were frequently made by the officials and newspapers. Usually they were so phrased or conducted that they appeared to cast a shadow of illegality upon most of the normal activities of the strike. For example, it was reported: "Strike agitators are thwarted" when they "find the County well patrolled today by deputies from the Sheriff's Office." (California, Oct. 4) Similarly:

CITES RIOT LAWS

While he does not expect any serious trouble out of the Kings county cotton strike situation, District Attorney Clarence H. Wilson pointed out yesterday that there are definite laws under which county officers can act to handle any possible trouble. Rioting or inciting to riot are amply covered in the state laws as is also refusal to obey an order from a peace officer to disperse a riotous meeting. If agitators force workers to leave their jobs against their will, they are subject to punishment for a high misdemeanor.

(pp. 19982–19983)

AFFIDAVIT OF O. W. MINER: POLICE HARASSMENT CONTINUES IN 1939

The previous documents explored the reasons for the hostility and distrust that many workers had toward law enforcement in the early 1930s. The following affidavit of farmworker O. W. Miner, made public by the La Follette committee, contains evidence of continued police harassment of agricultural workers in 1939.

O. W. Miner, one of several strike leaders among the farmworkers, tells about his attempt, along with other workers, to peaceably clear equipment from a bandstand so that they could obey the under-sheriff's orders to get off the platform. But before they could get down, the sheriff ordered a mob of vigilantes to "get the sons-of-bitches," and they were attacked with iron pipes, clubs, and tear gas.

FROM EXHIBIT 13072: AFFIDAVIT OF O. W. MINER
(In Hearings before a Subcommittee of the Committee on
Education and Labor, 76th Congress, Part 71; Washington, DC:
U.S. Government Printing Office, 1941)

STATE OF CALIFORNIA
Madera County, ss:

O. W. Miner, Road 13, Madera, California, being duly sworn, deposes and says (Between 8 and 8:30 Saturday morning, October 21, 1930) [His account follows]:

. . . By the time I got back to the park it was about two o'clock.

I remained in front of the bandstand about 10 minutes, then went up on the stand, when a commotion started out on the street. I saw some farmers gathering all around the park on all four sides. They was holding clubs, gas pipes, and different kinds of weapons and they all had white rags hanging from them. They was shouting, "Let's get the sons-of-bitches." I also heard them call the strikers "bastards" and other very vile names, and about everything they could lay their tongues to.

They kept closing and crowding up to the bandstand when the under-sheriff, Pickett, came over to the stand on the west and by the stairway and said, "All right, get off of that bandstand." We tried to protest to him to let us move the public address system out of the way, that we would get off. A young girl about 24, who was on the stand, said to the under-sheriff, "Just wait a minute, (pointing to the equipment on the stand) 'til we can remove this stuff." Just then Pickett called to some men who were about 75 or 100 feet away to come to the stand. Then one of the fellows on the stand said to Pickett, "You'd better wait a few minutes 'til we get this stuff off." Pickett then turned around, and by this time there was a crowd of about 250 men approaching from the north, and Pickett shouted, "Come and get the sons-of-bitches!" Then Pickett stepped back and the men rushed up the steps and on to the bandstand.

One of them threw a club and hit me right across the face, and one of the strikers standing next to me grabbed a chair and threatened them if they came up any closer. Then I grabbed a chair and we started shoving them, trying to get them off the stand. We knocked about four or five of them down with the chairs as they were coming up the steps. About four men were beating Anna Parker up on the other side of the stand. . . .

Then [an individual in the mob] turned around and came at me with a gas pipe. When he struck at me with the pipe, I knocked him loose from it with a chair and hit him over the forehead with it. When he dropped his gas pipe, he came after me with his fists.

Then the police started throwing tear gas into us and just then a fellow by the name of Eldon Cady, a cotton farmer I worked for a couple of years who lives west of town, rushed through and struck me with a gas pipe with a piece of wood stick in the end of it, and hit me with the end of it in the left eye. After Cady hit me, he grabbed the loudspeaker and picked it up and slammed it onto the floor and grabbed these mikes and started jerking at them.

After the gas started, I started to run off the stand and got my feet all tangled up in the wires on the floor and fell down. My wife was standing at the bottom of the east stairs and was screaming when she saw me fall. I got up and went off the west end of the steps and was so blinded by the lick in the eye and the gas that I couldn't see, and I staggered right out clear through the whole bunch of them to the end of the park. I felt around for my car because I knew about where I had parked it and finally found it.

I got in my car and washed my eyes out with a bottle of water that I had there, and Eldon Cady come up to the front of my car and said, "Get the hell out of the county and take your whole God-damned outfit; and get!" About 40 or 50 other men gathered around my car while he was talking to me, and I told him that it was all right for him to talk to me now, that I'd settle with him later. These other guys made threats that they was going to upset my car and beat me up. I asked them why in the hell they didn't get started, what they was waiting on. They didn't bother me and I backed my car out, pulled around on the east side of the park and pulled up alongside the sidewalks, and hollered to my wife to come on and get in the car. She was standing on the sidewalk crying and gasping from the gas. My wife came in the car and we drove home. Later, my wife, whose name is Ellen S. Miner, told me that a woman beat her and that someone else held her, and that a man hit her over the head with a club.

/s/ O. W. Miner.

Personally appeared before me this 14th day of November, 1939, O. W. Miner, Road 13, Madera, California, who swears that the above statement is true and correct to the best of his knowledge and belief.

Chas. F. Preciado,
Notary Public.

My commission expires June 2, 1943. (pp. 26280–26281)

LEAD STORY IN *NEW YORK TIMES:* THE DEATH OF PRETTY BOY FLOYD ON OCTOBER 23, 1934

The extent to which the small-town boy from Oklahoma captured the national imagination is shown in the paper's decision to run the account of Floyd's death as the lead story on page one.

The details provided by the FBI team who cornered Floyd were later disputed by one of the agents who was present. According to the agent, Floyd was only wounded in the leg at first, but instead of bringing him to justice, FBI agent Melvin Purvis ordered one of his men to kill him. The crime that made him a special FBI target, the Kansas City massacre, was very likely not committed by Floyd.

FROM "PRETTY BOY FLOYD SLAIN AS HE FLEES BY FEDERAL MEN"
(New York Times, October 23, 1934)

EAST LIVERPOOL, Ohio, Oct. 22—Charles (Pretty Boy) Floyd, one of the most notorious outlaws of the present era, was shot and killed on a farm seven miles from here this afternoon as he fled from Federal agents and East Liverpool police who were closing in on him.

The Chicago Department of Justice head, Melvin H. Purvis, nemesis of the late John Dillinger, was in at the end. Leading four Federal men and four East Liverpool policemen Purvis said he shouted a command to Floyd to halt. The bandit first darted toward a corn crib for cover, then, changing his mind, sprinted toward a wooded ridge. Machine guns and pistols barked and the desperado fell, mortally wounded in the body.

Upon reaching him, the agents found he held a .45-calibre automatic in his hand and had a second automatic in a shoulder holster. Neither one had been fired, though the magazines of both were full.

"Who the hell tipped you?" Floyd asked the officers. A moment later he said, "Where is Eddie?" "Eddie," the officers judged, was Adam Richetti, who was captured near Wellsville Saturday, when he and Floyd fought a gun battle with police.

The officers carried the desperado into the farmhouse of Mrs. Ellen Conkle, where he had appeared earlier for food.

Purvis bent close to Floyd, questioning him about the machine gun massacre of five men at the Kansas City Union Station in June, 1933. "I am Floyd," the dying bandit admitted, but to the last he denied complicity in the Kansas City killings. He lived about fifteen minutes after the burst of fire had sent fourteen bullets into his back and one into his side.

HAD MEAL AT FARMHOUSE.

The body was brought to an undertaking establishment in East Liverpool.

The outlaw's pockets yielded $120 in cash. Little else was found among his personal effects.

The killing climaxed two days of intensive man-hunting in this area by Federal, State and county officers after Floyd escaped in the gun fight with policemen near Wellsville.

This afternoon Floyd appeared at the Conkle farm and asked for something to eat. He received a meal, and after eating it asked Mrs. Conkle if she could arrange to get him an automobile to take him to Youngstown. She replied that she would have to wait until the men returned from the fields.

Floyd had been sighted on the farm by Arthur Conkle, brother-in-law of Mrs. Conkle, who notified the officers in East Liverpool.

When Purvis arrived with his Department of Justice agents and the four police officers, including Police Chief Hugh J. McDermott of East Liverpool, Floyd was trying to persuade S. L. Dyke, farm hand and brother of Mrs. Conkle, to take him to Youngstown.

Leaping out of their cars, the officers closed in on the gunman. Floyd started to run, but the officers' marksmanship prevented him from reaching the shelter of the woods.

• • •

FLOYD A WILL-O'-THE-WISP.

For a time it was believed that Floyd had made another of the spectacular escapes that have studded his notorious career. A posse of more than 100 Federal and local authorities hunted him through woods and thickets in this section, while officers in surrounding States were on the lookout for him, but the trail grew colder with no material clews [*sic*] being unearthed until the search suddenly ended in success this afternoon.

It ended one of the most sensational criminal chases in the history of the country, for Floyd had slipped through numerous Oklahoma man hunts in the early stages of his banditry, and more recently had eluded nation-wide searches with almost a will-o'-the-wisp ease. (pp. 1,2)

CHATTANOOGA NEWS: OSWALD GARRISON VILLARD ON PRETTY BOY FLOYD'S COLD-BLOODED MURDER

In the days that followed the killing of Pretty Boy Floyd, stories about the circumstances surrounding his death and the arrest of his partner, Adam Richetti, continued to appear in the pages of the *New York Times* and other newspapers, including the *Chattanooga News*. None of the stories inspired much confidence in law enforcement. Readers were struck by the fact that the FBI had hunted down Floyd primarily because of the Kansas City massacre, yet Floyd, who had denied any involvement all along, continued to deny it until he died.

Another story that placed the police in a bad light was an account in the *Times* about the arrest of Richetti. He was manacled hand and foot and thrown into a filthy jail, swimming in sewage, that had been condemned as unfit for human habitation. Then schoolchildren were paraded into the jail to stare at him as police enlarged on his criminal record and pointed out his present misery.

The story in the *Chattanooga News* that follows reveals the general attitude of many toward the FBI and especially what was regarded as law enforcement's reprehensible handling of Pretty Boy Floyd. Rumors also surfaced that FBI head J. Edgar Hoover was determined that Floyd not be taken alive because Floyd had too much information about law enforcement's collusion with mobsters.

FROM OSWALD GARRISON VILLARD, "COLD-BLOODED
MURDER"
(*Chattanooga [Tenn.] News*, November 13, 1934)

Is it not time to call a halt upon the Department of Justice's cold-blooded murder of gangsters? The other night I ran across two distinguished judges of the State of New Jersey. They asked me what I thought of the killing of "Pretty Boy" Floyd. I said that it seemed to me lynching, pure and simple. They replied that it was far worse than lynching because it was done by officers of the law, sworn to uphold the law and the orderly processes of the courts . . . and declared that so far from helping enforcement of justice in the United States it was hurting it. . . . They agreed with me that such a thing could happen in no other country in the world, except among the Nazis and others, who deliberately murder men and declare that they were "shot while escaping." They dwelt with particular horror on the pumping of thirteen bullets into "Pretty Boy" Floyd when he was surrounded and escape was impossible. They were convinced that the majesty of the law would have been much better served had Floyd been taken into court and sent to the electric chair by the regular procedure. . . .

A member of the younger generation asked me very seriously whether it was not better to exterminate outlaws as Floyd was killed than to have them running around the country killing and robbing. This was obviously beside the mark. That these men should be run down and imprisoned, or, if the law requires it, executed, is obvious. But when Government resorts to the methods of Messrs. Purvis and Hoover, it admits that it has sunk to the level of the gangsters, that the regular procedure has broken down, and that the Government's law-enforcement machinery is so weak that it has itself to resort to extralegal methods to rid the country of these public enemies. . . . (p. 2)

NEW YORK TIMES COVERS FLOYD'S BURIAL

The extent to which Pretty Boy Floyd intrigued, and was even idolized by, the public, is attested to by the thousands of people who attended his funeral. It is easy to imagine the fictional Joads among the 20,000 mourners and Ma Joad comforting Floyd's bereaved mother whom she said she knew as a neighbor.

Woody Guthrie, the famous Oklahoma folk song writer, reported that it was his custom in the mid- to late 1930s to sing at a number of camps for farmworkers in California. Invariably, he said, when he began to sing the song he had written in praise of Pretty Boy Floyd, "The Ballad of Pretty Boy Floyd," the camp would go wild with shouts of approval.

FROM "20,000 ATTEND BURIAL OF FLOYD IN OKLAHOMA"
(*New York Times*, October 29, 1934)

Preacher at Grave Blames
Forces of Environment for
Turning Youth to Crime.

SALLISAW, Okla., Oct. 28 (AP).—The bullet-riddled body of Charles A. (Pretty Boy) Floyd, Oklahoma's outlaw, was buried in a little hillside cemetery near the village of Akins today while a curious crowd estimated at 20,000 persons looked on.

His last resting place was a grave he reputedly had picked for himself more than a year ago with a remark to Mrs. Walter Floyd, his widowed mother:

"Right here is where you can put me. I expect to go down with lead in me—perhaps the sooner the better."

The mother, Mrs. Ruby Floyd; the outlaw's widow, his 12-year-old son, Jack Dempsey Floyd; four sisters and two brothers sat in a small arbor shielded from the eyes of the crowd as the simple casket was lowered into the grave.

The Rev. W. E. Rockett of the Sallisaw Baptist Church conducted the final services, assisted by the Rev. Owen White of the Akins Baptist Church.

"If heredity alone could direct the lives of our restless youth," Mr. Rockett said in a brief talk, "we in all probability should not be here on this sad occasion, but a stronger force, environment, steps in to defeat heredity. Thus ofttimes the example of consecrated mothers, fathers and grandparents are nullified by the evil forces of environment."

The thousands of onlookers stood about the cemetery and the crowd overflowed onto near-by pastures. Fences were torn down to make room for parked cars.

A steady stream of motor cars from twenty States came to the cemetery from Sallisaw. Some spectators came in wagons and buggies and others on horseback. A few came afoot. Farm women dressed in calico aprons appeared at the cemetery with babies in their arms. School buses brought children. Three women fainted and were nearly trampled. (p. 3)

TOPICS FOR ORAL OR WRITTEN DISCUSSION

1. Examine the language used by law-enforcement officers and guards in *The Grapes of Wrath* and in the historical documents included here. What does the choice of words indicate about their attitude? What was the likely effect of these words on a listener?

2. Write an essay on Tom Joad as an outlaw in order to explore the narrator's attitude toward Tom's law breaking.

3. Does the prevailing view of the narrator in *The Grapes of Wrath* agree with that of the minister at Pretty Boy Floyd's funeral? That is, is the outlaw made by society or by heredity? Discuss fully.

4. Make a list of the many aspects of a person's life and makeup that contribute to his or her becoming a criminal. Which do you think has the most impact? To what extent, if at all, is the criminal a victim? If there is sufficient disagreement among the students, debate the subject in class.

5. With the previous question in mind, turn to the question of capital punishment. Discuss whether capital punishment is ever justified. Is it defensible in only one or two instances? If so, which ones?

6. Write a research paper on the controversy surrounding the FBI in the 1930s.

7. If you were J. Edgar Hoover, head of the FBI, would you have made a deal with Floyd, guaranteeing him that he would not be executed if he surrendered? Consider the complex pros and cons of such a decision.

8. Watch some of the many gangster films made in the 1930s (such as *Little Caesar, Public Enemy*, and *Scarface* [1932 version]) and write reviews about the attitudes toward law and order and outlaws that they project.

9. Is the view of the law and the outlaw in the Great Depression exceptional because of the times, or can you document later or contemporary instances in which segments of the law-abiding population have had reason to distrust the police and have make heroes out of outlaws? After a class discussion, develop a written essay on a specific instance that exemplifies an attitude, similar to the one portrayed in this chapter, toward the law or toward a criminal. You may, of course, want to argue that the view in the Great Depression no longer prevails.

SUGGESTIONS FOR FURTHER READING

Bernstein, Irving. *The Turbulent Years: A History of the American Worker 1933–1941*. Boston: Houghton Mifflin Company, 1970.

Bruns, Roger A. *The Bandit Kings*. New York: Crown Publishers, 1995.

Culberson, William C. *Vigilantism: Political History of Private Power in America*. Westport, CT: Greenwood Press, 1990.

Girardin, G. Russell, with William J. Helmer. *Dillinger: The Untold Story*. Bloomington: Indiana University Press, 1994.

Guthrie, Woody. *Bound for Glory*. Garden City, NY: Doubleday, n.d.

King, Jeffrey S. *The Life and Death of Pretty Boy Floyd*. Kent, OH: The Kent State University Press, 1998.

Kooistra, Paul. *Criminals as Heroes: Structure, Power and Identity*. Bowling Green, OH: Bowling Green State University Popular Press, 1989.

Miller, Henry. *On the Fringe: The Dispossessed in America*. Lexington, MA: D. C. Heath and Co., 1991.

Prassel, Frank Richard. *The Great American Outlaw*. Norman: University of Oklahoma Press, 1993.

Wallis, Michael. *The Life and Times of Charles Arthur Floyd*. New York: St. Martin's Press, 1992.

7

After *The Grapes of Wrath:* The Life and Legacy of Cesar Chavez and the Farmworkers at the Close of the Twentieth Century

In some ways, the situation experienced in the 1930s by the Joads on California farms changed after World War II, but in other substantial ways, the plight of the farmworker remained the same, improving little from the time of the Joads to the end of the twentieth century.

Among the changes were the departure of many southerners and midwesterners from California farms to the growing defense industry and the return of Mexicans and Mexican Americans to a dominant place among farmworkers. The most significant change was the establishment of the United Farm Workers, an effective, farm labor union that won a voice for and improvements in working and living conditions for many farmworkers for the first time. In 1975, for the first time, the California legislature passed a law giving farmworkers protections that federal labor laws had failed to extend to them for the past sixty years.

There were improvements, but there were also new problems, some of which arose for the first time after the war, for example, the growers' hiring of temporary Mexican workers and using the Teamsters Union to undermine farmworkers, and the use of pesticides and the new problems that had simply not developed into issues in the Joads' day. Despite the reforms won by the United Farm Workers, many of the serious problems experienced by the

Cesar Chavez eulogizing a slain United Farm
Workers member. Reproduced courtesy of AP/
WIDE WORLD PHOTOS.

Joads continued for sixty years, right up to the closing years of the
twentieth century.

The story of farm labor in America after World War II is inextricably tied to an extraordinary figure, a farmworker named Cesar
Chavez. Chavez is exceptional for many reasons. Most apparent are
his accomplishments made in the best interests of farmworkers,
against incredible odds. He was a self-educated man without
schooling above the eighth grade, who acted with wisdom and
judgment in creating an effective grassroots alliance of workers of
many races, and marshalled effective national boycotts of farm
products to improve the situation of farmworkers. More than any
American labor leader, he was of the people, and in spite of the
national attention he received, he continued to see himself as a
Mexican American farmworker. From his poverty-ridden background, he rose to international prominence.

Above all, Cesar Chavez's greatness came from his character. No
leader in American history emerges quite so unsullied, so unam-
bitious for himself, so quietly self-effacing, so uninterested in
worldly goods. In Chavez, his gently ascetic and spiritual nature
was united with his thoroughly practical side. This is not to say
that he never made tactical mistakes, or that he was never criticized
by his friends and supporters, or that he was not truly hated by

many politicians and growers. Still, his motives always seemed unimpeachable, his morals without question. No person in American history so closely approaches sainthood.

The story of the farmworker after *The Grapes of Wrath* is inextricably tied to Cesar Chavez and his legacy. Chavez was born on March 31, 1927 near Yuma, Arizona. His background before World War II is similar to that of the Joads in many ways. Like Tom Joad's father, Chavez's father lost his land in 1937 as a result of the Great Depression, and was forced to take his family to California in search of work as a farm laborer. The instability of traveling from place to place, after having lived on their own ranch in Arizona, was especially hard on the children. All members of the family worked, making a grand total of one or two dollars a day, out of which they had to pay for some of the supplies they needed in the fields, as well as personal necessities. They lived in migrant camps in fifteen-by-fifteen-foot cabins made of tar paper and slats and shared an outhouse. At a grape ranch near Fresno, they were recruited by a labor contractor who eventually disappeared with every cent they had earned all season. In 1942, the family experienced working with the short-handled hoe, required by growers of certain crops, melons for example. This meant that the worker had to bend over double to thin the plants. For this backbreaking work, the children were paid eight cents an hour and the adults twelve cents an hour.

Chavez reported that his father, though unsophisticated in the ways of unions, was an ardent supporter of the smallest efforts to unite for better working and living conditions. The only tool the worker had was to withhold his labor, and this the Chavez family was willing to do on a number of occasions. In the 1930s and early 1940s Chavez's father joined several unions and participated in many strikes.

Even though the schools despised and mistreated the children of migrant workers, especially children of Mexicans, Chavez's mother insisted that her children attend school as often as possible. But in 1942, after completing the eighth grade, Chavez had to quit school to work full-time in the fields. Two years later, in 1944, at the age of seventeen, he joined the navy and served in the South Pacific.

In 1946, he returned to again work with his family in the California fields, and observed that the postwar years were ripe for union activity. Growers were stronger and richer than ever; they had amassed large empires that included canneries, processing plants, distribution centers, and retail businesses. One example was the Schenley Corporation, whose financial interests extended from grape growing to liquor distribution. The power of growers had become more entrenched through private boards that regulated agriculture exclusively to increase owner profits. By 1960, for example, thirty-five boards, with close to 1,000 corporate members, operated in California. To keep prices of food from going down, boards determined how much was planted and when surpluses were allowed to rot in the fields or destroyed.

Wage fixing was uncovered and deplored by the La Follette U.S. Senate committee, formed in 1937 to study the problems of labor, including violations of the civil rights of farmworkers. After World War II, however, wage fixing had again attained widespread usage. Growers presented a united front in keeping wages uniformly low.

The use of the hated labor contractors also reappeared after the war. With their return came all the old abuses. Contractors deceptively lured and contracted for far more workers than were needed in order to lower wages once workers was already in the fields. And contractors assumed the responsibility for feeding, housing, and transporting workers. They ran unsanitary camps and provided rotten food for which they charged a fee, refused to supply water so that they could make money selling drinks from concession stands set up in the fields, and were notorious for transporting workers in dangerous vehicles operated by untrained drivers. Fatal vehicular accidents were commonplace job hazards for the farmworkers. Moreover, contractors often disappeared with the workers' entire paychecks or pocketed the social security payments taken out of their pay.

One of the growers' chief strategies to avoid paying decent wages and providing decent living conditions was their use of the Bracero Program. During the war, when labor was often in short supply, growers imported young Mexican men to work temporarily at a given job before sending them back to Mexico. These young men were called braceros. The growers found that hiring braceros had a distinct advantage over hiring domestic workers in that they could work rapidly, did not insist upon receiving many of the benefits demanded by older domestic workers with families—like fresh water and toilets in the fields—did not bring with them the threat of unions, and could be immediately deported after their brief period of usefulness was over, or when they caused trouble. They could be housed cheaply in dormitories, were easily isolated from union organizers and strikers, and tolerated abominable living and working conditions. Braceros were also brought in to break strikes. So, even after the labor shortage of the war years was over, growers still kept the Bracero Program alive. In 1951, it was made official when Public Law 78 was passed by the U.S. Congress, officially sanctioning the importation of braceros to work in the fields on the specious assumption that there was a shortage of domestic farm labor. With the United States' and Mexico's endorsement, growers went to great lengths to keep from hiring domestic farmworkers. They paid them less, closed down family camps, and evicted domestic workers, and even drew attention to the poor working and living conditions to discourage domestic workers.

Given this situation, the Chavez family soon joined the most effective union for farm laborers at the time, the National Agricultural Workers Union, led by Hank Hasiwar and Mexican American scholar/author Ernesto Galarza. At this time, farmworkers included many blacks and whites from the deep South and Southwest, as well as Mexican Americans. Many, like the Chavez family, had managed to find a fairly stable home in one area, though most farmworkers continued to live in substandard housing—shacks, lean-tos, tents, and cabins, for which they paid upkeep. They had other grievances as well: in 1947, pay was around eighty cents an hour and there was absolutely no job security, even for workers with seniority.

Farmworkers had never been included in national labor law protections, and in 1949, a congressional subcommittee led by California congressman Richard Nixon, beholden to growers, recommended that farmworkers continue to be excluded from protections.

These conditions created increased labor unrest from 1947 until 1952, with the National Farm Labor Union targeting the DiGiorgio Corporation whose farms were near Arvin and Delano. (The National Farm Labor Union changed its name to the National Agricultural Workers Union in 1956.) In 1949, the union asked DiGiorgio (which had $18 million in sales in 1946) for a 10-cent-an-hour raise and recognition of a board to air grievances. However, those who went on strike were fired, braceros were brought in to harvest the grapes, pickets were attacked and some seriously wounded, union headquarters was fired on, and all modes of communication with the braceros were outlawed. When a film entitled *Spiders in the House*, made to present the workers' plight, was shown, DiGiorgio sued union leaders in a $2 million suit. The union, having no money for continuation of the strike or for its defense fund, had to call off the strike on May 9, 1950, without having achieved its goals.

Although the union was involved in other strikes during this period, its only success—and a significant one at that—was in seeing that the Bracero Program was eventually stopped. It was to this end that Ernesto Galarza devoted himself, believing that no gains would be forthcoming as long as Mexican workers could be shipped in to take the jobs of domestic workers and to break strikes. It took another fifteen years to phase out the Bracero Program. The result was that many growers then turned to illegal labor, but in the final analysis, workers' conditions and wages improved somewhat with the demise of the program. In August 1960, Galarza's National Agricultural Workers Union came to an end for lack of funding.

From 1946 until 1960, Cesar Chavez was reading extensively and studying with activists in the Catholic Church to arrive at his own philosophy. He joined his ascetic Catholicism, with its base in St. Francis of Assisi, to the nonviolent social action of the nineteenth-century American philosopher Henry David Thoreau, and India's Mahatma Gandhi. At the same time, he was being trained in methods of social action by observing Ernesto Galarza and listening to Father Thomas McCullough, a priest turned community organizer, who introduced him to Pope Leo XIII's encyclicals on the rights of labor. He went with McCullough to the camps and to the jails whenever he could. Throughout his life, Chavez would link his intense spirituality as a Catholic to his work as a reformer: fasting frequently for long periods of time to gain moral strength and to draw attention to the needs of the poor, reading and meditating, participating in public communions at the end of his fasts, envisioning his marches as holy pilgrimages, and choosing our Lady of Guadeloupe as a symbol of the movement.

Chavez's work with the poor began when he volunteered for the Community Services Organization (CSO), a nationwide group whose aim was to educate and organize the poor to find jobs, medical care, and other social services. His talent and dedication quickly brought him a paying job with the CSO. He eventually became National Director of the Community Service Organization for California and Arizona. Chavez and his assistant, Dolores Huerta, worked to educate the poor, to make benefits available to them, and to change legislation to help them. But they both became convinced that welfare and legislation were never going to get to the roots of the problem, which were poor wages and working conditions. In the Imperial Valley in 1950, for example, resident farmworkers were making from forty to fifty cents an hour. In Kern City, California, workers were paid six cents per sixty-five pounds of picked potatoes, with deductions for possible inclusion of debris, and for bags and bag ties. They received no pay for the hours they spent lugging the bags to the scales and standing in line waiting for their bags to be weighed. Chavez and Huerta believed that only an active labor union, run by the workers themselves, could get at the heart of the problem. In 1962, when Chavez failed to convince the CSO to move in this direction, he resigned his position, moved his growing family to Delano, California, near his brother, and began to work full-time for the farm labor movement, along with Dolores Huerta, members of his family, and another farmworker, Gilbert Padilla.

Chavez, in his very deliberate way, decided that the budding organization should not at first resemble a labor union. Nor should it include the word strike in its vocabulary. Instead, the group would begin with community organizing in as many areas as possible, charging dues to stimulate commitment, encouraging the workers to identify their problems, and putting them in leadership positions in every area. After widespread local meetings, the National Farm Worker's Association (NFWA) became official in 1962 with a membership of 300 families. At this time, the organization was able to establish three much-needed programs: a burial plan, whereby workers could be assured that family members who died would have a decent burial; a credit union; and a car parts cooperative.

Ironically, the association's biggest help at this time came not from the Catholic Church, which had inspired Chavez and of which he and most migrant workers were devout members (it was also the church of the growers), but from the Migrant Ministry, a Protestant organization established by the National Council of Churches. The association and the ministry worked as a single entity, except in one respect. Chavez believed it was vital to his association for its members to support themselves in the formative years, so he refused the substantial funding offered by the Migrant Ministry.

On January 21, 1963, the association held a convention to adopt a constitution. The most dramatic moment was provided by Chavez's brother, Manuel, who leaped onto the stage to unveil a striking red-and-white banner, the colors of Mexico, featuring a starkly stylized eagle.

The strategy of the growers had always been to segregate different nationalities from one another to foster tensions, but Chavez approached the sizable association of Filipino workers, asking for their cooperation. Larry Itliong, leader of the Agricultural Workers Organizing Committee composed of Filipino workers, readily agreed. It was this alliance that brought Chavez's association into a strike long before he had intended to become embroiled in such activity. In 1965, when Filipino workers supported by CID struck Delano grape growers for an increase to one dollar and forty cents an hour, the NFWA joined them, beginning the longest strike and boycott in agricultural history.

Three months after the strike began, it became apparent to Chavez that more than picket lines and work stoppages were needed to secure the union's demands because the growers were capable of neutralizing their efforts by bringing in scab labor and having the pickets outlawed and isolated. Union leaders fanned out across the country to promote a consumer boycott of nonunion grapes, focusing particularly on the Schenley and DiGiorgio Corporations.

To promote the goals of the strike and impress their unity on the California legislature, Chavez planned a 340-mile march, which he called a pilgrimage, from Delano to Sacramento, the state capital. The peaceful march, which began in March of 1966 and ended on Easter Sunday, was joined by thousands of people carrying the banners of the United States, Mexico, the Philippines, and the NFWA. The banner of Our Lady of Guadeloupe, the Masses held each day along the way, and the arrival of some 5,000 people at the steps of the capitol on Easter weekend, contributed to the religious nature of the march.

Nineteen sixty-six brought agreements with many Delano grape growers to hold union elections and meet other union demands, but the DiGiorgio Corporation continued to hold out, and complicated the negotiations by making a sweetheart deal with the Teamsters Union, without the participation of the workers. The Teamsters, in exchange for the grower's contract, were responsible for importing muscle men to intimidate NFWA pickets and keep them from communicating with scabs in the fields. Growers were inevitably pleased to have the Teamsters, basically because the union was satisfied with securing only short-term, modest wage increases with little input from the workers themselves, and could be depended upon to use whatever tactics were necessary to keep Chavez and his union out. But the NFWA, soon to become the United Farm Workers, was a more formidable threat to growers because it was run by the workers themselves for long-term economic and social changes.

As soon as the Teamsters entered the scene, carrying chains and pickaxes and firearms, the threat of violence escalated. To Chavez, who was fervently and steadfastly dedicated to nonviolence, the prospect of his own people being provoked into uncontrolled behavior was a nightmare. His dedication to nonviolence was an ironic response to the powerful and wealthy residents of a region that had controlled their employees by means of unspeakable violence in the 1930s.

After intense outside pressure, the Teamsters withdrew and in 1966 the DiGiorgio Corporation agreed to elections in which the workers chose the NFWA to represent them. The contract that followed based layoffs and promotions on seniority, set up a health fund, and granted unemployment benefits. Unfortunately, shortly afterward, the DiGiorgio Corporation was forced into a sale of most of its holdings and none of the buyers of its vineyards would agree to the contract the company had signed with the union.

Although the union had signed contracts with numerous growers, including the Schenley Corporation, the Giumarra Corporation, the largest of the Delano grape growers, refused to talk to the union. Plans were made to focus boycott efforts on Giumarra grapes. Soon, however, it came to light that Giumarra grapes were marketed under a hundred different labels, many lent to them by other growers, so the union had no choice but to boycott all table grapes.

By 1968, the strike had been going on for four years. Workers had been evicted from their homes, had lost their jobs, were being harassed by the police, and had been taunted and beaten by the

Teamsters. Chavez was fearful that his insistence on nonviolence would be ignored. At this time, he took a dramatic and unprecedented action by calling off all the pickets, sending some of the workers back to the fields, and then retiring to a monastic-like cell to fast, pray, and read the Bible and the writings of Mahatma Gandhi. Chavez announced that his twenty-five-day fast was an affirmation of nonviolence and that no social movement was worth the death of one worker or one grower. Mass and prayer vigils were conducted daily outside the Chavezes' hut where hundreds of people appeared daily on pilgrimages.

In the middle of his fast, the weakened Chavez had to be led to a court appearance necessitated by an action filed by the Giumarra Corporation that sued the union for picketing and boycotting the grapes from its company. One thousand farmworkers lined his path and kneeled in silent prayer. It was not the kind of public relations scene to promote the best interests of the growers or convince the public to ignore the grape boycott. Not surprisingly, Giumarra soon dropped the suit.

Chavez chose to break his fast in a Delano park in the presence of 4,000 supporters, including Robert F. Kennedy, with the taking of Communion served by a priest. But the ordeal had taken a toll on his health. He was immediately hospitalized for three weeks and then bedridden for eight months.

By this time, the public's boycott—now taken to a secondary level that included a ban of supermarkets that stocked Delano table grapes—was making serious inroads into growers' profits. And even though growers could have stopped the boycott at any time by agreeing to allow their workers to chose union representation through elections, they refused, capping their efforts with a multimillion dollar advertising campaign and strong support from conservatives like California governor Ronald Reagan and President Richard Nixon. In 1968, for example, President Nixon encouraged the passage of a farm bill that still left workers with no protections, prohibited secondary boycotts, and allowed the president to block serious strikes for eighty days. Bills were also introduced at the state and federal levels to make strikes and boycotts illegal during picking seasons. All these measures failed, but so did attempts to provide farmworkers with protections.

To shore up profits for the growers, the Defense Department became a strike-breaker by buying close to two and one-half million pounds of grapes a year to feed to soldiers. Instead of backing down, Chavez added another issue to the union's complaint against growers: their use of health-endangering pesticides, especially the cancer-causing Aldrin, which was found at eighteen times the maximum Food and Drug Administration (FDA) allowable levels in supermarket grapes. The union claimed that pesticides were especially dangerous to grape pickers and was able to provide statistics showing a much higher rate of cancer than the national average in the children of the grape pickers.

In early 1970, ten of the medium-sized corporations, followed by three of the larger grape-growing corporations, met Chavez with an offer to agree to the union's demands, even though other more powerful growers, State Senator George Murphy, and members of the California Farm Bureau had brought great pressure to bear on them to stand firm against setting the strike. Eventually, the other growers, including Giumarra, came to an agreement with the UFW.

It had been a long five-year strike. The wage gains seemed small, a 15-cent-an-hour raise to $1.80 and a promise of $2.05 by 1972. An added 12 cents an hour was added by the growers for health and welfare benefits. The most significant gains did not involve money but the power to make decisions about the laborers' working conditions: (1) the growers agreed to hire from the union hall rather than from contractors; (2) they agreed to set up committees consisting of owners and growers to monitor pesticide use; and (3) they agreed to set up committees of owners and employees to air grievances. Basic to these concessions was the growers' agreement to allow workers to hold elections to choose their own representatives in collective bargaining. Their options were usually the Teamsters Union, a company union, or the United Farm Workers (UFW). As growers and union members met together to sign the agreement, all those present realized it was an historic occasion: they were signing the first labor contract for farmworkers in the history of the United States. What had been commonplace for industrial workers for decades had finally reached at least some farmworkers in Delano, California.

Although the victory in Delano was momentous, Cesar Chavez's struggle was far from over. Lettuce workers in Salinas were having difficulty even as the grape strike in Delano ended. Some growers ignored UFW agreements and brought in the more grower-friendly Teamsters Union with rigged elections. The violence that ensued resulted in the arrests of 2,000 UFW members, beatings, and shootings, and two men killed. Chavez, still fervently committed to nonviolence, called for a reaffirmation of peaceful negotiations and asked for a new boycott—of lettuce. Toward the end of 1970, one of the lettuce growers took Chavez to court to call off the boycott. When Chavez refused, he was arrested and jailed on December 10, where he remained until Christmas eve, when a higher court ordered him released.

Throughout the 1970s and 1980s, Chavez met the opposition with his most effective tools: strikes, boycotts, marches, and pickets. He also undertook many long fasts to reaffirm nonviolence, to protest unconstitutional antifarmworker laws, to draw attention to workers' children dying of cancer because of pesticides, and to rededicate himself to his ideals of love and patience.

Nineteen seventy-five was a landmark year for farmworkers in that Chavez was successful in working with California governor Jerry Brown to enact the first law ever passed to protect agricultural laborers. The law guaranteed legitimate elections, collective bargaining, and protection of the rights of individual farmworkers. In the same year, a bill was passed giving unemployment insurance to farmworkers. Other legislation outlawed the short-handled hoe that had caused ruptured spinal disks and arthritis of the spine.

The laws were in place, but now Chavez had the problem of seeing that they were enforced. As less well-disposed politicians came to power, they packed oversight boards with growers and their supporters, so charges of union election violations were ignored, giving the edge to the growers sympathetic to the Teamsters Union. Growers often circumvented the spirit of the law when, for example, they forced workers to use their bare hands instead of longer hoes after the short-handled hoes were outlawed. They were also successful in using old trespass laws to keep the UFW from campaigning on their property before mandated elections, while welcoming the Teamsters. In 1975, the same year in which the first farm labor protection law was passed, the average annual salary for farmworkers was still under $2,000.

The stress of his mission, and his many draining fasts, began to take their toll on an already fragile Chavez. In the 1980s he had disagreements with some of his long-standing colleagues; the union was beginning to suffer losses under increasingly unsympathetic administrations in Sacramento and Washington, DC; and additional lawsuits were brought by growers. In 1993, as part of a never-ending battle, he traveled to Arizona to testify at a hearing during a grower's lawsuit against the union. A week before his testimony, he began another fast, explaining that his purpose was to gain moral strength. His friends, observing his exhaustion, convinced him to break his fast several days later. That night, on April 23, 1993, he died in his sleep at the age of sixty-six.

AT THE CENTURY'S CLOSE

While Chavez's legacy lives on in the form of the union he founded, the problems plaguing the farmworker also persist. In any reading of news stories, problems very much like the ones that the Joads and workers of the 1930s encountered, invariably surface. Housing conditions continue to be substandard, and the contractor system, with all its abuses, is still in operation. Child labor continues to be exploited.

Child Labor

At the close of 1997, the Associated Press published the results of an investigation into illegal child labor in the United States. The findings were astonishing: it found that 61,000 children between the ages of fourteen and seventeen were hired as field workers in violation of the law—that is, they were not working *for* or living *with* their parents. A total of 123,000 children were estimated to be performing farm labor. Reporters found children as young as twenty months being trained to work in the fields.

Unsafe and Unsanitary Housing

On July 9, 1998, the *Los Angeles Times* reported that a lawsuit was filed by the family of a farmworker who died on the property of a grower in San Diego County. The worker lost his life in a fire that started in one of the temporary, plastic-covered wood shanties that the employees had erected on the owner's land. The court ruled that owners were responsible—liable—when they allowed their workers to live in unsanitary, unsafe hovels near the fields. Tony Perry, the writer who filed the report, observes that "Substandard housing for workers in California agriculture has been a political issue for decades with laws and lawsuits aimed at ending the specter of farm workers living in filthy conditions. Still the problem persists" (Perry, "Farmer Faces Suit in Death of Worker," p. 3).

No Right to Unionize

In the summer of 1997, the UFW turned its attention to California's strawberry pickers, a nonunionized group described as having endured some of the lowest wages and harshest working conditions of any group of farmworkers. The Watsonville, California, growers had agreed to allow elections to determine which union the workers wanted to represent them. Then it was discovered that their choice was voting for a *company* union or no union at all. Workers sympathetic to the UFW were fired and blacklisted.

Violence and the Law

On June 24, 1998, UFW workers at one strawberry ranch were physically attacked by anti-UFW workers, chiefly the more highly paid truckers and foremen. Three workers were so severely injured that they had to be hospitalized. Neither the employees nor the police arrested or disciplined the attackers. In response, UFW president Arturo Rodriquez, Chavez's son-in-law, and Chavez's longtime friend and co-organizer, Dolores Huerta, held a march against violence, and maintained that the organization of a company union was a blatant attempt to squelch real unions.

In September 1998, the U.S. Labor Department reported that 77 percent of growers and labor contractors were in violation of worker protection laws. In a limited sampling of growers, the department found that hundreds of farm laborers were receiving less than the minimum wage mandated by law. The investigators also found significant safety violations and child labor violations.

Phony Labor Shortages and Illegal Workers

September also echoed conditions in the 1930s, 1940s, and 1950s, as growers complained of labor shortages and requested that the governor of California assign prisoners and the National Guard to help in the fields. The UFW, including Dolores Huerta, countered that there was no shortage of labor at all; the growers' complaints, they contended, were merely a ploy to get grower-friendly migrant worker legislation under consideration in the U.S. Congress, a bill that was stripped of the necessity for providing decent housing and insurance for the workers and that made it easier for growers to hire illegal instead of domestic workers.

Retaliation Against Union Members

A new story filed on September 25, 1998, indicates that up to September 1998, no farmworkers in Mendocino County, California, had ever been unionized. One of the growers explained that the county had never had labor problems, in part because malcontent workers were simply fired. In the summer of 1998, however, pickers contacted the United Farm Workers to help them improve their wages and to convince a particular grower to withdraw his insistence that they pay the tractor drivers out of their wages. The workers who voiced complaints about wages were escorted out of the vineyards by sheriff's deputies and told not to return. The growers also announced their plans to hire workers from outside the country, and the sheriff warned the workers that he would be present to stop any "trouble" when scab workers were imported.

The following documents enlarge on the situation of farmworkers since the publication of *The Grapes of Wrath* in 1939. First is a newspaper account of the end of Cesar Chavez's fast during the Delano grape boycott. The second includes selections from two 1997 Associated Press stories on child labor that it conducted. The third is a report on the situation of farmworkers, released by California Legislative Assembly Speaker Antonio R. Villaraigosa on September 9, 1998.

CESAR CHAVEZ AND THE IMPORTANCE OF NONVIOLENCE

A crowd of 4,000 supporters gathered in Delano, California, on Sunday, March 10, 1968, to celebrate Mass with Cesar Chavez. Chavez was breaking a twenty-five-day fast, which he had begun in large measure to undergird his followers' commitment to nonviolence. The event might have received little or no attention in the public press had it not been for the presence of Senator Robert F. Kennedy. Even so, few California newspapers included quotations from the brief statement composed by Chavez that was to be read by one of his followers. The *San Francisco Chronicle* was an exception. The following account, covered by one of its own reporters rather than a news service, captures the spirit and the importance of the event.

FROM "CHAVEZ ENDS SYMBOLIC 25-DAY FAST"
(San Francisco Chronicle, Monday, March 11, 1968)

From our Correspondent
Delano

Farm labor leader Cesar Chavez yesterday ended a 23-day fast symbolizing his commitment to non-violence by swallowing a hard piece of Mexican bread.

Looking drawn and weary, Chavez slumped in a a chair during a Roman Catholic Mass celebrated on an altar set up on the back of a flatbed truck.

A crowd estimated at 4000 gathered in a 20-acre city-owned park to celebrate the end of the fast by the 41-year-old labor leader.

Among those on hand was Senator Robert F. Kennedy (Dem.-N.Y.), who flew in from Los Angeles on a chartered plane.

"HEROIC"

"I am here out of respect for one of the heroic figures of our time—Cesar Chavez," Kennedy told the big crowd.

"I congratulate all of you who are locked with Cesar in the struggle for justice for the farm worker and the struggle for justice for Spanish-speaking Americans," he said.

"There are those who question the principle of everything that you have done so far—the principle of nonviolence. Let me say to you that violence is no answer," Kennedy declared.

The once-stocky Chavez began his fast to defuse a rising impatience with nonviolence among the members of his United Farmworkers Union.

STRIKE

The union's strike against grape growers in the hot, fertile San Joaquin Valley is 2½ years old and hundreds of imported strikebreakers still continue to toil in the dusty vineyards.

Some elements within the union have lately begun insisting that Chavez' Gandhian philosophy has had its chance and that it is time to switch to violence.

Chavez—whose weight dropped from 175 to 140 pounds during the 25 days—told the workers he wanted to demonstrate the error in the traditional Mexican-American belief in machismo, the test of manliness through violence.

"No union movement is worth the life of a single grower or his child, or the life of a single worker and his child," Chavez said.

"The test we believe in now is how much a man is willing to sacrifice, and how much he is willing to give, to secure a better life for himself and his children" said Chavez.

BREAD

The bread Chavez ate was from a loaf of "semita," a Mexican-style bread which was distributed after the Mass by clergymen from many faiths.

Last Wednesday, Chavez began taking bullion on his doctor's orders, then switched to unsweetened grapefruit juice. He was also taking carbohydrate pills to reduce the high blood level of uric acid threatening permanent damage to his kidney.

He had been looking forward to eating solid foods again, telling friends that his muscles were "twitching all over—they're hungry."

CHECK

During his fast, Chavez—the father of eight children—had been living in the office of an unopened service station west of here. He read two books, the Bible and a book on Mahatma Gandhi.

During the offertory of the Mass, Paul Schrade, head of the West Coast United Automobile Workers, presented Chavez and his union a check for $50,000.

The money will go to finance construction of a union headquarters. Chavez hopes eventually to establish a settlement for farm workers around the headquarters. (pp. 1, 10)

ASSOCIATED PRESS INVESTIGATION OF CHILD LABOR IN AMERICA

In 1997, the Associated Press (AP) undertook a study of child labor in America, first using statistics gathered by Professor Douglas L. Kruse of Rutgers University, and then by reportorial investigation of factories and fields. The study shows that child labor is still rampant in America—especially in the fields—sixty years after the publication of *The Grapes of Wrath*, and that labor laws mean very little to many small farmers and many big growers.

FROM DAVID FOSTER AND FARRELL KRAMER, "AMERICA'S
SECRET CHILD LABOR FORCE"
(New York, NY: Associated Press, December 14, 1997)

NEW YORK (AP)—Fifty-nine years after Congress outlawed child labor in its most onerous forms, underage children still toil in fields and factories scattered across America.

The poorest and most vulnerable among them start working before other children start kindergarten. Many earn wages below the legal minimum, often in exhausting, or even hazardous, jobs.

These children live in a world apart from most Americans, hidden from consumers and even the companies that buy the products of their labor. Yet those products can sometimes be as close as the local mall or the corner grocery.

In the past five months, The Associated Press found 165 children working illegally in 16 states, from the chili fields of New Mexico to the sweatshops of New York City.

They are children such as Angel Oliveras, 4, who stumbled between chili pepper plants as tall as his chin in New Mexico's fall harvest. Children such as Vielesee Cassell, 13, who spent the summer folding and bagging dresses in a Texas sweatshop. Children such as Bruce Lawrence, at 8 already a three-year veteran of Florida's bean fields.

The AP was able to follow the work products of 50 children to more than two dozen companies including Campbell Soup Co., Chi-Chi's Mexican restaurants, ConAgra, Costco, H. J. Heinz, Newman's Own, J. C. Penney, Pillsbury, Sears and Wal-Mart.

All the companies that responded condemned illegal child labor. Many launched investigations when told of suppliers employing underage children.

"If they are, that's against the law and they're gone—they don't supply to Campbell Soup Co.," said spokesman Kevin Lowery.

Although the number of children traced to any one company was small, there are uncounted thousands of boys and girls like Angel, Vielesee and Bruce. No one knows just how many because no one, the federal government included, has tried to count them all.

• • •

Employers saved $155 million in wages last year by hiring underage children instead of legal workers.

• • •

The 1938 law set age minimums designed to ease children into the adult world of work. Those minimums remain at the heart of federal child labor law:

Children must wait until age 16 to work in factories or during school hours.

Children under 14 are barred from most jobs except farming.

Children under 12 are banned from most farming jobs but can work on their parents' farm or on a small farm exempt from federal minimum-wage laws.

Children under 18, or under 16 on farms, are barred from a list of jobs deemed hazardous.

• • •

Despite agriculture's more relaxed labor standards, it was on farms that the AP most often found illegal child labor, including the most extreme cases: the youngest workers toiling the longest hours for the least pay.

Reporters saw 104 children working illegally in agriculture in the past five months—nearly three times the 35 that U.S. Labor Department inspectors witnessed nationwide last year, according to the department's computer records.

Underage children picked cucumbers in Michigan, green peppers in Tennessee, and apples in upstate New York. Their grape-cutting knives flashed in the sunny vineyards of California, and their head lamps bobbed in the gloomy mushroom sheds of Pennsylvania. They packed peaches into crates in Illinois and hoed sorghum in Lubbock, Texas.

On a simmering July day near Bowling Green, Ohio, Pasqual Mares looked sadly at his 10-year-old daughter Laura, her back bent over a row of cucumbers. In a full week of harvest work, Mares said, he and his wife and their two working children had earned just $120—far below the normal minimum wage.

"Someday, I want my children to be treated like human beings, not like animals," he said. "It's not right that the children work. But we have to do it."

In a New Mexico field, Maria Perez watched her 10-year-old son Victor pick chilies. "I like him to work in the fields with me because I want him to learn that this work is hard, hot and laborious," she said. "I want him to hate this, to stay in school and to study hard so he doesn't have to do this work."

Victor was one of 35 children under age 12 seen picking chilies in the fields of New Mexico and west Texas. Laura Mares was among 34 kids under 12 spotted in Ohio's cucumber rows.

In the bean fields near Homestead, Fla., the Lawrence kids—Bruce, 8, Angie, 10, and Benjamin, 11—were among eight children under 12 picking beans one November morning.

"No kids in the field—especially when we've got reporters here," a crew boss at one Homestead field yelled out. Surprised parents said it was the first they'd been told that children weren't allowed.

Some employers on whose property the AP saw underage children working denied breaking the law, even when presented with photographs of the activity. Others blamed the kids and their parents.

"We tell them that we don't want children in the fields," said Tim Reynolds, whose family runs the farm where Laura worked. "But you know, migrant laborers want their kids out there. They get more produce picked."

Far from being anomalies, those young faces are windows into a larger, seldom-seen population of child workers, say those most familiar with child labor, including migrant-education workers, union organizers, priests and school teachers.

"They are in the dark alleys of the big cities," or "down a dirt road," said Linda F. Golodner, co-chairwoman of the Washington-based Child Labor Coalition.

LOST CHILDHOOD: THE ASSOCIATED PRESS LOOKS INTO A HIDDEN WORLD

As part of an Associated Press series on child labor in America, Verena Dobnik and Ted Anthony visited fields, factories, and homes of workers to see this "hidden America" for themselves. They also interviewed some of the children who work. The following excerpts hint at just how pervasive the problem is and how devastating these conditions are for the children, physically and psychologically.

FROM VERENA DOBNIK AND TED ANTHONY, "FROM FIELDS AND FACTORIES, CHILDREN'S VOICES EMERGE"
(New York, NY: Associated Press, December 9, 1997)

NEW YORK (AP)—They are children, yes. But is this childhood?

She sweats into the soil of a vast Ohio field. A baseball cap keeps the sun and her unruly dark hair from her almond eyes. Adult rubber gloves engulf the small hands that snap cucumbers from their vines. Her name is Alejandra Renteria. She is 6.

· · ·

Some are very young. Others are approaching adulthood. From America's fields they harvest onions, peppers, mushrooms, beans, berries, pecans. In garment factories, they iron pants, hang shirts, trim clothing. In meat-packing and egg-producing plants, in sawmills and furniture factories they toil.

Among them are an estimated 61,000 child field workers, ages 14 to 17, who live apart from their parents, according to an unreleased U.S. Labor Department survey. In thousands of cases, their parents aren't even in the country. In all, about 123,000 children in that age group work in America's fields, the survey said. Younger children in the fields are an all-but hidden, untracked work force.

· · ·

Federal law bars children under 16 from working while school is in session. Outside school hours, anyone 14 or 15 may work in farm jobs that the U.S. Labor Department deems safe. Younger children, those 12 or 13, can work only on farms and at a few other specific jobs.

Many of the children working in America are frequently underpaid, often unaccompanied and largely unprotected—a shadow generation made prematurely adult, moving from coast to coast, border to border.

Listen to Mercy Gandarilla, 10, kneeling in a cold New Mexico field since 6 A.M. Dew has soaked her shirt and a deep cough has taken her voice. "Cutting the chili," she rasps. "I like it—in the sun."

Listen to Omar Cruz Gonzales, 15, who rises at 2:30 A.M. to pick mushrooms for 12 hours in a windowless Pennsylvania shed. He sees no sun until midafternoon. "I have to work," says Omar. "The dollars are here."

Listen to Jaime Guerrero Jr., who loads crates of cabbage six days a week in Delaware. Three years ago, when he was 12, he heard his arm break as a conveyor caught his sleeve. "I'll do something else someday," he says.

These children are sometimes punished financially for small mistakes: Omar's employers, for example, occasionally withhold his pay if he drops or dirties mushrooms.

"Farmers used to own slaves. Now they rent them," says Diane Mull, executive director of the nonprofit Association of Farm Worker Opportunity Programs in Arlington, Va. "The agrarian myth is dead."

• • •

Why do they live these lives?

Some kids want spending money to buy into the consumer culture they see as necessary to being American. But many, especially migrant children, work because their parents don't earn enough.

"If adults were paid a living wage, we wouldn't have child labor," says Ann Millard, a Michigan State University anthropologist who studies migrant labor. Three out of four migrant families say they earn $5,000 or less yearly according to a national database of 54,000 families compiled by Mull's group.

Near Homestead, Fla., sisters LaKesha Brooks, 11, and Marie, 10, are already training the family's next breadwinner—their sister, Angelica, just 20 months old. "She can pick the beans one by one," LaKesha says.

Eluding rarely enforced laws, these workers bypass the modern Western concept of children as virtually a separate society—one to be protected, educated and prepped for adulthood rather than forced into it.

When Jose Madrid picks chilies in New Mexico's blistering heat, he dreams of Colorado mountains covered with vanilla ice cream.

But he is pragmatic beyond his 11 years. "I'm not good at math," he says, "but I'm good at money." Jose finishes the day exhausted and falls into a bottom bunk, his feet caked with mud. He hopes the rickety top bunk won't collapse on him. His mother can't afford a new bed; together they make about $30 daily.

Jose's cousin, Victor Perez, 10, trembles as he lugs 25-pound buckets of peppers. "I'll pick chilies when I grow up, because what else do I do?" he says. His mother, working nearby, wipes away a tear.

And near Ohio cucumber fields, the five members of the Mares family live in a one-room shack with no running water. The children fantasize about what many American kids take for granted—"our own house, with my own room," says Fabiola Mares, 12.

For them, even normal childhood friendships aren't easy. When Laura Mares, 10, received a rare invitation to a classmate's birthday party, "she couldn't go," says her mother, Elvira. "We just didn't have the money to buy a gift."

In Bowling Green, Ohio, American flags grace nearly every block of Main Street. Those who work the surrounding farmland rarely venture into this college town. They are moving specks in the lush landscape, forgotten among red barns, white steeples and stretches of corn, tomatoes and wheat.

This is where Alejandra, the 6-year-old with the oversized rubber gloves, spent the most recent summer of her childhood. She and her family rode 1,000 miles from Florida in a faded green Oldsmobile to pick cucumbers.

Alejandra's toenails are painted green. "I like green because grass is that color. And I want to be a grass, cause it gets watered every day, and it's cool."

Her father, Marcelo Renteria, a 30-year-old with a third-grade education, voices a hope that has driven immigrant America for generations. "I want the kids to study," he says, "so they don't end up like me."

Alejandra wants to work with computers, and her 9-year-old sister wants to be a teacher. But for now they must help the family survive.

"When I grow up and have kids, my kids will not work in the fields," says Jose Madrid, the boy who dreams of ice cream-covered mountains. "It's not a good place for children."

• • •

"I won't be doing this forever," says Jackie Villegas, a 17-year-old girl from Florida who has been picking produce for six years. "I have plans."

Alex Ledezma, 11, harvests sorghum, cotton and onions near Lubbock, Texas. Though he misses weeks of school each year to follow the crops, he has reached sixth grade. He makes $2.25 an hour hoeing. He wants to become a policeman.

Beside the sorghum plants that tower above his head sits a van that carries his family and the hoes to the field. On its rear window is a sticker. It says, "I believe in America."

ONGOING FARMWORKER PROBLEMS
REVEALED IN CALIFORNIA IN 1998

In September 1998, a study of farmworkers conducted for the California legislature was released by State Assembly Speaker Antonio R. Villaraigosa. The result of a fact-finding report designed to support new legislation, this press release reveals that many of the problems faced by the Joads in *The Grapes of Wrath* are still suffered by workers some sixty years later. Income levels, poverty rates, health care, working hours and conditions are substandard. The findings brought to light by the report prompted the introduction of bills designed to ease the ongoing problems.

FROM ANTONIO R. VILLARAIGOSA, " 'FARMWORKERS IN
CALIFORNIA' GIVES BLEAK PICTURE OF FARMWORKER LIFE"
(Assembly Speaker Antonio R. Villaraigosa,
45th Assembly District, speaker@assembly.ca.gov,
For Immediate Release: September 9, 1998)

ASSEMBLY SPEAKER'S REPORT SHOWS THE DIFFICULT LIFE OF
CALIFORNIA'S FARMWORKERS

Sacramento, CA—A study that shows California's farmworkers work harder, for less pay, and poorer living conditions than virtually any other employment group was released today by Assembly Speaker Antonio R. Villaraigosa (D-Los Angeles). The study was commissioned by the Speaker from the nonpartisan California Research Bureau (CRB) of the State Library. Titled "Farmworkers in California" the study surveys, among other factors the economic, educational, health, insurance and housing status of farmworkers—showing that, within most variables, the plight of farmworkers in California is more dire than that of other California workers.

"Farmworkers are among the hardest working members of our community—but they do not receive equal treatment. They carry a crucial burden—and they carry it with dignity, grace and strength. California leads the nation in agricultural production, and farmworkers are the linchpin in the whole process," stated Villaraigosa.

"We are moving past the old, crude stereotypes, to realize that farmworkers work harder, for fewer rewards, and at greater peril, than virtually any other occupational group. In turn, it is our responsibility to see that their basic needs are adequately addressed in the Legislature. We have made progress in protecting farmworkers rights, particularly in this year's budget battles—but this study graphically illustrates that we have far to go before achieving fairness," added Speaker Villaraigosa.

Farmworkers, according to occupational data from the Census Bureau, as analyzed by the CRB, are found on the extreme low-end of the spectrum in per-capita income for individuals and families, and in health insurance coverage. The CRB analysis also shows that farmworkers have the highest instance of living below the poverty level, and work among the longest hours of all occupational groups.

HIGHLIGHTS

Income Levels

The CRB analysis of Census Bureau data shows that approximately eighty percent of California's farmworkers earn less than $10,000 a year—and half earn below $5,000. Farmworkers' family income is the lowest of all occupations studied. The Employment Development Department further reports that farmworkers frequently earn below the minimum wage, and often must pay for transportation, lodging and food at prices set by their employers. Farmworkers frequently must take extra jobs and pool their resources to meet their family's fundamental needs.

Poverty Rate

As stated above, farmworkers frequently labor for substandard wages, consequently they have a high instance of falling below poverty levels. In the census comparison, farmworkers have the highest poverty rate of any surveyed occupation. Thirty eight percent of workers are below the federal poverty level.

Rate of Health Insurance and Quality of Health Care

Forty percent of farmworkers are uninsured (and their families are often uninsured in greater numbers)—one of the lowest insurance rates of any occupational groups. In addition, farmworkers experience difficult barriers to receiving health care, given their lack of transportation, limited free hours, language barriers, and other obstacles. Furthermore, there are substandard sanitary conditions on many job and housing sites. Several studies of agricultural communities have found a higher incidence of malnutrition and frequent risks of exposure to pesticides, painting a dismal picture of the quality of farmworkers' health, and more distressing, the health of their families and children.

Work Hours

Eighty percent of California crops are considered "labor intensive." In addition to the difficulty of the labor, farmworkers are found to work extremely long hours. Of occupational groups studied, farmworkers have the second highest rate of working more than 46 hours a week.

Working Conditions

According to data submitted in 1997 by the Division of Labor Standards Enforcement in California, of 455 agricultural employers reviewed, 130 were cited for child labor, workers' compensation violations, cash payment, and minimum wage violations. In addition, nationwide, an estimated 800,000 farmworkers lack adequate shelter. Although there are many laws and regulatory agencies designed to oversee working conditions for farmworkers and other occupations, there are numerous violations and official oversight is irregular.

In terms of legislative remedy, the legislatively approved 1998–99 budget package provided for a number of farmworker protection measures:

- Restored funding for foodstamps for all non-citizens, including farmworkers,
- Restored funding for SSI/SSP for all non-citizen immigrants,
- Provided $9 million for Rural Demonstration Projects under the Healthy Families Program,
- Provided $2 million for Naturalization Assistance,
- Added $1 million for the Self-Help Housing Program,
- Included $16.9 million for Migrant Childcare,
- Added $5 million for Rural Clinics and Migrant and Seasonal Farmworker Clinics, $3 million for Rural Health Grants, and $6 million [for] the Farmworker Housing Grant Fund. These last provisions, unfortunately, were vetoed by Governor Wilson.

"I am proud of the farmworker assistance and protection measures offered in the 1998–99 budget. Clearly, we need to continue and strengthen our efforts to offer assistance—to protect this vital, hardworking, and vulnerable group. Such protections will ensure the well-being of the farmworkers, who will, in turn, ensure the well-being of our state's economy," concluded Speaker Villaraigosa.

The CRB provides objective, nonpartisan research to the State Legislature. The Speaker would like to thank the CRB, and particularly Alicia Bugarin and Elias Lopez, for their timely and exhaustive analysis of this important issue. The report can be found on the California State Library website at www.library.ca.gov/ under CRB reports.

TOPICS FOR ORAL OR WRITTEN EXPLORATION

1. Write a paper comparing Cesar Chavez's and Jim Casy's attitudes toward violence.

2. A number of Chavez's followers were becoming so frustrated in 1968, that they contemplated meeting violence with violence. Debate the question of whether nonviolence is a viable course of action in situations like those faced by the Joads.

3. Conduct some research on agricultural workers' living and working conditions in rural areas nearest your home. Investigate some of the elements similar to those Assembly Speaker Villaraigosa looked into in California. Write up your findings.

4. Steinbeck devotes considerable attention to the children in *The Grapes of Wrath*. Write a paper about the impact on the Joad children of the life they are forced to lead. Are there any problems in common with the findings of the Associated Press?

5. After reading some books or articles on the United Farm Workers, write a paper speculating on the reasons for its success rather than that of the unions that came and went so quickly during the Depression.

6. Visit the UFW web site to read newspaper articles about the 1998 strike by strawberry pickers in Watsonville, California. Are there any similarities between this strike and those that occurred in the 1930s? Try to pinpoint the ongoing problems between unionism and growers in California.

7. Try to get an idea of what percentage of California farmworkers are not organized. Are they primarily in one area or in one type of agriculture? By computer and snail mail, compare the reasons for failure to organize given by the UFW and by the growers in a particular area.

8. Organize a debate about whether any action is needed to improve the lives of farmworkers and, if so, what that action should be.

SUGGESTIONS FOR FURTHER READING

De Ruiz, Dana Catherine, and Richard Larios. *La Causa: The Migrant Farmworkers' Story*. Austin, TX: Raintree Steck-Vaughn, 1993.

Dunne, John Gregory. *Delano: The Story of the California Grape Strike*. New York: Farrar, Straus and Giroux, 1967.

Ferris, Susan, and Ricardo Sandoval. *The Fight in the Fields*. New York: Harcourt Brace and Co., 1997.

Galarza, Ernesto. *Farm Workers and Agri-business in California, 1947–1960*. Notre Dame, IN: University of Notre Dame Press, 1997.

Goldfarb, Ronald L. *Migrant Farm Workers: A Caste in Despair*. Ames: Iowa State University Press, 1981.

Gonzales, Juan L. *Mexican and Mexican American Farm Workers*. New York: Praeger, 1985.

Griswold del Castillo, Richard, and Richard A. Garcia. *Cesar Chavez: A Triumph of Spirit*. Norman: University of Oklahoma Press, 1995.

Levy, Jacques E. *Cesar Chavez: Autobiography of La Causa*. New York: W. W. Norton, 1975.

Loftis Anne, and Dick Meister. *A Long Time Coming: The Struggle to Unionize America's Farm Workers*. New York: Macmillan Publishing Co., 1977.

London, Joan, and Henry Anderson. *So Shall Ye Reap: The Story of Cesar Chavez and the Farm Workers Movement*. New York: T. Y. Crowell, 1970.

Matthiessen, Peter. *Sal Si Puedes: Cesar Chavez and the New American Revolution*. New York: Random House, 1969.

Moore, Truman E. *The Slaves We Rent*. New York: Random House, 1965.

Nelson, Eugene. *Huelga: The First One Hundred Days of the Great Delano Grape Strike*. N.p.: Farm Workers Press, 1969.

Perry, Tony. "Farmer Faces Suit in Death of Worker." *Los Angeles Times*, 9 July 1998, p. 3.

Taylor, Ronald. *A Study in the Acquisitions and Use of Power: Chavez and the Farm Workers*. Boston: Beacon Press, 1975.

Young, Jan. *The Migrant Workers and Cesar Chavez*. New York: J. Messner, 1972.

Web Site:

The Official Web Page of the United Farm Workers of America: www.ufw. org.

Chronology

1920	18th Amendment passes and Prohibition begins.

As part of an ongoing "Red Scare," radicals Nicola Sacco and Bartolomeo Vanzetti are arrested for a bombing on questionable evidence and are executed in 1927.

Eugene V. Debs is nominated by the Socialist party for president of the United States and runs his campaign from jail.

Farmer Labor Party also meets to chose a presidential candidate.

Warren G. Harding elected president of the United States.

Europe, getting back on its feet, begins to depend less and less on American farm products and prices in the United States begin to fall.

The upper levels of U.S. society begin a decade of reckless investing and high living.

1921 For the workingman, wages begin to be cut in major industries because production is far outstripping demand. Industry routinely uses the stretch-out, demanding more work in less time.

President Harding orders Eugene V. Debs released from prison.

1923 Harding dies amid personal and economic scandals.

Calvin Coolidge sworn in as president.

U.S. Steel adopts an eight-hour day, setting the trend for other industries.

Supreme Court rules that state labor laws are unconstitutional.

1924 A constitutional amendment is offered to the states regulating child labor, but an insufficient number of states adopt it. By 1950, with ratification by only twenty-six states, the amendments dies.

Senator Robert La Follette of Wisconsin is chosen as a presidential candidate by the Conference for Progressive Political Action.

Calvin Coolidge elected president.

1920–1929 The economic situation continues, permitting wild speculation and lavish spending by the privileged few, and decreased wages for labor and loss of land for the farmer.

1927 Cesar Estrada Chavez is born near Yuma, Arizona.

1928	Herbert Hoover elected president.
	Worker discontent in the West leads to the formation of the Cannery and Agricultural Workers Industrial Union (CA-WIU), which folded in 1935.
1929	By August, big industries are feeling declines, but over-priced stock prices continue to rise.
	In late September, the market begins to decline. By October 23, panic has set in.
	On October 24, the market is in total collapse as 13,000,000 shares are unloaded and banks begin to close.
	Formation of TUUL.
	On October 29, "Black Thursday," another 16,000,000 shares are dumped and the Great Depression begins.
1930	Hawley-Smoot Tariff Act passed to aid American capitalism. It helped industry but hurt farmers. It caused Europe to raise tariffs, and created general unrest and instability in Europe.
	State Department prohibits immigration of workers to help U.S. unemployment, which reaches 4,500,000.
	Bank of the United States, one of the largest banks in the country, closes its doors.
1931	In September and October, 827 more banks close. Between 1930 and 1933, 5,000 banks close, wiping out $9,000,000 in savings.
	Al Capone, a notorious gangster whose career was advanced by Prohibition, is sentenced to eleven years in prison.
	Citizens stage a hunger march on Washington.
	Farmers' revolts begin across the Midwest to protest mortgage foreclosures. They are usually armed and fearless.
1932	On May 29, 17,000 veterans march on Washington, DC, to demand the full value of the Bonus Certificates they had been promised.
	On July 28 and 29, the starving bonus marchers who had camped out in Washington, DC, are attacked by the army, under the command of Douglas MacArthur, Dwight D. Eisenhower, and George S. Patton. Two policemen and two veterans are killed. Many people suffer serious injuries.

On November 8, Franklin D. Roosevelt wins the election for president by a landslide.

Unemployment reaches 13,000,000.

An estimated 250,000 people lose their homes this year.

Wages are 60 percent less than they were in 1929.

Unemployed workers in Detroit fill shopping carts with groceries and leave without paying.

On November 11, Charles "Pretty Boy" Floyd robs the bank in his hometown of Sallisaw, Oklahoma, in broad daylight.

1933

On March 5, Roosevelt declares a four-day bank holiday to slow panic and runs on banks to withdraw funds. He also halts the export and hoarding of gold. Within three days, 1,000 banks reopen.

On March 9, Roosevelt begins his Hundred Days of reforms. Before the year is out, much legislation is generated to alleviate the nation's suffering, among which are: the Civilian Conservation Corps (providing 250,000 jobs for young people); the Federal Emergency Relief Act (with immediate grants to states for relief projects); the Agricultural Adjustment Act (relief to farm owners); the Tennessee Valley Authority (providing public money to build dams and power plants for electricity); the Federal Securities Act (a Wall Street watchdog); the National Employment System Act (supporting state employment agencies); the Home Owners Refinancing Act (to provide mortgage money); the National Industrial Recovery Act (encouraging voluntary free trade, but ended by the Supreme Court in 1935 and reversed later); the National Labor Relations Board under Robert Wagner of New York; the Civil Works Administration, which provided 4,000,000 jobs.

On December 5, Prohibition ends.

More than 1,000 mortgages are foreclosed every day.

Agricultural workers launch more strikes and sit-downs in 1933 and 1934 than at any time in history. Among the thirty-one documented strikes in California alone are the cotton strikes in October 1933, in the San Joaquin Valley, resulting in three deaths, many arrests, woundings, and deportations. As a result, Mexican farm laborers throughout California are forbidden to work in the fields and native workers from the South and Midwest are conscripted.

1934   Other legislation to help farm owners introduced that do little for the small farmer and farmworker.

Strikes continue in California fields, with little monetary gains and much violence on the part of growers and law enforcement.

In May, dust storms ravage the Midwest and the Southwest, blowing away 300,000,000 tons of topsoil in farming country. Citizens begin leaving for California in large numbers.

Growers' associations in California grow in strength and conspire to fix wages, squelch union activity, and improve the growers' image.

In June, Congress passes the National Labor Relations Board that oversees the fights of workers, but exempts farm laborers.

On July 16, a general strike of all workers in the country begins in San Francisco, ending in death and violence as the police move in to break up peaceful demonstrations.

On July 22, John Dillinger, the FBI's Public Enemy Number 1, is shot and killed in Chicago.

On October 23, Pretty Boy Floyd is shot down by the FBI.

1935   The Supreme Court rules that the National Industrial Relations Act is unconstitutional.

In July, the National Labor Relations Act gives workers the right to vote for the representatives who will bargain on their behalf. It also gives workers the right to join a union. Farmworkers are excluded from this act.

On August 14, the Social Security Act passes, but migrant farmworkers are again excluded from this act.

In November, John L. Lewis, head of the United Mine Workers, becomes the courageous leader of the new Congress of Industrial Organization (CIO).

1936   In May, one of the worst of many strikes this year occurs in the lettuce fields of Steinbeck's home area of Monterey, California.

Steinbeck enters the public arena as a champion of the migrant farmworker in California with the publication of his novel *In Dubious Battle*, and a series of news articles for the *San Francisco News*.

Roosevelt wins another term in office.

On December 30, one of the longest major strikes of the decade occurs when the United Auto Workers walk out at General Motors. The strike lasts until February 11, 1937.

1937   A devastating epidemic of flu breaks out among farmworkers in California, with 6,000 documented cases.

Strike activity in large industries escalates with demands on U.S. Steel, by workers. Chicago police kill ten strikers.

The Supreme Court rules that the NLRA of 1935 is constitutional.

Indicating a condition of long-standing among workers in California, the California Immigration and Housing Authority orders thirty shanties in Vidalia condemned as unfit for human habitation.

Woody Guthrie, born and bred in Oklahoma, moves to California where he works as a farm laborer, writes songs, and is active in social and political arenas.

This may be the year the fictional Joads strike out for California.

Senator Robert La Follette begins congressional hearings (Committee on Education and Labor) into the abuse of labor by growers in California. The hearings continue into 1940.

The Chavez family, having lost their Arizona farm, become migrant workers in California.

1938   This is the year of the greatest population in California of Farmworkers from other parts of the country.

In January, torrential rains hit California. Many migrants are found homeless, sick, and soaked to the skin. Conditions are very like those depicted in the last chapters of *The Grapes of Wrath*.

California demands that migrants be returned to their native states.

In June, Congress passes the Fair Labor Standards Act. Farmworkers continue to be excluded from the 40-cent-an-hour minimum wage and the forty-four-hour work week.

In October, a new wage-hour law excludes migrants.

1939   Publication of Steinbeck's *The Grapes of Wrath*.

Publication of Carey McWilliams' *Factories in the Field*.

Publication, with growers' association backing, of M. V. Hartranft's *Grapes of Gladness*.

1940   In November, Roosevelt is elected to a third term.

An award-winning film is made of *The Grapes of Wrath*.

1941   On December 7, Pearl Harbor is attacked, beginning U.S. involvement in World War II.

On December 11, Germany and Italy declare war on the United States.

La Follette is unsuccessful in getting Congress to include farmworkers under various acts that guarantee laborers decent hours and wages, protection for children, and the right to organize.

1942   Cesar Chavez finishes eighth grade and begins working in the fields full-time.

1944   Roosevelt is elected to an unprecedented fourth term.

Cesar Chavez joins the Navy and fights in World War II.

1945   On April 12, Roosevelt dies and Harry S. Truman becomes president.

World War II ends after the dropping of atomic bombs on Hiroshima and Nagasaki.

After four years of refraining from strike activity, laborers begin striking for better wages. There is heavy activity throughout the 1940s and 1950s. Among the larger unions that walk out are the United Auto Workers, the Western Electric Telephone Workers, the United Steelworkers, the United Mine Workers, the Railroad Trainmen and Locomotive Engineers, and the Telephone Workers.

1946   On April 29, farm prices are reported at an all-time high.

Cesar Chavez returns to California to work with his family as a farm laborer. He makes forty-eight cents an hour in the apricot fields.

Labor unrest occurs in the DiGiorgio Corporation, which has $18,000,000 in sales this year.

1947   Taft-Hartley Law passes over Truman's veto. In giving states the right to outlaw closed shops, a blow is delivered to organized labor.

1948   Truman wins another presidential term.

1949   Farmworkers for DiGiorgio Corporation are unsuccessful in negotiating a raise. A strike is called.

A Senate committee, chaired by Richard M. Nixon, recommends that farmworkers continue to be excluded from labor laws.

Strike of cotton workers begins in California.

1950   On June 26, U.S. troops are committed to Korea.

Potato pickers strike in California. Violence and lack of funds forces them back to work.

Cesar Chavez becomes a student of activism in the fields and joins the Community Service Organization (CSO), becoming a full-time social activist.

1951   Public Law 78 is passed, formalizing an already informal agreement with Mexico to allow young Mexicans to be trucked into agricultural fields on a per-job basis. This is known as the Bracero Program, a move that impedes the labor movement's attempts to improve working conditions for farm laborers.

1953   Dwight D. Eisenhower sworn in as president.

1955   Minimum wage increased to one dollar per hour.

Chavez family is involved in National Agricultural Workers Union led by Ernesto Galarza.

AFL and CIO unite, forming the AFL-CIO.

1956   Eisenhower reelected for second term.

1960   John F. Kennedy elected president.

Survey finds that majority of farmworkers receive poverty-level wages, have no indoor toilets, and receive no vaccinations or medical care. Many have no refrigerators.

1961   Minimum wage increased to one dollar and twenty-five cents an hour.

1962   Chavez organizes the National Farm Worker's Association (NFWA) in Fresno, California.

John Steinbeck receives the Nobel Prize for literature.

1963   Federal government mandates a gradual end to the Bracero Program that Galarza has fought against for many years.

1964   John F. Kennedy is assassinated. Lyndon Johnson becomes president.

Vietnam conflict escalates into a full-scale U.S. commitment of armed forces.

1965   Domestic farmworkers in Delano, California, are paid one dollar an hour, a salary out of which they have to support themselves during the four winter months when there is no work. Illegal workers and the last of those in the Bracero Program are paid at a government-mandated rate of one dollar and forty cents an hour.

Chavez and the United Farm Workers join the CIO-supported Filipino farmworkers in a strike against Delano, California, grape growers.

Boycott of Delano grapes begins across the United States.

1966   United Farm Workers begin a 340-mile pilgrimage from Delano to Sacramento.

1968   Chavez undergoes a 23-day fast to encourage nonviolence in the strike. The fast ends in a Mass celebrated by 8,000 people, including Senator Robert F. Kennedy.

Robert F. Kennedy, a strong supporter of United Farm Workers, is assassinated.

John Steinbeck dies.

Richard M. Nixon is elected president. Earlier, as governor of California, he had lent support to programs in the interest of the growers as opposed to the workers.

1970   Grape boycott ends with the first contracts for farmworkers in U.S. history.

Lettuce boycott begins to force free elections among workers.

December 10–24, Chavez is jailed for refusing to stop the boycott.

1974   August 8, Nixon resigns and Gerald Ford becomes president.

Fifty thousand illegal workers are imported by San Joaquin Valley growers to break a strike called by Chavez's United Farm Workers.

1975   With the help of California governor Jerry Brown, Chavez and the growers agree to the first legislation of any kind that offers farmworkers some protections and bargaining rights.

1976   Jimmy Carter is elected president.

1980   Farmworkers see difficulties on the horizon when Ronald Reagan, one of California's ex-governors most openly antagonistic to their cause, is elected president.

1984	Reagan reelected.
1988	George Bush elected president.
1992	William Jefferson Clinton elected president.
1993	Cesar Chavez dies on April 23.
1998	A study by the California legislature finds that half the state's farmworkers earn less than $5,000 a year and work more than forty-six hours a week, when employment is available. In 1997, one hundred and thirty growers are cited for violations in the areas of child labor, workers' compensation, cash payments, and minimum wage violations.

Index

About the Author

CLAUDIA DURST JOHNSON is Professor Emerita at the University of Alabama, where she chaired the English Department for twelve years. She is series editor of the Greenwood Press "Literature in Context" series, for which she has authored several other books. She is also author of *To Kill a Mockingbird: Threatening Boundaries* (1994) and *The Productive Tension of Hawthorne's Art* (1981), as well as numerous articles on American literature and theatre.